The Abyss

The Abyss

*Bridging the Divide between
Israel and the Arab World*

Eli Avidar

ROWMAN & LITTLEFIELD
Lanham • Boulder • New York • London

Published by Rowman & Littlefield
A wholly owned subsidiary of The Rowman & Littlefield Publishing Group, Inc.
4501 Forbes Boulevard, Suite 200, Lanham, Maryland 20706
www.rowman.com

Unit A, Whitacre Mews, 26-34 Stannary Street, London SE11 4AB

First edition 2011

Editor: Shachar Alterman
Translator from Hebrew to English: Chaya Naor
Editor of the English translation: Julie Phelps

British Library Cataloguing in Publication Information Available

Library of Congress Cataloging-in-Publication Data

Avidar, Eli, author.
[Tehom. English]
The abyss : bridging the divide between Israel and the Arab world / Eli Avidar.
pages cm
First (Hebrew) edition 2011.
Includes bibliographical references and index.
ISBN 978-1-4422-4547-1 (cloth : alk. paper) — ISBN 978-1-4422-4548-8 (electronic) 1. Arab-Israeli conflict—History—20th century. 2. Arab-Israeli conflict—History—21st century. 3. Arab-Israeli conflict—Diplomatic history. 4. Arab-Israeli conflict—1993— —Peace. 5. Arab-Israeli conflict—Psychological aspects. 6. Al-Aqsa Intifada, 2000– 7. Israel—Foreign relations—Arab countries. 8. Arab countries—Foreign relations—Israel. I. Title.
DS119.7.A86713 2015
956.04—dc23
2014046336

∞™ The paper used in this publication meets the minimum requirements of American National Standard for Information Sciences Permanence of Paper for Printed Library Materials, ANSI/NISO Z39.48-1992.

Printed in the United States of America

To my dearest
Ornit, Liron, Omri, and Ophir

Contents

Introduction

It was the early days of the second Intifada, September 2000. Talks between Israel, under Ehud Barak's leadership, and the Palestinian Authority, headed by Yasser Arafat, were once again at a standstill. Israel's frustration, again, with the Palestinian campaign of terror came to a head in a show of force by Barak—a volley of missiles fired from helicopters at the *rais*'s headquarters in Ramallah. That did no good. Barak's standing with the Israeli public was declining rapidly. As the elections drew near, the bloodshed increased.

On December 6, 2000, when I was head of the Israeli foreign ministry's delegation to Qatar, I received a surprising phone call at my office. It was from Muhammad Jiham Qa'wari, Qatar's foreign minister's chief of bureau, who was known not only for his religious stringency but also for his hostility toward Israel, and primarily for his unwillingness—perhaps more than any other Qatari—to accept the presence of Israelis in his state. The content of the call, however, was even more surprising—Qa'wari informed me that his boss, the foreign minister of Qatar, Hamad bin Jassim, wanted to set up an urgent meeting in Europe with Israeli's foreign minister, Shlomo Ben Ami. He repeatedly stressed that this meeting and its contents had to be entirely secret.

"I'll do my best," I replied. As soon as the conversation ended, I contacted Alon Pinkas, head of Ben Ami's office. After consulting with the foreign minister, Pinkas told me that he'd be glad to accede to the request. On the morning of Monday, December 11, 2000, I met with the members of the delegation that had accompanied the foreign minister to the airport. It included his strategic adviser, Dr. Haim Assa; his political adviser, Alon Ushpiz; and Israel Hasson, the former deputy chief of the Israel Security Agency (ISA), also known as the Shabak, who had been a member of the delegation to the Camp David talks. Later Hasson moved over to the oppos-

1

ing political camp and was elected as a Knesset member on the Israel Betanu ticket. Today he is a Knesset member in the Kadima party. The delegation was flown to the secret meeting on a small private plane, which had to stop in Italy to refuel for the flight to Paris.

Shortly after takeoff, Foreign Minister Ben Ami asked me what I thought would happen at the meeting. I believed that Qatar was very interested in playing a key role in mediating the Israeli-Palestinian conflict. As a rule, I explained to the foreign minister, Qatar also attempts to position itself as a mediator in disputes between various Arab countries. I assumed that at the meeting the Qatari minister would suggest several confidence-building measures that would lead to an Israeli-Palestinian summit meeting in Qatar.

After hearing my views, Ben Ami nodded and immediately turned to Haim Assa and Israel Hasson, who were sitting next to him, and said, "I want to meet Arafat in Ramallah."

"Shlomo," Israel Hasson said, "why would you want to meet with that man? It'd be a waste of time."

"I want to look him straight in the eye and try to understand why he doesn't want to wrap it up and sign a peace agreement with us."

"Shlomo, it's a waste of time; that man doesn't want to sign an agreement," Hasson said.

"Nonetheless," Ben Ami replied, "I want to see the whites of his eyes when I hear his answer."

When we landed in Italy to refuel, I discovered that, despite all efforts to keep the meeting a secret, news of it had leaked. While we were still in the air, CNN had reported that the Israeli foreign minister was on his way to a secret meeting in Europe. To my surprise, Ben Ami did not seem to be disturbed by the leak. I was concerned that we might arrive in Paris only to hear that the Qataris had canceled the meeting because of the leak, but that was not the case.

When we arrived in Paris, CNN had already reported that the Israeli foreign minister had come to the city for a secret meeting with an "Arab leader." During the official handshake between the parties, in the Qatari foreign minister's suite, Bin Jassim said sarcastically to Ben Ami, "Mr. Foreign Minister, I'm happy to meet you and glad you found the time for this meeting. I heard that you came to Paris for a secret meeting with an Arab leader."

Ben Ami's only response was a slight smile.

The meeting was opened by the Qatari foreign minister: "Mr. Foreign Minister of Israel, the present situation in the Middle East places the entire region in great danger, and we Qataris are interested in helping to calm the waters before the situation spirals out of control. I am in close contact with Abu Mazen [who was at the time one of the two deputies of Yasser Arafat] and I also spoke to him prior to this meeting. Of all the Palestinian leaders, I have the greatest esteem for him, and his oldest son Mazen also worked with me in Qatar."

I had gotten to know Mazen Abbas well during my stay in Qatar. For some time, I had also met with him on the opposite side of the net in our weekly tennis match. During those matches, Abbas Jr. often spoke of his despair at the failure of the Camp David summit and his anger at Arafat's attempts to remove his father from the circle of the senior leadership after he had severely criticized the *rais*'s conduct at Camp David. To my sorrow, Mazen Abbas, an amiable man, died in Qatar on June 15, 2002, of a heart attack.

"The truth is," the Qatari foreign minister went on to say, "I don't understand what went wrong at Camp David."

According to him, the Palestinians claimed that the problem involved the division of the Old City. Ben Ami replied that he did not understand what had gone wrong either, especially since President Clinton had suggested the division of the Old City, with the Muslim and Christian quarters to be under Palestinian control, and the Jewish and Armenian quarters under Israeli control.

"You're right," the Qatari minister replied, "but the Palestinians complained about the Armenian quarter."

"If we had to make some accommodation, we would have expanded the Palestinian area to include the Armenian quarter, even though most of that quarter is populated by Jews."

"And what about the Temple Mount?" the Qatari minister asked.

Ben Ami replied, "We said the Temple Mount would be under Palestinian control. The only thing we asked in the framework of the agreement was that it contain wording to the effect that the Jewish people has a historical and religious connection to the area under the Temple Mount, so that no changes would be made there without our knowledge and consent."

The Qatari foreign minister said, "Sounds logical. And what about the problem of the refugees?"

At this stage, Ben Ami's tone of voice suggested he was losing patience, and he replied, "We were prepared to enable the reunion of families of up to 200,000 refugees coming to the territory of the State of Israel [the 1948 territories], and I am telling you," he added, his face reddening and his voice rising, "that in order to end the conflict, we were ready to expand that quota to 400,000 refugees."

At this point, everyone in the room fell silent. They all realized how generous and far-reaching the Israeli proposal had been. Then the Qatari minister asked his Israeli counterpart, "And what do you want from the Palestinians?"

Before Ben Ami had a chance to answer, all of us—Israel Hasson, Haim Assa, and myself—spoke in unison: "We want the end of the conflict."

We had not coordinated our reply in advance, but I suppose our joint chorus reflected the sincere wish of each and every Israeli: that whenever a peace agreement is signed with the Palestinians it will include a declaration about the end of the Israeli-Arab conflict.

Again the room was silent, and after a few seconds, the Qatari minister replied, "This is something I cannot give you; no one can. Sign a peace agreement with the Palestinians," he went on to say, "and we, as presidents of the Organization of Islamic Conference, will do our best to persuade the Muslim states to come to the signing ceremony in Washington.

"I estimate that about twenty moderate states, like Azerbaijan, Uzbekistan, Turkey, Jordan, Egypt, and others, will accede to our request, but not all the Muslim states will come. That's how it is, despite the fact that the president of Iran, [Mohammad] Khatami, told me personally that Iran would support any agreement the Palestinians entered into, since Iran believes that the Palestinians know what their national interest is [this was before the extreme period of Mahmoud Ahmadinejad]. But in my view, Iran and Saudi Arabia would not come to the ceremony. After the agreement is signed, there will be a long period of calm in the region, and maybe in another fifty years another conflict will erupt that will make everyone forget the Israeli-Arab conflict. We'll wait fifty years," the Qatari foreign minister said.

Then I remembered what the president of Egypt, Anwar Sadat, had said when he signed the first peace agreement between an Arab state and Israel: "We'll leave the full peace for the coming generations, they'll decide on that."

Just then, the penny dropped. Bin Jassim's response, more than any earlier statement I had heard or read from an official Arab source, brought home sharply to me the depth of the misunderstanding between us and our neighbors in the Middle East. Like all the members of the Israeli delegation, I hadn't understood why Israel had made the most generous offer ever made by any Israeli government—until that moment I and many others hadn't known how far-reaching that offer was—and why it was turned down without any hesitation.

At that moment, I decided to embark on a private journey to try to find out what was causing all of Israel's efforts vis-à-vis the Palestinians and the Arab world to fail. This book describes the conclusions and insights I arrived at during that journey.

* * *

In 1985, the Israeli government sent me to an Arab country for the first time. This was the time of the "Lebanese mud," and I was handling agents in the intelligence section of the Liaison Unit for Lebanon. The second time was in 1999, when I was appointed head of the Israeli delegation to Qatar. I very soon ended up—along with my colleagues in the foreign ministry—struggling around the clock to maintain Israel's image and its international standing after the Al Aqsa Intifada broke out.

I managed to get a lot in during those years. I served as a handler of agents in three zones, completed my BA and MA studies in Middle Eastern history, was hired by the foreign ministry and served on three different continents, was Ariel Sharon's adviser when he was foreign minister, and founded the Smart Middle East Forum. During all that time, again and again, I came up against a wall of misunderstanding between us and our neighbors, which was often expressed in absurd ways and had tragic implications. This book is a modest attempt to find a way out of this dialogue of the deaf.

* * *

Even before the peace process began, Israeli public opinion was divided into two opposing camps. One camp believed there was a solution to the Israeli-Arab conflict, which depended mainly on Israel's readiness to make territorial concessions. The pessimists in this camp held that since Israel was not ready to take painful decisions about such concessions, the conflict would only end with the aggressive intervention of a third party (the United States? the world?) that would impose an agreement on both parties.

The opposing camp held—with the same degree of self-conviction—that the solution to the conflict did not lie with Israel's moves or concessions, because Israel had no real partners in the Middle East for a peace agreement. According to this view, a true peace with our neighbors was impossible, because the "Arabs" wanted Israel's annihilation and the conflict was based on ideological and religious beliefs instilled into our neighbors by force of a "tyranny of thought" that rendered any significant change in their perceptions impossible.

These two positions, which were supposedly totally antithetical, vied with each other—mainly in the political arena, but sometimes even escalating to violence—to win over Israeli public opinion. Deep down, however, they shared the same basic assumption and suffered from the same blindness. They both related to the Arab world—the partner or the "no partner"—as if it were one faceless, static, unchanging entity.

The doves related to the Arabs as a mirror image of the voters for Meretz, a left-wing social-democratic political party, as pragmatic peace seekers who were only waiting for the moment when they could sign a peace agreement with us, in triplicate, so they could open hummus bars for us in Damascus and Hebron. The hawks, on the other hand, were convinced that the same Arabs were waiting for us with a knife between their teeth.

Both of these positions fail to understand—even after a hundred years, of good and bad experiences, of living as neighbors—that there is no such thing as "Arabs." Because they are even more divided in their views and attitudes than we are, so before we get to the bottom line—peace or all-out war—we need a process of confidence building, of mutual recognition, and a complex dialogue that will last for years.

We are in a rush. We want our partner to give us peace now, a big hug, or, alternatively, to immediately show his "true face." This is a state of mind that relates dismissively to the journey taken and only sanctifies the outcome. The expert in Middle East affairs, Dr. Shimon Shamir (formerly Israel's ambassador to Egypt), calls that "brutal pragmatism."

As I have already emphasized, at the end of the meeting between the Israeli foreign minister and his Qatari counterpart in the winter of 2000, I felt profoundly frustrated. That frustration, shared with me by no small part of the Israeli public, stemmed from the gap between the huge step that Israel had taken toward the Palestinians and their absolute refusal to accept the peace initiative. If that was the situation, what awaits us?

Frustration, however, is not a good adviser. After that meeting, I did not jump to the obvious conclusion that Arafat's real face had been exposed and that it was never turned toward peace. I wasn't interested in Arafat's real face; it had never been a pretty sight anyway. I was only interested in whether it was possible to gradually create a new reality here, to lower the flames and prepare the ground with the patience of a farmer waiting for rain—in order to reach a sober, mature reconciliation, free of any illusions and sentiment. I was also interested in whether we bore some responsibility, what the lawyers call "contributory guilt," for having fueled the arrogant obstinacy of the Palestinians during the negotiations.

In our haste, were we too weak when we ought to have been strong and too belligerent when we ought to have been generous?

* * *

The thoughts that evolved in my mind throughout the thirty years of my public service and my studies coalesced into a general concept about how we actually behave in the Middle East and how we ought to behave.

These insights grew sharper with the increasing number of times I entered rooms in which intelligence and diplomatic discussions and work were going on, rooms closed to the general public. My theoretical studies, as well as my practical experience, combined to strengthen my conviction that an alternative kind of discourse for the Middle East needed to be formulated, one in which we look at our partner straight in the eye, without patronizing him but also without idealizing him in the name of some romantic, utopian notion of brotherly love. That was what motivated me to write this book.

If I had to come up with a fitting, to-the-point motto for this entire book, I would say, "Israel, speak Arabic!" Only if we become wholly familiar with the culture of the opposing parties—their motives, quandaries, and sensitivities—can we know who we are dealing with. Only by speaking in their language can we learn to deal with them successfully. To understand how to do this correctly, we need to know where we've gone wrong until now. The Middle East is a volatile arena that changes quickly and to the extreme, but some fundamentals do not change. The major part of this book, then, is devoted to several of our most common errors in the past and maybe some lessons for the future.

The first chapter deals with the bubble we have lived in as a small state within the Middle East. The State of Israel, I will argue, acts in total isolation from the region in which it exists, from the regional culture and the traditional philosophy of the peoples of the region. Our absolute ignorance in these areas gives rise to a dialogue of the deaf, and it's important to think about that.

The second chapter is about one by-product, which is an especially extreme one: the isolationist approach. It is the policy of one-sided measures that comes to the forefront every time the Israeli leadership despairs of its Arab partner. In the Israeli view, a one-sided policy—such as the withdrawal from Lebanon or the disengagement in Gaza—is an expression of strength, since we "don't ask them, we just take the right decision." However, our neighbors actually perceive it as a sign of fear and weakness. Instead of encouraging them to move forward in the peace process, it causes the most extreme among them, and, unfortunately, the more moderate as well, to cast doubt on our ability to survive in the region, and encourages them to react by escalating the conflict.

One aspect of the cultural and conceptual rift between us and the Arab world is manifested in the irksome striving of the Israeli side for normalization and the speed with which Israel tries to impose "a new Middle East" on those who only yesterday were its bitter enemies—even before a political agreement is signed: a perfect, new Middle East that looks like an ad for the yummiest hummus. This urgent rush for normalization increases the other side's suspicion of us, causing it to entrench itself even more deeply in its position.

I learned this lesson thoroughly during my diplomatic service in Qatar. There I also learned how it's possible to replace our ravenous appetite for normalization with more measured, modest steps, which are also far more effective.

In addition to issues of tact and patience, it is also impossible to discuss normalization without clarifying whether Israel is sincerely interested in becoming a part of the Middle East, and what price it is ready to pay. That is the subject of the third chapter.

In recent decades, economic sanctions have become a popular weapon with the international community. Economic pressure, Western states and others believe, is likely to soften an adamant adversary, or even to lead to a change of government that will serve the interests of the boycotting states. The fourth chapter will examine the effectiveness of this weapon in Middle Eastern conflicts, particularly in relation to the economic siege that Israel has imposed on the Hamas government in Gaza. It will also deal at length with conclusions that can be drawn regarding the sanctions imposed by the international community on Iran.

An especially painful case of a bridge we unwittingly lost is our relations with the Shi'ite community in Lebanon. Until recently, this community was one of the moderate streams of Islam, and we possessed the means and the opportunities to make it our ally. Instead, it became a bitter enemy of the State of Israel and now calls for an armed struggle against Israel as a solution to the problems of Islam. The dynamics that led to this lamentable outcome will be addressed in the fifth chapter of this book.

One of the claims being voiced more frequently in recent years—as the negotiations become deadlocked and worldwide terror escalates—is that we are in a "war of civilizations." According to this approach, we are now in the midst of a worldwide culture war between different civilizations, particularly between the "West" and "Islam," and in this war, Israel is the front-line bastion of the West. The obvious conclusion is, then, that there is no chance for political negotiations because the conflict goes deeper than disagreements about territory and originates in a religious commandment.

In the sixth chapter, I will show that the very attitude toward Islam, with all its complexity and variety, as a single threatening entity, is a kind of self-fulfilling image. I will already state now that I believe that the Muslim clergy, who putatively despise Western culture in general and us in particular, actually can serve as a bridge for a dialogue and perhaps even for reconciliation (excluding the now growing radical fundamentalists), and the same holds true for our rabbis.

Chapter 7 is dedicated to hope. Hope that it is possible to get out of our fixated mode of thought, and that through a deeper familiarity with and understanding of the other side, with the help of a little emotional intelligence, we can begin doing something to restore trust with our neighbors, to improve our standing in the Middle East, and to revive political negotiations at a reasonable pace while setting realistic goals. I believe that Israel can find its place in this contentious, turbulent region, if the country only learns how to speak in the region's language. I hope I will also be able to convince you, my readers.

Which of us is not familiar with the sense of despair we feel after the failure of negotiations or a horrible act of terror? There isn't an Israeli who hasn't said or thought in such situations, "There's nothing to be done; there's no solution; it's so depressing." And yet, as understandable as this attitude is, it does not constitute a plan of action. There is nothing more disheartening than despair itself. The statement "There's nothing to be done" is merely an expression of mistaken, automatic behavior. We obstinately stick to old patterns of thought instead of looking for new solutions. We do not learn from our past mistakes, and in the end, we are surprised, or just give up, when once again we end up in a deadlock.

If, instead of trying to bend the Middle East to fit our measurements, we would learn to navigate through it, listen to the myriad voices rising from the variety of peoples living in it, and learn to identify among them our potential allies and turn to them, with confidence but also with humility—then we might discover that we are not a "villa in the jungle," as Ehud Barak (former Israeli prime minister) so depressingly put it.

Our failure to listen attentively to voices of the region we live in often causes us to adopt simplistic generalizations about that same "jungle." The Middle East is not a single entity, nor is it one culture or one system. What is good for Mauretania is not necessarily good for Iraq or Yemen. The Arab world, if we can even call it that, is not homogeneous. Rather, it is a huge mosaic of states, streams, organizations, and people. This distinction also holds true for the religion of Islam. It is not uniform either, and it encompasses ethnic groups, streams, and factions that often despise each other far more than they hate Israel.

One of the important rules of the game in the Middle East, which I learned mainly during my service in Qatar, is that when interests are involved, each state is unto itself. The bombastic declarations about a united Arab world and a binding all-Arab policy become worthless once conflicting interests arise between the various elements in the Middle East.

The State of Israel needs to learn the Middle East game of interests and understand the various interests that can cause the most extreme states to become moderate, and, unfortunately, the other way around, too.

A good example is Qatar, which in the mid-1990s was considered a progressive country that aspired to change the traditional discourse in its area as well as in the Middle East in general, structuring balances within its foreign policy to maintain strong ties to the West as well as extreme organizations and states in the Muslim world and, over the years, becoming an ardent supporter of the Muslim Brothers in Egypt and in other parts of the Middle East. The country also became the greatest financier of the Hamas movement and its terror infrastructure in Gaza without anybody realizing it.

In this book, I also stress the need to act with modesty in the Middle East. Throughout the years, Israel has been characterized by arrogance and condescension toward its neighbors. In time of war, that condescension was expressed in disparagement for our enemy's military capacity. In the time of talks, it took the form of telling the peoples of the Middle East how to run their lives, how to educate their children, how to build their economy, and how to decide on their political establishment.

The Jews are the chosen people in the Bible and I am proud to be one of them, but no one authorized us to be the instructing people, the educating people, the defining people, and the enlightened people. Only if we understand that we are living in a geographical region that has a tradition, a culture, science, and philosophy thousands of years old, will we acquire the degree of modesty we need in order to intelligently find our way around the region and avoid having every proposal we make come up against a stone wall, and every gesture we make interpreted as an attempt at an imperialistic takeover.

Before we look at our neighbors, we would do well to look at ourselves. When the founding fathers established the modern State of Israel against all odds, they believed everything was possible. They were weaker than we are, lacking nearly everything, surrounded by a huge sea of enemies without a significant ability to defend themselves. But they were not dissuaded and they founded the state that Jews had dreamed of for more than two thousand years.

Paradoxically, recent years, a time of strength, progress, and economic prosperity, have brought with them the notion that "there is nothing to be done." How did we get to a situation in which our faith in our ability to change stands in an inverse ratio to our wealth, power, and progress? In September 2008, I met with an ardent Jew by the name of Yehudah Hubashi, a man committed to the state from its establishment and throughout all of its trials. After hearing me sum up the issue briefly, he said, "Listen, when we were weak, we were strong."

* * *

I wrote this book to sound a warning bell, to awaken us from the deep sleep we have fallen into in recent years since Israel has grown stronger economically and scored successes in many walks of life. Despite these successes and our desire to influence events in the Middle East, our isolationist, one-sided, patronizing behavior and our blindness to the mentality of the region have doomed us to remain outside the playing field—but influenced by what happens inside it each and every moment.

If Israel wants to survive and prosper in peace, we have to get into that field as players. The people who can do this are not the ones who see our neighbors through a rifle sight, but those who know them through literature and philosophy, through handshakes and direct contacts. I am very hopeful that this discussion will lead the Israeli and the Western reader to conclude that it is possible to conduct ourselves differently, in a smarter way, in the Middle East.

* * *

I began writing this book before the riots that spread in winter 2011 and spring 2012 from Tunisia to Egypt, from Bahrain to Saudi Arabia, and from Yemen to Syria. Like many people with a theory, I also observed the events with concern, afraid that the facts might spoil my story. To my satisfaction— mingled with some sorrow, I admit—I did not have to throw away my manuscript; in fact, I hardly had to change a word. The revolts in Tunisia, Egypt, and Libya; the riots that were halted at the outset in Saudi Arabia, Bahrain, and Jordan; and those still going strong in Syria as I write these lines taught me a lesson or two about one's actions in the Middle East and underscored other lessons I had internalized in the past. It is too early to know where this trend will take the region, but already now I believe it is possible to extract several lessons from it.

The first lesson is that a full democratic revolution in the Arab world has not yet taken place, and it's doubtful whether it will soon. In Egypt, for example, the riots meant to overthrow Hosni Mubarak empowered the Muslim Brotherhood, which at the time was the only organized force among the opposition movements. After Mohamed Morsi's election as president in June 2012, and his enforcement of sprouts of Sharia law, he was ousted a year later when riots took place throughout Egypt in July 2013; in 2015, Abdel Fattah el-Sisi serves as the president, after his victory in the last elections.

With all the symbolism of Tahrir Square, the people have not taken hold of the reins of government. Yet the second lesson is that the United States has lost, perhaps for good, its position as a significant, even-handed mediator because of the way it turned its back on Mubarak and his government, its support for the Muslim Brotherhood against the army, and its well-intended but misplaced dissatisfaction with el-Sisi's election as president (although he is turning out to be one of the most impressive leaders who has come into power in the region in recent years).

Moreover, the deafening silence of the United States when riots in Bahrain and Saudia were suppressed revealed (more than any damaging document published in WikiLeaks) how biased and interest based its policy in the region is, how limited its understanding of Middle Eastern politics is, and how fickle a friend Americans are even to the Arab leaders most faithful to them. In the case of Egypt, the United States' disloyalty to Mubarak did not earn them a speck of gratitude or respect from the demonstrators. When former secretary of state Hillary Clinton came to Cairo after Mubarak's fall and asked to meet with the representatives of the demonstrators in Tahrir Square, her outstretched hand was rejected and she had to leave the country without meeting with any of them. If Israel wants to renew talks with Arab states in the immediate neighborhood as well as those farther away, the country can rely less than ever before on the services of the United States. Israel will have to do it alone.

A third lesson is that just as there is no such thing as "the Arab world," there is also no such thing as "riots in the Arab world." Other than the timing, very little is common to the riots that took place in Egypt in the last three years and the ousting of Mubarak and Morsi, the tribal war in Libya, and the ousting of Muammar al-Qaddafi.

Then, of course, there is the selective manner in which the world reacted to the violation of human rights and the shooting of demonstrators in countries like Tunisia, Syria, and Egypt, in contrast to similar offenses in large oil-supplying countries like Saudi Arabia and Bahrain. At first glance, the demonstrations look alike to the television viewer, but the reality is far more complex, and so is the policy that should be adopted in each and every case.

A fourth lesson is the role of Israel in the events—the nation has none. The "Arab world," Israelis were again surprised to realize, is preoccupied mainly with itself. Each nation has its problems; every people has its troubles. Any attempt to involve Israel as a unifying glue by inventing a conspiracy theory of one kind or another, like the one promoted by Syrian president Bashar al-Assad at the start of the riots in his country, has not yet succeeded. Israel should continue to maintain media silence in relation to riots in any Arab country, friend or foe. Israel needs to do so to avoid providing ammunition to its enemies, but also because a degree of humility is required. These are not our quarrels, nor are they our struggles for freedom. Each nation will decide its own fate, whether we like it or not. That does not mean that Israel has to remain silent when events directly involve the country, or forgo channels of communication with Arab countries. It only obliges us to stay carefully within the bounds of good manners and restraint, which is also required of us in calmer times.

In my view, the last lesson is the most important one. We must learn to speak Arabic, in order to understand and to be understood. Only when we are completely fluent in this culture, in all its complexity and nuances, can we navigate intelligently and safely in a place that is too often unstable and turbulent. We must speak Arabic not only behind closed doors, with Arab leaders and statesmen—who are often as practiced in the language of international diplomacy as our politicians and statesmen—but also with the Arab multi-channel media and, through it, with the Arab peoples—whether they want this dialogue or regard us with hostility and suspicion—just as we have related and still relate to them. Because wherever there is no dialogue, only fear and cannons will speak.

Eli Avidar
February 2015

Chapter One

A Dialogue of the Deaf

Are the grievous failures in our negotiations with the Arab world the result of a breakdown in communications?

What is not clear to us? What is not clear to them?

One of the questions of the "what would happen if?" genre that keeps crop-ping up, disturbing scholars, politicians, and the public at large, which has been following the foundering political negotiations in the last two decades with concern, is this: To what extent does the human factor influence these failures?

Did the whack on the back that Ehud Barak gave Yasser Arafat at Camp David really make a difference? And what would have happened if another man, more pragmatic and open minded, had headed up the Palestinian dele-gation? How meaningful is the personality of the leader and the chemistry between him and his adversary-partner on the other side? Is the muddle we got ourselves into in the Middle East only a tragedy of misunderstandings, or, in other words, "a dialogue of the deaf"?

Far be it for me to decide on this fundamental question that historians and political scientists have been grappling with for generations. Moreover, as far as the relations between Israel and the Arabs are concerned, beyond the personal chemistry between the leaders, the conflicts are truly deep and difficult to resolve. My firm belief in the importance of the human element, as well as my optimism about our ability to find paths to the hearts and minds of our enemies, actually developed in the Israel Defense Forces (IDF), at the beginning of my service as a case officer in unit 504 of the Intelligence Corps.

Chapter 1

THE AGENT WHO WASN'T IMPRESSED
BY THE YAD VASHEM HOLOCAUST MUSEUM

It was in 1986. As soon as I completed the case officers' course (one that trains officers to recruit and handle agents), on my first day at the central command of unit 504, I was asked to go to the office of the commander at the time, Lieutenant Colonel E.—an impressive, authoritative man. He handed me a bunch of car keys and a folder bearing the heading, "Operation File—Top Secret."

"These two will always be with you, one alongside the other," my new commander said. "One is a tool and a status symbol; the other represents the purpose for which you came here." Before I had a chance to glance at the contents of the folder, I learned from the sector commander that the project involved was one that had not yet been successfully completed—a potential recruit that two handlers had not been able to recruit.

"Knock yourself out with this guy, and good luck," Lieutenant Colonel E. said, before going back to leaf through the pile of papers on his desk.

I went back to my desk in the office that would be mine for the coming three years. I opened the folder and spent three hours perusing it, trying to learn how I might succeed where others had failed.

When I finished reading, one of the old-timer officers sitting near me asked, "So, what do you say?"

I answered, "I'm going to change the rules of the game with this guy."

My officemate grinned and said, "Don't feel bad if you don't succeed. The file you got is like the ones we got on our first day. The object is to confront you with a nearly impossible mission."

I gathered up my belongings and that same evening went back home, the details in the folder spinning around in my head like an unwinding film.

One of the first things I noticed while reading the hundreds of pages in the folder was the repeated note that the candidate was interested in working with the unit—namely, he had expressed his desire to join our setup of agents, but each time the two previous handlers attempted to recruit him, they had come up against a problem.

The problem, as I understood the reports and the assessment, was what the candidate had said about terrorist acts, remarks that sounded overly harsh to Israeli ears. This was a man who defined those who carried out terrorist acts in Israel by means of remotely activated explosive devices as "cowards." It was clear that he thought actions carried out by suicide bombers were "brave"—not exactly the first man you would want to recruit for the Israeli security services. When my predecessor took him on a tour at the Yad Vashem museum in an attempt to change his attitude, he lashed out at him: "Why did you bring me here? Why are you showing me what others did to you? After all, you do worse things." Another fact I learned from the folder was that this man's religious views were very extreme; those of Hamas paled in comparison.

But despite all of this disheartening information, I noted that concealed beneath all of his provocative statements was a man who nonetheless was interested in working with us. Otherwise, he would not have volunteered to meet with people from the unit. He had held dozens of futile meetings with my predecessors, and still had not stopped coming or disappeared.

In addition to my man's extreme attitudes, at a certain stage a new problem appeared. During one of the meetings with my predecessor, he said, "If you want me to carry out the mission, you'll have to pay me a million and a half dollars and deposit the money in advance in a bank account I open. Otherwise, I'm out."

The last document in the folder was a short interim report written by my predecessor, summarizing the important points to be taken into account at any future contact with that Palestinian. The report ended with a slightly bitter comment: "I don't know who will replace me on this operation, but whoever it is, I wish him luck."

When I closed the folder, I put it back into the archive and never opened it again. Before I fell asleep that night, I decided to "forget" everything I had read and get to know the man. I felt that I had to meet with him as soon as possible and clarify the matter myself.

The first meeting took place in a military government compound in Judah and Samaria. Before I could get a word out, the man told me he was no longer interested in meeting me or anyone else from the unit.

"I met with all the ones who came before you," he went on to say. "You're not serious."

I found no reason to argue with him, and simply replied, "My name is Captain So-and-So [I didn't give my real name but a pseudonym that every intelligence handler receives]. I've read about you and I want to meet with you. I'll wait for you this coming Tuesday at 1800h at a certain place in the city. If you arrive—fine. If you don't, then in the name of the 'office' [the pseudonym of the unit], I wish you the best of luck." With those words, I escorted him outside.

Like a Swiss watch, on Tuesday the candidate arrived right on time. For me that was a sign that his resolve to cut off contact with us was not exactly set in stone. After a brief walk, we came to the building containing the apartment where members of the unit met with its agents.

While he settled himself in an armchair, I asked him to join me in a meal. He declined. A few minutes later, when the food was already on the table, I invited him again to eat but he refused again.

"You're being impolite, but I'm going to eat anyway," I said and began eating, noting his shocked look. While I was chewing, the man launched into a series of accusations against the members of the unit who, he said, had ignored his financial demands, were not serious, and had wasted his time. I didn't respond. I told him that this meeting was not for the purpose of work, but just to become personally acquainted.

"Maybe you could just tell me a bit about yourself so I can get to know you," I said.

"I'm not interested in telling you about myself," he replied curtly.

"No problem," I said. "I'll tell you about myself."

I started telling him my life story, completely ignoring his growing anger. "I was born in Alexandria in 1964," I began. "We came to Israel in 1967. My father worked at various jobs when we came here. Listen, it wasn't easy coming to a new country when you're used to having four servants in the house—three nursemaids and a woman to do the laundry—and a driver, too. Then you come here, look all around, and there's no one there."

That guy sat across from me, looking astonished but not saying a word. I went on telling him about my family life in Egypt, how every day at noon the driver would come to pick up my mother, my sister, and my brothers and drive them to the restaurant in a private sports club, whose members came from the elite of Alexandria and included foreign diplomats and heads of foreign corporations.

As time passed, I saw it dawn on him that my story was true, and he began to show a lot of interest in it. When I finished about an hour later, I got up, extended my hand, and thanked him for having come to the meeting and listening to my life story.

"Is that all?" he asked, amazed. "Don't you want to talk about other things?" (alluding to an attempt on my part to recruit him).

"No," I replied. "I invited you here so I could get to know you and I'd be glad to meet you next week as well. Same time, same place."

The man gave me a stunned look. I could have sworn I heard him say to himself, "Who's this idiot they dumped on me?" Before walking out of the apartment he said to me, "I'm not coming anymore."

I answered curtly, "It's okay if you don't come, but I'll be waiting for you next Tuesday. Same time, same place."

A week later the man turned up at the place and time I had fixed. This time, too, I opened the meeting with a meal. I did not invite him to eat, but just handed him a *pitta*. He tore it in two, handed me a half, and began eating. After we ate a bit, I asked him, "Do you want to tell me something about yourself?"

The man replied, "No."

"That's okay," I said.

Then I took a videocassette out of my bag and inserted it into a player under the TV in front of us.

"What are you doing?" he asked while I was still fiddling with the player.

"Last time I told you my life story, and you don't want to tell me yours now. So I brought a good movie to enjoy while we eat." At this point, the room began to fill with the melody from the theme song of the movie about the famous Egyptian singer Mounira El-Mahdeya: "*Yaaa yaa yaama Yaamantna waaheshni we rohaq rohaq rohaq . . .*"

The movie told the life story of El-Mahdeya, who was Umm Kulthum's rival at the start of her career. It was an old black-and-white movie that portrayed the glamorous, glittering Egypt of the days before Gamal Abdel Nasser's revolution. The man looked at me as if I were mad.

An hour and a half later, when the movie ended, I got up, shook his hand, said good-bye, and added, "I'll wait for you next week. Same time, same place."

He said nothing and just went on his way.

The following week, while we were eating, the Palestinian's wall of silence began to show some cracks. During the evening, I learned he was indeed a man who held very extreme religious views, and that the only reason he had considered cooperating with Israeli intelligence was that he hated the country where a relative of his lived. He hated it even more than he hated Israel. Each of us knows how to find some justification for our actions, and I certainly did not intend to argue with him about that.

At this point, I understood that it was a mistake to think that anyone willing to serve as an agent has to necessarily show complete loyalty to Israel, to sing the Hatikvah anthem or recite from the texts of Theodor Herzl. It does not work like that, just as it did not work in Afghanistan between the United States and the Taliban. The only reason the Taliban agreed to cooperate with the U.S. Army against the Communists was their hatred for the latter. So a week after the Soviet Union withdrew from Afghanistan, the Taliban turned against the United States.

In other words, a Muslim Arab who becomes an agent of an arm of Israeli intelligence does not become a pro-Zionist. He cooperates on a certain level, but he does not give up his national and religious identity, and that is actually a good thing, because agents lacking in personality and backbone are no good to us.

After that first meeting, I met with the candidate alone another four or five times. We talked into the night about every imaginable subject but intelligence and espionage activity. Only then, when I felt we had established a form of communication, did our meetings move on to practical matters.

During those preliminary meetings, I did not ask him his positions or his opinions about terrorist acts; I did not ask him to identify with the Jews and, as a result, never gave him an opportunity to express his extremist views. I did not ask him what would happen if the Muslims were to rule here, so I would not have to hear that they would slaughter all the Jews. I simply devoted all of my time and skills to finding a frequency on which I could communicate with him straight from the shoulder, unpretentiously, naturally, and honestly, because insincerity never produces any results in such situations.

As time passed after Israel entered the territories in 1967, Israeli society developed a patronizing attitude toward the Palestinians. The Palestinians were very sensitive to that, rightly so, and it was very difficult to come to any understanding with them under those circumstances. I did not believe that this condescending attitude would serve our purposes, and, more important, I do not believe it is justified. From the outset, I treated the Palestinian as a partner, and only after he tested me and was convinced of my sincerity was a basis for cooperation established between us.

Although all the reports written about him stressed that he was an extremist Muslim who was not recruitable, I was glad to find that such was not the case. He understood that he could rely on me, that I related to him as a person and not as a means to an end, that I did not ask him or expect him to give up his religious or national identity, and that we respected each other. The day he returned from his mission, bringing with him the target's consent to assist us, was one of the happiest, most satisfying of the entire period of my service.

I was not the only case officer to behave this way, and certainly not the first. One of the pioneers and developers of this approach was Colonel (Res.) M., considered to this very day to be one of the best case officers and recruiters of agents in the unit. During my service, I never met him personally, but his name was always in the background. In unit 504, the handlers go out to the field escorted by a security detail. These men are noncommissioned officers (NCOs) in the IDF, who are not only important and very professional but also the ones who serve as the unit's "collective memory." They used to tease us, the young officers, saying we would never understand the essence of the job, and they also told great tales about M.'s exploits.

One of them, the late D., one of the finest professionals, took me under his wing as his own "project" as soon as I came to the unit: "You new officers, you smart guys, will never understand what it means to really handle an agent."

"Tell me," I asked him one day, and he said, "M. handled John Doe. He was the unit's best agent. Thousands, maybe even tens of thousands of Israelis owe him their lives. When the agent came to a periodical meeting that lasted several days, M. would stay with him in the apartment. He would debrief him for hours, and when he saw that the agent was tired, he'd say, 'Yallah, let's take a break.' They'd change clothes and go out for a game of backgammon. M., the commander of the sector, would wear shorts, a white undershirt and flip-flops, and play with the agent for an hour or two. By that time, the guy was ready to bring him the moon. Do you get me, smart guy?" D. asked, raising his voice as if he had lost all hope for me. The truth was that

I did understand him; I understood every word, and everything he said was deeply engraved in my memory.

Quite a few of the Palestinian agents recruited by M. back in 1968 were still serving in the unit when I got there in 1986, eighteen years later. One of the main agents I handled was one recruited by M.—a man who had linked his fate with ours in 1968 and kept his promises until the day he died. Some of the handlers who arrived after M. tried to change the terms of the agent's work and get him to do things he had not agreed to from the outset, but he always refused. On more than one occasion, this caused a serious problem, and M. had to come to pacify the agent and restore good relations between him and his new handlers.

I admired that agent. I handled him for three years, and during our meetings, which lasted several days, I listened raptly to his stories and experiences, beginning from the time the IDF entered his hometown in 1967. He was a walking history book, covering a time period nearly erased by now from the Israeli consciousness.

At one of our meetings, I asked if he would agree to carry out an operation that deviated from what we had agreed upon. The request came from the highest echelons of the Intelligence Branch, and I knew these were cases that had previously led to quarrels with agents, after they adamantly refused. I asked him cautiously for his opinion. I didn't order him to do it. I didn't try to coerce him. He looked at me for several seconds, and a slight smile flittered across his face. He understood what I had asked him and knew it deviated from his past assignments. He asked several questions, requested some details, and then said, "I'll do it and bring you results at our next meeting."

When I tried to make the assignment easier for him with different technical devices, he replied, "Don't help me with devices that will just make me look suspicious. I'll do it my way; don't worry."

The veteran agent did, in fact, carry out the mission. Thanks to him, a great risk that the elite units of the IDF usually encounter was removed. If anything went wrong in a military operation of that kind, there were liable to be many casualties, an international crisis, and innumerable inquiry commissions. But that man was a genius.

Nineteen years after our last meeting, when he had already died of old age, I went to look for the owners of the apartment in which I had met with him. I remembered that on the wall of the room there had been a picture by the Swiss artist Carla Goetz. It was an oil painting that depicted, with surprisingly appropriate symbolism, a secret meeting.

I had gazed at that painting for hours while the agent was interrogated by various other people. I asked the owner of the house about the picture, and he told me it was in the attic, probably in bad shape.

"Bring it to me," I asked.

He brought down from the attic a creased, dusty canvas, and my face lit up. I purchased the oil painting, sent it to be restored by an expert, and from then to this very day, it hangs in my office in memory of that dear man I had the privilege to work with and learn from.

While writing this chapter, I wanted to meet with M. to glean from him the secret of his success. In early July 2010 I contacted him, and we arranged to meet two hours later in his office in the Sharon region. He turned out to be an impressive man, lacking in any pretentiousness or need for self-aggrandizement. When I asked him what the secret of his success was, he smiled and replied, "I respected them; I never lied to them; I never made them a promise I didn't intend to keep; I never patronized them; I never backed them against the wall. I took an interest in them and their families, not only in their work. It was a genuine interest, not just something I felt obliged to do.

"They repaid me by being ready to do everything for me. But you know what? They knew I'd do anything for them. I didn't learn to behave that way in a course I took or from some experienced instructor. I learned it from my late father, who lived most of his life in Iraq. When I was offered the job in 504, I asked for forty-eight hours to think about it and went to talk to my father. That's the advice he gave me, and it was the principle that guided me and served me well, not only in the unit and in other military positions, but as a way of life."

Two hours later, when I was about to leave his office, M. tossed a question at me: "Do you know who would sit in my office and ask me that same question you asked?"

"No," I said, "who?"

"Yitzhak Rabin," he replied. "He saw that after I left the unit, a model of cooperation with the local Palestinian leadership had been built in the sector where I served, one that didn't exist in the others. So he would sit in my office for hours, trying to understand why we were successful."

* * *

The reason I wrote about my initiation as a handler of agents in unit 504 and about Colonel (Res.) M. was not to give myself a pat on the back, but to show that the human element is really important, maybe even decisive.

Even when the opening conditions are bad, when you are sitting opposite a man who hates you and your people, and you want to convince him to act against the interests of his own people, you can still find common ground and create a productive dialogue without twisting his arm. On the other hand, even when a person or a group of people are interested in cooperating with you, it may come to nothing because of a lack of communication, the absence of any chemistry, or the condescending attitude of one of the parties.

And if that is the case in a complex, clandestine act involving loyalty, nationalism, and religion, it is doubly true in the event of a political negotiation between Israel and its neighbors. Although the secret recruitment of an agent is not like negotiations between heads of state or leaders of countries in the region, the one thing common to both is that it is very difficult to achieve mutual trust and very easy to lose it.

In the chapter titled "The Influence of Culture and the Israeli Aspect," from her book *The Dynamics of Negotiations—from Theory to Application*, Professor Amira Galin, an expert in organizational behavior and negotiation, notes that cultural differences are major elements in the problems that crop up during any negotiation.[1] She claims that the diverse styles and disparate discourses between the parties lead to suspicion and anger, which escalate objective crises. Knowledge of the other party's culture and an understanding of how he conducts negotiations can make the process more effective and save it from ending in a deadlock.

In his 1990 book *Culture and Conflict in Israeli-Egyptian Relations*, Professor Raymond Cohen, of the Department of International Relations at the Hebrew University of Jerusalem, examines how the cultural difference between Israelis and Egyptians has affected the dialogue between the two states since the signing of their peace treaty. He noted in particular that "mistrust, misunderstanding and pride have precluded direct contact and then hindered negotiation,"[2] which continued to emerge between them, even three decades later.

Cohen asserted that the quality of the communication between the leaders of the two sides is of crucial importance to the success or failure of the diplomatic process. In the case of Israel and the Arab world, it is possible to write a one-hundred-volume encyclopedia replete with examples that illustrate the breakdowns in communication—land mines, some of which Israel continues to stumble over time after time. I will try to briefly touch upon some of the major differences in approach.

NEVER BE THE FIRST ONE TO SPEAK

I was privileged to hear an edifying example of the complexity of diplomatic etiquette in the Middle East from an Orientalist, Professor Moshe Sharon, one of my teachers in the department of Middle Eastern history at the Hebrew University. His students completely filled the large lecture hall of the department to hear his riveting lectures, largely due to his ability to link events from Arab and Islamic history to the behavior of Arab and Muslim leaders in the modern era. It was Professor Sharon who showed us time after time that the behavior of the Arab world was based on a thousand-year-old cultural and philosophical foundation. But I also learned from him that to understand the other side does not necessarily mean accepting his positions and deferring to him. Sometimes the exact opposite is true.

At the end of October 1980, several months after the peace treaty was signed, the president of Egypt, Anwar Sadat, invited Yitzhak Navon—the fifth president of the State of Israel—to be the first Israeli president to visit Egypt and speak to the Egyptian parliament. Before Navon's trip, Professor Sharon asked to meet with him to give him some tips about culture, respect, and discourse in the Arab world.

"At official events in an Arab state and at every official event elsewhere, in which a senior Arab person participates, always make sure that he is the first to speak," Sharon told Navon. "Never be the first speaker."

Then Sharon told Navon the story of the arbitration and negotiation of Abu Musa al-Ash'ari and 'Amr Ibn al-'As. In the seventh century, a controversy broke out between Ali Ibn Abi Talib, the nephew of the Prophet Muhammad, and Mu'āwiyah ibn 'Abī Sufyān, the ruler of Damascus, over the throne of the caliph, then the leader of the entire Muslim world.

The two decided on an arbitration. Ali was represented by an older, highly respected religious scholar by the name of Abu Musa al-Ash'ari, while Mu'āwiyah was represented by 'Amr Ibn al-'As, a shrewd man whose nickname was "Dahiyat al-'Arab" ("the catastrophe of the Arabs").

According to the story, after the two representatives had sat alone and agreed that Ali should be the next caliph, they went out to the crowd that filled the square to await the results of the arbitration. 'Amr Ibn al-'As suggested that Abu Musa al-Ash'ari speak first, since he was the older and more respected of the two. Al-Ash'ari, gratified by the compliment, began by telling the crowd that he and Ibn al-'As had discussed the matter in depth and had arrived at an agreed decision. At this stage, al-Ash'ari gave the second speaker the honor of announcing the decision. Ibn al-'As continued from that point and said it was decided that . . . Mu'āwiyah Ibn Sufyān would be the caliph.

Al-Ash'ari was stunned, his breath caught in his throat, but Mu'āwiyah's supporters cheered and shouted with joy, and the caliphate was taken from 'Ali. This is actually the origin of the schism that later gave rise to the Shi'ite faction, and it teaches an important lesson: Never speak first.

Professor Sharon told this story to his students and—several years earlier—to President Navon. He also had more topical examples. He told Navon about quite a few occasions on which Menachem Begin and Sadat met and decided on joint projects. At the press conferences, Sadat also allowed Begin to speak first and announce their decisions, while he only said that they had had a good meeting and did not commit himself to anything. Sadat understood that Begin was a man to whom honor was important and would regard the suggestion that he speak first as a gesture made by Sadat. But Begin was not aware of the tradition on which Sadat based his gestures and the true motivation underlying them. Navon took the advice to heart.

When he returned from Egypt, Navon met again with the professor, to close the circle. "Sadat and I came to some agreements," Navon told Sharon. "We agreed to renew the railway line from Lod to Cairo, to make use of this and that, and at the end of the meeting, when we were about to go into the hall where the press conference would be held, Sadat turned to me and said: 'Since you are my guest, I'd like you to enter the hall first and to be the first to speak as well.' Then I recalled what you told me, and said to Sadat: 'Mr. President, I am the guest and you are the host, so I would be grateful if you were the first to lead us to the hall and deliver your words first.'"

The negotiation between the two lasted several minutes. It was definitely a battle between two equal rivals.

On one side was a courageous Egyptian president, born in the village of Mit Abu al-Kum on the banks of the Nile, son to a father of Egyptian-Arab origin and a mother of African origin, a man well versed in all the Egyptian customs and etiquette, possessed of rich political and diplomatic experience. Sadat began his political career as a member of the Free Officers group, which led the military coup in Egypt in 1952 that unseated King Farouk. Later he served as the deputy of the legendary president Gamal Abdel Nasser and, after his death, became the president of Egypt.

On the other side was an Israeli president, no less likeable, very experienced in Israeli political life, scion of one of the oldest Jewish families in Jerusalem, descended from the prominent Talmudist and Kabbalist from Morocco, R. Chaim ben Moshe Ibn Attar, known by his epithet *Or hakhayyim hakadosh* ("The Sacred Light of Life"). One only needs to read the speech Navon delivered before the leadership of the ruling party in Egypt to understand that the man is fluent in all the intricacies of Arab culture and philosophy, which he absorbed from his father, who maintained warm relations with his Palestinian neighbors in the Old City of Jerusalem.

The battle was a close one. Surrounded by dozens of people waiting impatiently for the next part of the ceremony, the host and his guest employed their finest skills to persuade the other to take the first step.

"Finally," Navon said, "when Sadat understood that I was not going to give in, he suddenly said: 'Why do we need to talk to the journalists now? Let's take a trip to visit the village of my birth.'"

And that is what happened. The press conference was canceled, and the two presidents went on a tour on the banks of the Nile. The world, however, was still waiting to hear the results of the historic meeting between the presidents, and the representatives of the media, who accompanied the two throughout the tour, were asking for their pound of flesh. When the tour ended in Sadat's village, Sadat and Navon again found themselves embroiled in the same argument: Who would be the first to speak?

At this stage, Navon told Sharon, when he understood the polite argument had reached an impasse, that it might even adversely affect the entire visit, and that Sadat would not hesitate to cancel the press conference altogether, he decided to give in and speak first. But while they were standing in front of hundreds of journalists from all over the world, including the major media of all the Arab countries, it was Navon's turn to throw down the winning card. Ignoring the official rules of protocol, as soon as Navon began speaking, he turned to Sadat and said, "We have decided to revive the railway line between Lod and Cairo, isn't that so, Mr. President?" Sadat, who was caught unprepared, had no choice but to nod again and again.

President Navon's resourcefulness was only one example of the way in which knowledge of the other side's cultural language and an understanding of his sensitivities can be helpful to us without necessarily requiring that we yield on matters vital to us. From my experience as a case officer and a diplomat, I have always believed that we have someone to talk to, whether they are Palestinians, Egyptians, Syrians, Lebanese, Jordanians, or other Arabs, and the only question is how to go about it.

The challenge is to learn how to talk with the peoples of the Middle East, to know their culture and the ideological foundations underpinning their worldview. And we need to learn to listen to what they say and understand their words through the cultural context of the region, and not through the prism of our own cultural context.

It is critically important to understand the rules of discourse in the Middle East, not only in order to achieve an overall solution to the conflict and to bring about peace but also as a vehicle for wise, stable, and nonaggressive behavior that will make it possible to quickly extinguish any conflagrations that erupt as a result of a breakdown in communication, and, even better, to avoid becoming embroiled in any unnecessary conflicts.

THE PUBLIC AND THE PUBLIC SERVANT

Most Arab cultures sanctify the collective—the extended family, the group, or the nation—as the basic principle of their existence and the main framework of their lives. The needs of the group determine the values, expectations, and even the degree of autonomy of the individual. The name of the game is conformism; everyone has to be "on the same page." Israeli culture, on the other hand, does not recognize the principle of tribalism as a source of identity and loyalty. In Israel, as in Western countries, education is oriented toward individualism, stressing each person's independence and right to act freely in pursuit of happiness.

The difference between a collective society and an individualistic society is also manifested in the way each judges its members. Arab culture is generally one of honor and shame. There is no greater injury to a man than an affront to his honor. One of the major reasons for many instances of violence in Arab society is the desire to avenge a wrong and to restore the honor of a family or individual.

To prevent such affronts, Arab culture has developed an enormous degree of sensitivity to others, a fear of offending their honor, and a supreme attempt to maintain social order. Consequently, the language and behavior is replete with manners and niceties, all aimed at creating a safety belt of courtesy to avoid social accidents.

In Israeli culture, in contrast, the individual is not so dependent on the approval of the collective and, consequently, is less vulnerable. It is a far more direct society, free of any rigid formalities or etiquette. Its members are strong willed, competitive, and so accustomed from infancy to the blunt speech of their fellow citizens that they are almost immune to insult. The typical Israeli will not allow an insult to divert him from pursuing his goal, nor will he waste time flattering others. The distinction between a collectivist society that exalts the value of honor and an individualist society that sanctifies the goal may be banal and all too familiar, but its implications in a negotiation are apt to be very surprising.

An Israeli conducting a negotiation tends quite often to act rather independently, as far as the mandate he has been given allows him to, based on his own interests and those of the group he represents. An Arab conducting a negotiation will feel he is much more bound by the collective he represents, so he is in no hurry to undertake too much responsibility for weighty decisions without first ascertaining that he has the authority to do so. This idea holds true not only for officials and ambassadors but also for government ministers, presidents, and kings.

Very rarely does an Arab spokesman pull a reply out of his sleeve before consulting with the members of his group. When he does come up with a quick reply, it is usually insinuated and oblique, not unequivocal. Israelis often perceive this behavior as an attempt to "pull the wool over their eyes." We tend to wrongly interpret the Arab speaker's words and intentions and, consequently, react with suspicion and even hostility. It is interesting that our representatives, who often come to the negotiation table after being chosen by the people in democratic elections, feel that they can freely make hard decisions that might be viewed as a lack of commitment to the voters, while their Arab counterparts, most of whom have not been elected (at least until recently), nonetheless (perhaps actually because of that) are so apprehensive about their public image at every stage of the negotiations.

Arab representatives and Arab society as a whole believe that failure to faithfully represent their side in the talks might lead to the loss of their status in the group. The statements by an Arab spokesman will always reflect the positions of the state, of the party, of the ethnic group, or of the organization in whose name he is acting, in the most extreme way. The Israeli spokesman, on the other hand, will always carry out his mission in a more flexible manner. The Israeli addresses his words to the outside world; the Arab always addresses his first to the members of his group.

A remark by former foreign minister Shlomo Ben Ami provides a good example of this. He candidly describes his conduct during the negotiations with the Palestinians in 2000: "At different junctures of the negotiations, I undertook the initiative for steps that went beyond 'my guidelines,' and I was criticized for that by the other members of my team. I knew I was acting in the spirit of the Prime Minister's intentions and his readiness for a compromise, as I understood them. He did not send me to parrot his words, and I would not have accepted that assignment."[3]

WHAT IS SPOKEN OUTSIDE;
WHAT IS SAID BEHIND CLOSED DOORS

On December 27, 1977, Begin met with Sadat at Ismailia, Egypt. It was evident from their first meetings that while Begin was enthusiastically proposing plans and a vision of peace between the two peoples, Sadat was presenting chilly, tougher positions. After some time, the members of the Israeli delegation realized that the Egyptian president was first delivering those speeches to the members of his own delegation. At a certain stage, someone advised Begin to meet Sadat alone, without any of the delegates. As one of his advisers put it, "so the two old men will sit and talk alone." And, in fact, after they had several private meetings, they did make significant progress in their talks.

But the gap between the public conduct of the Arab side and the leader's tendency toward moderation in private meetings has an inverse side, and that is also important to realize. In 1992, when I was participating in the foreign ministry's cadet course, I was attached as a trainee to the Palestinian section of the ministry's Center for Political Research. As part of my duties, I engaged mainly in reading intelligence material and the Arab press. This was the time of the Oslo process, and one day I came across a newspaper item about a meeting held at the Palestine Liberation Organization (PLO) Executive Committee at which the organization's positions vis-à-vis the Oslo process were discussed. The item, which contained quotes from the meeting, stated that the PLO regarded the Oslo agreement as a way of achieving "*Itifakia.*" I was stunned. It was not a leak from a closed meeting, but an official statement issued to the press after the meeting ended.

Anyone unfamiliar with the intricacies of Arab discourse may find it hard to understand what amazed me. After all, *itifak salam* is a peace agreement, and how much difference is there between *itifakia* and *itifak salam*? But since I have spoken Arabic from an early age and am sensitive to the great significance of these nuances, I knew that the meaning of the word *itifakia* is a "minor agreement," one that is less binding, not a real agreement. I drew the section head's attention to the item and told him that, in my view, the PLO leadership was trying via this nuance to inform the Palestinian public that they were not planning to reach a full peace agreement, but at the most a partial, nonbinding one. The section head listened and said he would convey that view to the higher echelons in the office. I was very agitated when I met him the next day and asked him how the higher-ups had reacted to my remark, but he replied, "It didn't interest anyone."

Although I was merely a cadet, that reaction really angered me. Even though he had not invited me into his office, I went in anyway and asked for an explanation. His reply astonished me and left me frustrated for a long time: "I spoke to my friend in the office of the deputy foreign minister, and he said, 'Semantics do not interest us; we don't care if they want to write one word or another, or what it means. As far as we are concerned, they can call it a football field. We are only interested in what will actually take place.'"

At that point, even before I left the offices and got a taste of work in the field, I understood that there was a problem of perception in the highest echelons of the Israeli foreign ministry relating to the difference in approach between us and the Arab world. I learned firsthand that those making decisions on our side did not comprehend that what the other side says in public may not always reflect their opinion, but is always binding and irrevocable.

In addition, Israeli leaders have a nearly inherent tendency to maintain an aura of secrecy. The Israelis always prefer a dialogue behind closed doors, barring the media and the public, to an open, public dialogue broadcast on the radio or in the form of public lectures. The representatives of Arab countries, however, will always publicly express their positions and present the state of the negotiations from their vantage point, particularly those things the other side is being asked to carry out.

Here is a typical example from Gilead Sher's book *The Israeli-Palestinian Peace Negotiations 1999–2000: Within Reach*: "From then on, I avoided making any statements to the media at the end of the meetings, while Erekat went down to the journalists to provide them with little more than the 'photo op' and handshake that each meeting begins with."[4]

That pattern is a familiar, well-known one. Nonetheless, time after time I come across decision makers who maintain that the statements of the Palestinian leadership to the media are not important because they are intended for internal politics. However, my long years of experience have shown that in a negotiation with an Arab partner, what is said behind closed doors is actually far less important and meaningful than what the Arab leaders say in public. What an Arab leader says behind closed doors is not binding, while every word he utters to the media commits him and continues to commit him for many years, which is the very opposite of the Israeli case.

When our basic interpretation is wrong, and we assume the other side will behave the same way we do, then we are actually closing our eyes to all the warning signs and developing unrealistically high expectations that could easily be lowered and adjusted if we would only read our neighbors' newspapers seriously.

On January 23, 2011, this thesis gained further support. Al-Jazeera published 1,600 Palestinian Authority documents on the peace process and negotiations during the Ehud Olmert administration. The Authority was in an uproar, and Saeb Erekat spoke on Al-Jazeera, bursting into a fury on a live broadcast. Time after time, he refused to answer the interviewer's questions about whether these were genuine or false documents. After a few futile attempts, the presenter stopped the broadcast and stated that Erekat understood that the documents were authentic and that he had no answers. The leaked documents were internal and had never been brought to the public's knowledge, so the Palestinian leadership was caught unprepared, "with their pants down." Why? Because the Palestinian Authority did not report to the Palestinian public on the progress made, nor did it explain the constraints that obliged it to compromise. Months of negotiations between Saeb Erekat, head of the Palestinian delegation to the talks, and Foreign Minister Tzipi Livni were accompanied by statements issued by Erekat about the Israelis' unwillingness to make progress in the talks and, at the same time, by silence on Livni's part. This was blatantly seen in the last Israel-Gaza negotiations in August 2014 in Cairo, where the joint Palestinian negotiation delegation to the cease-fire included representatives of Fatah, Hamas, and Islamic Jihad. Each had their own spokesman, which influenced the negotiations and international media coverage of the process, while Israel once again chose to say nothing, allowing the void to be controlled by others.

Later in this chapter, we will see that Palestinian leaders cannot make any compromises unless they manage to persuade the public that they were forced to do so and that there was no other alternative. Al-Jazeera set a trap for the Palestinian Authority: it arranged a simulation of meetings with actors playing the roles of the participants. This gave the spectators the feeling that the heads of the Authority had willingly relinquished their positions regarding historical assets. The Palestinian fury, followed by Saeb Erekat's resignation, proved to us that the Palestinian leadership did not want to be seen as having made concessions without first obtaining the backing of the public and the media.

SIGN, YOU SON OF A DOG!

The Israeli and/or Western sides are repeatedly frustrated in negotiations with Arab partners because of their tendency to put off as long as possible signing any binding document. This tendency is systematic and consistent. In the numerous meetings I had over the years with Arab representatives—in my military service and diplomatic or business positions—I noticed that the Arab side always prefers to avoid as far as possible bringing things to a final resolution, or even to sign drafts. However, as far as we are concerned, a deliberation that does not lead to a signature is meaningless.

In conversations with several Arab diplomats during my service in Qatar and other places, they told me that this behavior stems from the Arab perception that if they sign an agreement or end a process, the options are limited, while if they leave an item unresolved they have more freedom of action in the future. The peoples of the Middle East, therefore, love to leave all their options open and generally do so while emphasizing the unresolved topics so they can put off signing the completed agreement. For example, Ben Ami complained about Arafat, "Arafat will always see the empty half of the glass, and would always give his interlocutor the feeling that no matter how many concessions he made, he was still in debt to him."[5] When relating to the right of return of the Palestinian refugees, the former foreign minister stated, "At no time would Arafat ever acknowledge that as far as he was concerned, solving the problem of the Lebanese refugees would 'close' the issue of the right of return. Arafat never 'closed' any topic."[6]

Arabs believe that the objective of any dialogue (political, business, or otherwise) is first of all to develop a personal and social relationship between the parties, in order to create a personal commitment between them. Signing any document not only severs these relations but also commits the parties vis-à-vis more senior officials or those whom they were representing. In contrast to the "short-and-to-the-point" approach of the Israelis, the Arab culture of discourse endorses the statement "the more said, the better." Every discussion in the Arab world, no matter what the topic is, will also include the presentation of a number of options, at the end of which several modes of action will be presented, in order to enable the decision makers a broad field for maneuver in the future. The decision maker in the Arab world will never be content with two possibilities, as the Israelis have learned in their contacts with the Palestinians.

The man who perfected this approach into an art, and dragged the Middle East down into the depths of despair and bloodshed, was, of course, the head of the Palestinian Authority, Yasser Arafat.

On May 4, 1994, the Cairo agreement between Yitzhak Rabin and Arafat was signed in Egypt. It included the transfer of the Gaza Strip and the city of Jericho to the Palestinians. The last-minute crisis was broadcast live, nearly leading to the cancellation of the signing ceremony in front of fifteen hundred guests from abroad, when Arafat refused to sign the maps appended to the agreement and demanded some changes in them. Pressure was brought to bear on Arafat during the live broadcast, and the president of Egypt, Mubarak, went so far as to force him with a curse: "Sign, you son of a dog!"

Finally Arafat signed, but he first had to show his people that he had no other alternative, and that he did not sign willingly. On July 1, 1994, when he arrived in the territories following that agreement, the journalists lashed out at him, asking how he—the leader of the Palestinian struggle—could have signed an agreement that made him the mayor of the cities of Gaza and Jericho.

"International pressure was brought to bear on me, there was Arab pressure and Egyptian pressure, and I was forced to sign," Arafat explained, and the journalists accepted that explanation.

But what Hosni Mubarak—who knew the man well and knew how shrewd he could be—understood, Ehud Barak did not understand in 2000. At Camp David, when he made the head of the Palestinian Authority the most generous offer ever made by an Israeli government to end the conflict, the Israeli prime minister, truly believing his offer could not be refused, said to Arafat, "Take it or leave it."

Arafat did not blink. It was clear to him that Barak was threatening him with an unloaded gun, and as long as he had a choice he had no intention of making do with that offer. Arafat was not backed into a corner at Camp David 2000, primarily because there was no corner there at all. Barak himself, vigorously pushed by President Clinton, improved his generous offer several times during the conference and continued doing so at the Taba summit in January 2001. Those were the last days of Barak's term in office and a few days before the eruption of the second Intifada buried the peace process for many years along with his political career, while Arafat faded into the Mukata.

Barak, it turns out, proved that Arafat was right to wait for a better offer, and Arafat finally proved that he was wrong to misunderstand how far it is possible to stretch the Israeli border.

"Barak did not really want peace," Ashraf al-Ajrami, the former Palestinian minister for prisoner affairs, said to me on November 14, 2009, when we were attending the Israeli-Palestinian Forum in Turkey held under the auspices of the Van Leer Institute. "If Barak really wanted peace, he had a thousand ways to make Arafat sign the agreement. Barak was stronger than Arafat, Israel was stronger than the Palestinians, and if Barak truly had wanted to, he could have forced Arafat to sign." I smiled at him and in my heart thanked him. Al-Ajrami had solved a puzzle that had troubled me since the failure of the Camp David summit and the generous and desperate offers Israel made in its wake. Why did Arafat persist in his refusal? A Palestinian leader, al-Ajrami's words taught me, cannot sign an agreement that is less than 100 percent, unless he is forced to do so and can prove to his people— preferably in a theatrical gesture like the one at the Cairo summit—that he had no choice but to sign. Clinton's logical talks with Arafat about the harm to Palestinian interests[7] and Barak's vain threats during the summit did not really force Arafat to sign. He only understood that he could still get more concessions.

It is a fact that although no agreement was reached at Camp David, Arafat never threatened to leave the conference. Why should he if he was getting more every minute?[8] If Barak had taken off his gloves and told Arafat— when still at Camp David and with U.S. backing—that if he refused the Israeli offer, he and his people would be expelled on the first ship back to Tunisia, and Israel would renege on all the agreements ever reached with the PLO—maybe things would have been different, but we will never know.

Did anyone learn from that lesson? I am not sure. On September 2, 2010, at a peace summit, the phase of direct talks between Israel and the Palestinians opened. Barack Obama, Abu Mazen, and Benjamin Netanyahu participated, and King Abdullah of Jordan and President Mubarak of Egypt were present.

In the weeks leading up to the summit, Abu Mazen declared at every possible forum that he was not interested in attending the summit. He consulted with the Arab League, which supported him and authorized him to go to the summit. That did not suffice, and Abu Mazen kept claiming that the United States was pressuring him vigorously, until the U.S. government stated that it was not pressuring him at all. The United States did not understand that Abu Mazen had to explain to his people why he was going to a summit without any commitment by Israel to freeze the settlements over the green line, particularly in the absence of any Israeli commitment to begin negotiations where they had left off. By denying it was bringing pressure to bear on him, the U.S. government weakened Abu Mazen's legitimacy instead of strengthening it.

The same week that Al-Jazeera exposed documents relating to the Israeli-Palestinian negotiations during Olmert's term of office as prime minister, Olmert published a chapter from his book about what went on in those talks. He described the last meeting he had with Abu Mazen on September 16, 2008. At that time, Olmert responded to all the issues and presented Abu Mazen with a detailed map outlining the borders of the Palestinian state, something no other Israeli prime minister had ever done. At that meeting, Abu Mazen said he had to think about it, and Olmert told him, "It's hard for me, too. Pick up the pen and sign." The two parted and decided that their advisers would meet the next day. Olmert summed it up as follows: "From that day, I never met with Abu Mazen. The map remained with me."[9]

BORDERLESS

Just as they are very reluctant to sign documents, our neighbors resist mark-ing any boundaries. The saying that "good fences make good neighbors," so popular in Israel, does not sit well with the Arabs. Israel is a sovereign state, but one that is also persecuted and attacked repeatedly, and to feel safe, it needs clearly defined fences. As a people whose collective memory is largely based on defense against assailants, we have developed an approach that unequivocally defines the territory. When we are still in first grade, we take care to draw a line in the middle of our desk so the pupil sitting next to us will know where the uncrossable boundary lies.

The Arab world, in contrast, largely views these fences as a limitation that impedes freedom of movement. At a dinner, I broached the subject to an Egyptian guest, who said, "You know what? I never thought about that, but when I go on a jeep trip in the dunes of western Egypt, I don't know where the border is, and my GPS is the only thing that shows I have crossed into Libya."

I did not conduct an academic study to find the reason for our neighbors' dislike of clear boundaries and our insistence on them. I assume that it originates in the Bedouin nomadic culture, in which the horizon was the only border, as well as in less distant times when movement in the Middle East from state to state was freer, even though not entirely without its dangers.

In any event, any time the subject came up in talks I had throughout the years with Arabs from different countries in the Middle East, I learned that the very mention of the word *border*, to say nothing of the establishment of a concrete, impassable border between states, is really repugnant to them.

In quite a few Arab states in the Middle East, the border dividing them is no more than two adjacent barriers on a road and two sentry booths next to them. There are no fences, no intrusion-tracking roads or any other obstacle. Syrian Bedouin shepherds cross the international border between Syria and Iraq every morning to let their herds graze in Iraqi pastures. The border between Syria and Lebanon is also invisible, to our regret. In fact, in the entire Middle East, only two states have constructed fences on their bor-ders—Israel and Saudi Arabia.

The former did so for obvious reasons, while the latter began to fence off its border in 2004 to prevent the entry of tribesmen from Yemen who crossed into Saudi Arabia to carry out looting raids. Two years later, fearing that the chaos in Iraq would spread to its territory and endanger the kingdom's stabil-ity, Saudi Arabia also built an 814-kilometer fence along its border with Iraq. But other than the Saudi fences and ours, the Middle East does not favor borders, fences, or walls—either physical or conceptual—and we would do well to remember this sensitivity when we come to the negotiating table, even if we do not have to take it into account in the end.

PEACE IS RELATIVE

Another problem that keeps cropping up in contacts between Israel and the Arab states is the way the parties perceive the agreements between them, even after they have been signed. Arabs tend to relate to the letter of the agreement and nothing further, but Israel tends to view agreements as far more than their content.

One example was the Israeli claim toward Egypt regarding the smuggling of ammunition by Hamas into the Gaza Strip through the Egyptian border. Israel was incapable of understanding how Egypt, a state that had signed a peace agreement with Israel and had declared that Egypt attributed great importance to maintaining proper relations with Israel, could at the same time allow a terror organization to smuggle through its territory weapons intended to harm Israel, its friend.

In Egypt's view, during Mubarak's time in office, however, turning a blind eye to the smuggling of arms into the Gaza Strip was not contradictory to the peace agreement Egypt had signed with Israel. From Egypt's point of view, not only is the state not obliged by the peace agreement to cooperate with Israel against the Palestinian effort to wage war, but in that instance the smuggling also served another of Egypt's interests—weakening Israel. It was only when the Mubarak government felt that the unguarded border between Sinai and the Gaza Strip was serving Egyptian Muslim extremists that it began to harden its stance and limit the tunnels, but never to the fullest extent possible. During Mohamed Morsi's time in office, the smuggling continued and was even supported; only at the beginning of 2014 did the Egyptian government begin to take steps to prevent smuggling into the Strip, under Abdel Fattah el-Sisi's instructions, first as defense minister and later as president. He did this in view of the problematic cooperation with Hamas that the Muslim Brotherhood enjoyed during the riots.

This Egyptian approach during Mubarak's time was, of course, perceived by Israel as an unacceptable violation, but it is typical of the multidimensional world of the Arab states—a perception according to which Egypt can sign a peace agreement with Israel and serve as the Arab driving force behind the Israeli-Palestinian peace process, while, at the same time, it has the right to torpedo moves to bring Israel closer to other Arab states, whether in the Gulf or in North Africa.

In Egypt's view, Egypt can cooperate with Israel in efforts to persuade the United States to provide foreign aid to Israel and to Egypt, but in the same breath also can object to Israel's participation in joint research projects of the European Union (EU). Egypt can comply with the peace treaty with Israel and also serve as Israel's main critic when calling for the reactor in Dimona to be opened to inspectors of the International Agency for Atomic Energy, since Israeli nuclear superiority is opposed to Egypt's interest. This remains el-Sisi's policy today. Egypt will cooperate with Israel in those areas in which Egypt has a real interest, and not for the sake of friendship or peaceful relations between the two countries.

On May 24, 2010, at a meeting of the Likud faction in the Knesset, Prime Minister Netanyahu clearly expressed the Israeli approach, when he stated that Palestinian participation in the proximity talks and, at the same time, its intensive activity to prevent Israel's acceptance into the Organisation for Economic Co-operation and Development (OECD, into which Israel was later accepted) reveals its insincerity in relation to any progress in the peace process.

In Netanyahu's opinion, the Palestinians ought to honor the momentum achieved in the talks and not attack Israel at the same time. He did not understand why, when his government was making considerable concessions, especially freezing construction in the settlements, as a condition for moving forward, the Palestinians were paying them back by opposing Israel's membership in the OECD.

However, from his own point of view, Abu Mazen's approach is also justified. If we in Israel are conducting peace talks, they become the be-all-and-end-all. We no longer attack, and claims against the other side—in security, economic, and social areas—are not heard. All of this is done in order to maintain the positive momentum. Even when the other side violates agreements, we "swallow" the violations and do not react harshly. The Palestinians, on the other hand, can hold proximity talks, but if it is in their interest to block our acceptance into the OECD in order to weaken us, they will simultaneously try to do so.

The Palestinians will talk to us and in the same breath will ask Arab states to submit proposals denouncing us to the United Nations, will launch a campaign to boycott goods from the settlements in order to further delegitimize them, and will continue to employ all possible means of pressure as if there were no negotiations. As far as they are concerned, there is no connection between these things, because of that multidimensional approach so deeply rooted in their culture.

In 2011, Jordan could also maintain far-ranging diplomatic and strategic links with us in a state of peace, but that did not prevent King Abdullah from attacking Israeli policy in interviews for the international press, when he wanted to situate himself and Jordan as important players in the Middle East.

Although it is hard for Israel to accept this approach, we need to understand it arises from a foundation on which the policy of the peoples of the region is based. It is not something personal against us, and we have to learn to live with this basic condition, to cope with it, and to maneuver around it in order to achieve Israel's most important national interests.

Arab states conduct a multifaceted diplomacy, replete with contradiction. The Middle East never existed in shades of black and white, and we cannot expect the other side to behave like us. We have to become effective players, not naive or one-dimensional, in the regional and international diplomatic game. Nonetheless, we have to stop overlooking the violation of agreements by the negotiating partner out of our desire to maintain a positive momentum. The other side has never done so and probably never will.

SHOOT OR EMBRACE

Israel is a multifaceted, multilingual country, with an ancient, rich, and color-ful culture. But when we deal with an outside element, and certainly one with which we are in a conflict or controversy, our cultural wealth fades into dichromatic black and white. We either love our opposite number or hate him. We shoot at him or embrace him. Israelis also know how to resolutely change their position to the other extreme as soon as the situation changes and a new reality is created. That may be cognitive flexibility, or perhaps it is naiveté that stems from our fierce desire to achieve peace. African heads of state were depicted in Israel as enlightened, outstanding leaders so long as they maintained diplomatic relations with Israel, but as soon as they severed those relations, those same leaders became wild cannibals. I have no doubt, for example, that on the day we sign, *inshallah*, a peace agreement with Syria, after the situation there is secure and a stable government is in power, we will regard that country overnight not as a bitter enemy but as our dearest friend.

But I am afraid that will not be the situation on the other side of the fence. For the Syrians, as for most of the residents and leaders of Arab states, no political agreement has the force to erase the scars of the past. The Syrian people will have a hard time removing all traces of the years-long hostility toward Israel from their national consciousness. That is how it was with Egypt.

Immediately after the peace treaty with Egypt was signed in 1979—and actually with Sadat's visit to Israel in 1977—most Israelis managed to set aside their strong feelings of hostility toward Egypt. At one stroke, we forgot the horror stories of the Israeli prisoners of war who returned from the Egyptian prisons. We forgot the appalling incidents of the Egyptian civilians who fell upon Israeli pilots as soon as they touched the ground after their planes were shot down, lynched them, and then inhumanely mutilated their bodies. We forgot and hurried to tour the pyramids.

One visit to Israel and a ceremony on the White House lawn was all we required to replace our sense of loathing with feelings of affection, with songs of peace and endless efforts to promote relations with the leading Arab country.

I confess that I was also swept up at the time with a sense of optimism, not only because that was the worldview I was brought up on but also because I understood that in the Middle East—one of the most politically complex and unstable regions in the world—everything is possible. Nonetheless, as a native-born Egyptian, I had no doubt that the feeling that the Israeli public's elation did not reflect the situation on the other side.

Still, the encounter with the reality was painful and discouraging. I cannot forget how in the summer of 1980—before the ink had dried on the document signed by Anwar Sadat, Menachem Begin, and Jimmy Carter—I found my mother terribly upset and offended. A group of my parents' friends, who had also been born in Egypt, had just returned from a trip searching for their Egyptian roots, one of the first of such excursions to take place. Their local guide took them on a tour to the quarter where Cairo's celebrities lived. When they came to the home of the well-known actor Farid Shawki, everyone on the bus became very excited.

For the average Israeli, that name does not mean much, but for those who regularly watched the Friday afternoon Egyptian movies on Israeli television, Shawki was their idol. In Egyptian films of the 1970s, he was the ultimate actor. He would occasionally exchange blows with ten men at the same time, and his typical tactic in those fights was a fierce butt of his head (*rasiaah*). When he grew older, his cinematic image changed from that of a reckless youth to a wise, responsible family man. Every father in Egypt wanted to be like him, every Egyptian mother wanted to have a husband like him, and every naughty Egyptian boy thanked the Lord each morning that his biological father did not at all resemble the character portrayed by Farid Shawki in the movies.

For those same Israeli-Egyptian travelers, Shawki was an admired figure, whether they left Egypt in 1948 with the establishment of the State of Israel or in 1954–1956 after the Young Officers revolution, or at any other time. When the Egyptian guide said he would try to arrange a photograph with the famous actor, emotions on the bus ran high. At once, everyone moved to the right side of the bus, watching closely as the guide walked slowly to the front door of Farid Shawki's home, and even saw their idol open the gate after a few rings of the bell. They heard their guide make his request, and then they saw Shawki looking with contempt at the bus and heard him say unhesitatingly, "I am not interested in having my picture taken with Israelis."

My mother was not present at the time and just described to me what she had heard from her friends. But her volatile reaction reflected the feelings of humiliation and bitter disappointment of the members of that Israeli group.

Disappointments of that sort, produced by the displays of hostility and hatred encountered by Israeli visitors to Egypt, became daily occurrences. I am not sure what is more natural: the Israelis' disappointment at the enemy's adamant refusal to become a lover overnight, or the repugnance of the Egyptians, certainly of the most famous among them, at the bear hug of the Israeli hurry to reconcile all differences.

Some would say that it was a nasty way to behave, if not outright anti-Semitic, but it is important to understand that in the case of Shawki, as in other instances, outer appearances do not necessarily reflect personal attitudes. In Egypt and in the entire Arab world, Shawki is perceived as a national symbol. Direct contact with Israelis is apt to tarnish that image and cause him irrevocable financial damage. It will take many years, probably decades, to change the mood in the street, and Arab celebrities will change their approach only after their fans do, not before.

The gap between the Israelis' overzealous urge to "wipe" hummus with pita bread and eat fava beans in Cairo and the Egyptians' wariness and resentment toward the invaders from the north armed with cameras has provided endless opportunities for misunderstandings.

During the first year of my brother Rafi's service at the Israeli embassy in Egypt, a friend of the family, also a civil servant, visited him. On his first day in Cairo, he asked Rafi to help him locate the house where his wife was born and grew up. He wanted to have his photograph taken there to surprise her. My brother, who had already spent several months in Egypt, explained to his acquaintance that it was highly probable that the present residents in the house would not welcome his visit. The man insisted, and my brother finally gave in.

The next day, the two traveled to the house, located in the exclusive quarter of Heliopolis. My brother, who had learned firsthand the local sentiment toward Israel, exited the car but left the keys in the ignition and the motor running. After he rang the bell, the door opened and the two Israelis were met by a tall, corpulent Egyptian wearing a white, wide *galabeya*.

"*Efendem?*" (How can I help you?) the man asked. In fluent Arabic with an Egyptian dialect, my brother explained to the Egyptian who they were and the object of their visit. The man listened patiently and then responded, "Wait here for a moment, please."

The door closed and the two Israelis remained standing there. My brother, who was uneasy, looked through the peephole. He will never forget what he saw. While the two of them thought the Egyptian had gone to check out something with another resident in the building, the man had gone over to a large cabinet in the living room from which he removed a long two-barreled shotgun. That was all my brother had to see. While running away, the two had a glimpse of the Egyptian waving the rifle at them, yelling at the top of his lungs, "*Ya Welad, el-Kalb 'awzeen tistawlu 'ala beyti?*" (You sons of dogs, you want to take over my house?)

* * *

One of the major exponents of the optimistic mood that pervaded the Israeli public in the years after the signing of the peace treaty with Egypt was Ezer Weizman, in later years the seventh president of the State of Israel. On more than one occasion, he said that the day when Israelis can drive to Damascus and eat hummus there will be the happiest day of his life.

When I once asked a Palestinian acquaintance how the Arab world regards a statement of that kind, he replied, "For you Israelis, hummus is the ultimate symbol of peace, but I don't see Jordanians traveling to Damascus to eat hummus, or Egyptians traveling to Sudan or Libya to eat hummus, although there are peaceful relations between those countries. You Israelis have a romantic view of life, but I suggest that you sober up. After you sign a peace treaty with Syria, it will take years until you can eat hummus in each other's country. With the Egyptian people, the most forgiving of all Arab nations, it will still take a long time." For us Israelis, it is easy to forget and change gears completely, but, as I pointed out, it's not like that in the Arab world.

HASTE IS FROM THE DEVIL

In the study of cultures, two opposing methods of perceiving time have been identified. One is a monochromic view of time, prevalent among individualistic cultures, such as those in the West. It attributes a great deal of importance to the element of time. These cultures end one action before beginning another. In the polychromic perception of time, characteristic of collective cultures, meeting time schedules is of far less importance, and several actions can be carried out simultaneously.

The difference between these two perceptions is visible in any negotiation, whether political, commercial, or personal. Israel is at the center of the axis between these two perceptions. Unlike Americans, for example, we do not tend to be strict about sticking to schedules, and sometimes we get to the date we have chosen as the time for ending a process and decide to postpone it. But generally we are in a hurry, and tend to think that the faster we act, the better.

But for Arabs, in contrast to Israelis, patience and unhurried deliberation are the healthy, correct way of thinking and behaving. They perceive the limitation of a process in time as an error that can result in hasty, rash decisions. The saying that represents this perception is a byword throughout the Middle East: *Al 'Ajalah min al-Shaytan* (haste is from the devil).

In August 2008, shortly after I founded the Smart Middle East Forum, I met with my colleagues to write the basic principles of the Forum. One of the sections in the document dealt with the cultural differences between us and the Arabs, particularly when carrying out regional projects. At a certain stage, I asked my friends, "How would you interpret and analyze a declaration by an Israeli prime minister about a political plan to implement a peace agreement with Syria in phases over a thirty-year period?"

All those present, without any exception, said that the plan would be an attempt by the prime minister to delay the implementation forever and actually a ruse, so that he can find a pretext in the future to back down from the agreement.

Then I asked them, "And how would you react if the prime minister declared that the peace agreement with Syria would be implemented within a year or two?" Everyone agreed that would indicate that the prime minister seriously intended to achieve true peace with Syria.

When I posed these two questions to several Arab friends, their replies did not surprise me. An agreement implemented in a year or two was perceived by them as hasty and erroneous. One implemented over thirty years, on the other hand, seemed to be serious, real, and wise.

A few days before the direct talks between Israel and the Palestinians began, on September 2, 2010, I could not help smiling when I read a quote from an unidentified source in Washington who told an Israeli, "Sign an agreement and implement it within ten years." Maybe someone there had finally found a way that could be acceptable to both sides.

In Arab culture, a one-hundred-year-long struggle cannot end overnight and the enemy cannot become a loved one at once. Such a change is possible, if at all, only within the Arab family. More than once, we witnessed a sudden improvement in the relations between two Arab states, whose leaders had been hurling curses at one another for months or years, and abruptly concluded they had to end the animosity. Those two heads of states would meet, hug and kiss each other in public, and their spokesmen solemnly explain that these are two sister states, that the conflict began from an unfortunate misunderstanding, and that other countries had gone out of their way to foment the quarrel between them.

There, too, however, if we dig a little deeper, we will find a layer of hostility that refuses to go away, since forgetting is not the strong point of the Arab people. Israel is not a member of the family, so any change toward the country will always be slower, and never, heaven forbid, hasty.

OLD IS GOOD; NEW IS BAD

Israeli society sanctifies the new. For the people in Israel, who built their state in sixty-six years, every new project, every new city, every new settlement is a reason to celebrate. Israelis value new and innovative ideas and even see them as a sign of cultural superiority, while they view anything that is constant and not up-to-date as a regression.

The other side does not necessarily share this approach. "I do not like our policy or the way our administration acts," a Qatari senior official once told me candidly when I was head of the Israeli delegation in Qatar. "One day we are on the side of Iran, and the next, we're on the American side. One day we announce a national project, and the next, a different one. Today the Qatari government is ruled by people who are too young. They run our country impetuously, immaturely, and unwisely. Look at what is happening in Saudi Arabia. No one is appointed as a minister if he is under the age of sixty-five or seventy, and only after he has proven that he is experienced, is not rash or reckless in his thinking and behavior."

In the view of that Qatari, the Saudi government's mature, slow-moving, unchanging conduct was immensely preferable to the speed and innovation that characterized Qatari policy at the end of the twentieth century. In his eyes, deliberation and constancy attest to wisdom, good sense, and discretion.

That was not the first time I had come across these differences in approach. In winter 1992, when I was a cadet in the foreign ministry, my eye was caught by editorial attacks in the Arab press against the Israeli most closely identified with the peace process—the then foreign minister, Shimon Peres.

The attacks focused on the concept that Peres was then vigorously promoting "a new Middle East." This was written in an editorial in the Egyptian *Al-Ahram*: "The Israeli Foreign Minister is already building a 'new Middle East.' Israel has been in this region about fifty years, and she already knows what is good for us, the Arabs. We, who have 7,000 years of Pharaonic civilization in Egypt and 5,000 years of Sumerian civilization in Iraq, do not need his advice regarding our economy or the education of our children. He, Peres, wants to destroy everything and build a new Middle East here in the image of Israel and to turn the territorial conquest into an economic and cultural conquest."[10]

I could not comprehend that hostile attitude. How could the writer of the editorial have attributed such negative intentions to a worldview that says "let us build here a better place for our children"? But it is understandable when you examine the attitude of Arab culture to tradition. In the Arab world, young generations are educated on the importance of the heritage and glorious past of their countries. The future is of merely secondary importance, and is generally left to the grace of God, while the present is not important at all. Consequently, the great challenge facing Arab leadership when implementing a significant change is to try to present it as a natural continuation and to conceal its innovativeness as far as possible.

A distinct example of this approach occurred in 1970, the last year in the life of the former Egyptian president, Gamal Abdel Nasser. Nasser, who from every possible stage called for the annihilation of Israel and the refusal to enter any negotiations for peace with the country, always tended to go with the Soviet camp and reject the U.S. peace initiatives as illegitimate. Suddenly in July 1970, he decided to change direction and to accept the second Rogers plan—a U.S.-backed plan to end the conflict with Israel on the basis of the return of territory.

On July 18, when Nasser informed the heads of his party of his decision, they asked how he thought the public would react. Nasser reassured them and said that soon an article would be published in the Egyptian press explaining to the Egyptian people that there was nothing new in the Rogers plan.[11] Several days later, after Nasser announced his acceptance of the second Rogers plan, his close associate, Mohamed Hassanein Heikal, published an article justifying the decision and explaining that acceptance of the initiative was not a new move.[12] As far as Nasser was concerned, as long as Egyptian public opinion was persuaded that no change in policy was involved, but rather a continuation of the tradition, he would have no problem.

We should learn this lesson before announcing new, revolutionary initiatives and placing our negotiating partner in a truly distressing situation. I discuss this topic at length in the third chapter, "A Demon Called Normalization."

CONCEDING GRACIOUSLY

Every language contains the value system, perceptions, approaches, and modes of behavior of its speakers. Modern Hebrew, unlike Arabic and English, is characterized primarily by its tendency toward directness. Israelis love to get straight to the point and say whatever is on their mind.

Israelis like to speak *dugri* (talk straight), a word derived from Arabic. This enables them, among other things, to maximally exploit time and advance toward the next objective, since there is a lot to be done and time is short. This tendency, however, is often perceived by the foreign listener—be he American, European, or Arab—as bluntness, vulgarity, or even as "social trespassing," which is liable to bring the conversation to an abrupt end (the very opposite of what Israelis want to achieve with this approach).

In Arab culture, the tendency is just the opposite: to be roundabout, to be obscure, to use etiquette and honorifics—whether out of fear of offending the other party's feelings or to try to gain time and avoid making commitments. The Arabic language, a very rich one, serves this purpose very well. Arabic speakers devote much thought to every expression, statement, or declaration that they utter.

The attitude toward the verbal skills of the speaker also differs in the two cultures. In Israeli eyes, a man who uses lengthy sentences and flowery language is regarded as rather weird. Abba Eban, for example, was unfortunately perceived as foreign to Israeli society because of his elegant language. In Arab culture, in contrast, a person who speaks an elevated, educated language is esteemed. One outstanding example is that of Hussein, the late king of Jordan, who delivered speeches to his people in such high-flown Arabic that many of his listeners clearly did not understand, and yet they all appreciated the erudition reflected in his speech.

Moreover, Israeli leaders are not in the habit of publicly praising leaders of foreign countries, certainly not those of Arab states. If you ask an Israeli leader why he does not openly commend a friendly country in the region, he will probably reply, "We speak with them frankly in our talks and they know exactly what we think about them," or "After all, the nature of our relations is clear to everyone and there's no need to speak about that." Arab leaders, on the other hand, have often, in their rich language, extended compliments to one Israeli leader or another.

A few years ago, I asked an Israeli who was about to be appointed as a minister why he does not publicly compliment Egypt or Jordan as a means of tightening ties between the states. He was astonished by my question and replied, "You're mad. Do you want people to think I'm a leftist?" I asked how saying something nice to the Jordanians about their level of education, quality of environment, or economy was likely to make him a member of Peace Now in the eyes of the Israeli public.

"You may understand that," he said, "but the Israeli public doesn't."

I have to admit that is not an unusual attitude in Israel. Many others have answered that question in the same spirit. Israelis regard graciously conceding anything to another person as fawning and a sign of weakness. In January 2000, just before the direct negotiations with Syria, Prime Minister Ehud Barak said that Hafez al-Assad is a "strong, serious and reliable leader,"[13] and he was sharply attacked for that. That was not how his words were received in Arab society. Consequently, I believe Israeli leaders would do well to be more gracious to our neighbors in their speeches and lectures (and that does not mean we should not criticize them whenever necessary).

In the region we live in, much can be gained by gracious, forbearing behavior. The various Arab countries publicly express all of their positions on a regular basis. Our blaring silence is in many instances perceived as weakness and in others as pretentiousness and condescension.

As a result of nuances in style, even when an Israeli leader decides to relate publicly to an Arab country or leader, he errs and ends up cursing instead of blessing. In mid-2008, rumors spread that the president of Egypt was fatally ill and that his son Gamal was going to succeed him (then no one imagined that Mubarak would be ousted during his lifetime in 2011). It was clear to everyone that Mubarak was indeed ill, but nothing was known about his exact condition. At a government meeting held after these rumors reached Israel, Prime Minister Ehud Olmert said, "I want to send from here, from

Jerusalem, to the president of Egypt, in my name, the name of the government and people of Israel, wishes for a complete recovery and a speedy return to the best of health."

No one denies that Olmert was one of the warmest, most sensitive prime ministers Israel ever had. He was also a professional politician, with whom I had the privilege of working during his visit to Hong Kong. I also do not doubt that he wanted to wish a speedy recovery to a friend and important ally. But when I heard the wording of the message on the noon news on Kol Israel, I smiled sadly. "Do you remember that?" I asked Israel Maimon, the Cabinet secretary at the time. "Do I remember? Of course I do. I was sitting next to him when he said it."

I knew that the prime minister was sure he had done the right thing. The overwhelming majority of Israelis would have agreed, as well as most Americans and Europeans, if his words had been translated into their languages. But in Arabic, they sounded totally different. It is not polite to wish the president of a neighboring state a recovery and, by doing so, to confirm the fact of his illness, which had been officially denied.

If Olmert had wanted to win the hearts of the Egyptian populace as well as Mubarak's, he should have made a statement along these lines:

"I have been asked about the state of President Mubarak's health. I think there are too many rumors in the air, and I want to say to you that President Mubarak is eighty years old and plays squash for an hour each day, while I, who am sixty and run about six kilometers a day, am incapable of playing squash even one hour a week. I think that Mubarak is in good health, and I look forward to talking to him in the coming days."

When I read this wording to Israelis, they thought it was funny and strange. They said it did not sound diplomatic, that it was ingratiating and made the speaker look ridiculous.

In contrast, an Egyptian businessman whom I met in Tel Aviv reacted at once with enthusiasm: "Wow, hearing a message like that, all of Egypt would have applauded Olmert."

Unquestionably, our miserly reluctance to make public gestures, our suspicious attitude toward the gracious behavior of others, and our adamant disregard for the centuries-old etiquette and social formalities practiced in the region we live in are likely to make us fail every sociometric test in the Middle East.

* * *

Since Israel's appearance as a state on the map of the Middle East, over sixty years ago, the country has experienced many ups and downs in its relations with the nations of the region. Until the peace treaty with Egypt in 1977, Israel was totally isolated, ostracized by all the Arab states. During this period, Israel developed the patterns of behavior of a tough, independent power that, on its own, shapes the reality in which it lives. Israel is a nation that adopted the axiom "It doesn't matter what the gentiles say, what counts is what the Jews do," and it certainly was not especially impressed by the flowery phrases, threats, and propaganda of its Arab neighbors.

In 1977, the rules of the game changed. Israel was invited—although not necessarily with open arms and certainly not by all the players—to join the circle of those talking to one another. Since the start of the contacts with Egypt, significant developments took place in our relations with the Arab states, but in general Israel continues to behave in isolation from events in the region. Instead of taking the trouble to learn the language and customs of the region, we insist all too often on acting erroneously, misinterpreting the intention of the other side and being misinterpreted by it.

The height of this dialogue of the deaf was, in my view, in the failure of the Camp David conference, where Arafat rejected Israel's most generous offer when he was pressured to give an immediate, unequivocal answer, but did not believe the Israeli ultimatum was genuine. This opened the door to the second Intifada and another decade of conflict and bloodshed.

I heard Shlomo Ben Ami give vent to his frustration with Arafat on a flight to the secret meeting in Paris. He said, "Arafat is a mirror image of the Palestinian street, not a leader. A leader influences the people and makes them follow him, while Arafat checks out the street and acts accordingly."

I thought highly of Ben Ami as foreign minister, and I will never forget how he personally contacted the various emissaries in the Arab countries and took an interest in their well-being during the second Intifada, a time of serious security problems. Neither before nor after his term in office was that the usual practice. He also knew how to work in coordination with the employees of the ministry in the home office and in the delegations, and showed his concern for his employees. But I believe Ben Ami was rash in his scornful assessment of Arafat and his view of what makes a leader.

Despite all the justified criticism of the Palestinian *rais*—often bordering on hatred, which is also justified—it is impossible to accuse him of not understanding his public. After all, Ben Ami's term in the foreign ministry and Barak's in the prime minister's office were very brief, while Arafat managed to remain head of his movement and his people for dozens of years, until his death, and even afterward was regarded there as a hero. So he was, in fact, a leader—a cynical leader, no question about that, but still a leader.

That fact also needs to be taken into account when coming to negotiate or to grapple with a partner like him.

Despite everything that has been written about the Camp David conference, it is still difficult to estimate the part that the human factor played in the failure of the talks and other negotiations held before and after Camp David. I only want to point out that a common basis for a dialogue is a precondition for progress (although not necessarily a sufficient one). A lack of chemistry can lead to a lack of trust, which in turn can block any real attempt to negotiate.

The following are seven points that briefly sum up the important conditions for a productive and effective dialogue between us and the Arab peoples:

1. Every peace agreement between Israel and an Arab state should be regarded as a meeting of common interests, and in no case as a blending of interests.

2. In our neighboring states, there is no such thing as a cognitive totality that dictates a one-dimensional policy. They can hug and quarrel, cooperate and contend at one and the same time, while we either love or hate, shoot or hug. Even after signing a peace agreement, the other side will not hesitate to act against us (within the limitations of the formal agreement) if that serves his interests. We, on the other hand, tend to sacrifice important interests for the sake of "maintaining the momentum."

3. In the Middle East, haste is from the devil. Speed is perceived as ineffective and even dangerous. A long process based on many stops along the way to check the situation, on orderly thinking, and on natural progress is the only kind that will gain approval. As a matter of fact, processes in the Middle East never "end." Instead, they gradually fade, or lose their importance over the years, but no one determines the time of their death.

4. Arab leaders will avoid making public statements that will be held against them in the future. Anything said in public is binding, but from their perspective what is said behind closed doors is less binding.

5. Israel's failure to publicly react to certain issues, like monks who have taken a vow of silence, is viewed in the best case as a foolish mistake on Israel's part in forgoing its right to express its opinion. In the worst case, it is regarded as arrogant disregard for the issue and Israel's neighbors.

6. The Arabs perceive reality as open to change. History has proven that the greatest powers that ruled large parts of the region from the seventh century came and conquered but eventually left. Hence no "facts on the ground" are seen as irreversible.

7. "After all, it is clear to them." No, it is not clear! What is clear to us is not necessarily clear to them. The Arab side carries out agreements to the letter and has no intention of meeting us halfway on matters not written in agreements, unless it serves their own interests.

* * *

If we recognize the sensitivities of the other side, understand his fear of rapid changes, of clear borders, and of a "too close" proximity, and if we note his tendencies to act demonstratively in front of his public, that does not mean we accept all of his positions and accede to all of his demands. We can take account of some of these sensitivities in order to build confidence; some we can use as leverage to improve our situation in the negotiations, while in regard to others, we need not blink. But if we learn the language of the region, instead of waiting for it to learn ours, we can advance our important aims much more effectively and prevent useless bloodshed resulting from misunderstanding.

We do not live alone in this region. We are not big enough or strong enough to impose our worldview. It is not smart to behave with arrogance that leads to failures, and to repeat that behavior time after time and to keep failing. Life teaches us that habit produces confidence, even if that habit is bad and harmful, and we have to stop, check, and change when necessary.

"It is impossible to solve a problem by using the same kind of thinking we used when we created it," Albert Einstein once said.[14] Two opposite world-views—based on ancient cultural foundations—do not enable us to hold a fruitful dialogue with our neighbors. Such a dialogue is possible only when the sides have learned the way of the other. An excellent example of a leader who did that is Hussein, the late king of Jordan, who had a good knowledge of the Israeli mentality and knew how to navigate between our leaders, and who arrived at a productive dialogue with them despite the crises and difficulties that confronted the relationship between the two countries. We need someone like Hussein on our side.

Chapter Two

Unilateral Steps

When Israel withdraws unilaterally from Lebanon and Gaza, Israelis believe the country is demonstrating strength. That is strange, because the entire Arab world calls it weakness.

On May 24, 2000, after an eighteen-year-long presence in Lebanon, the Israel Defense Forces (IDF) withdrew from the land of cedars, by order of Prime Minister Ehud Barak. It was a lightning operation. The name it was assigned—Forbearance—seemed rather cynical to me, given the way in which it was carried out. It was the first time Israel gave in to an ultimatum she had imposed on herself: on the eve of the 1999 elections, while negotiating with Syria, Ehud Barak, chairman of the Labor Party and its candidate for the prime ministership, promised the Israeli public that he would pull the IDF out of the security zone within a year, with or without an agreement. In the meantime, the negotiations with Syria failed, and the date drew nearer. Barak's decision to withdraw from Lebanon unilaterally, before Israel could get the international community and the moderate Arab states on board so they would guarantee its success, was one of the hastiest, most ill-fated decisions Israel has made since its establishment, but definitely not the last. Many Israelis, including myself, wanted a withdrawal, but the way it was done was detrimental. We feel the shock waves from it to this very day.

The decision to pull out was imposed on the defense establishment. Senior officials vigorously opposed the unilateral withdrawal of the IDF, in the absence of any guarantees or understandings regarding the sovereignty in south Lebanon, or any political arrangement with the Syrians. The greatest fear of the Intelligence Corps and other intelligence and evaluation groups was that, in the event of a withdrawal without any arrangement on the ground, Hezbollah would grab control of the evacuated areas and carry out attacks against the Israeli settlements along the border. Some warned that it would surely lead to a war with Syria, but Barak insisted on keeping his promise and carrying out his decision no matter what the cost. At first, it seemed that the prophecies of doom were exaggerated, but it quickly turned out that all the fears were justified, all the dire warnings had come true, and the situation grew even worse than predicted. The change was not in the form of daily attacks, but in a strategic equation on Israel's northern border. Hezbollah took over southern Lebanon, proclaimed itself the victor, received legitimation from the Arab world, and was massively supported by Iran. In January 2011, a new Lebanese government was sworn in, in Hassan Nasrallah's spirit and under his influence.

The unilateral withdrawal from Lebanon became a strategic move that changed the face of the region and redefined the balance of power in it to one totally different from what we had known until then, and not in our favor. Our worst, most extreme enemy—whether Hezbollah in Lebanon, the Palestinian rejectionist organizations (Hamas and Islamic Jihad), or hostile states such as Syria and Iran—received a gift from heaven.

The tragedy here is that Barak really was right, at least in principle. Israel definitely had to get out of Lebanon, but the way Barak chose—a unilateral and hasty retreat—that made the IDF look as if it were fleeing in fear, abandoning those who had been our allies in Lebanon from the end of the 1970s, the soldiers of the Southern Lebanon Army and their families, still resonates in the Middle East.

Because Ehud Barak and other Israeli leaders were shortsighted, they tried to solve complex regional problems with military tactics. Barak was "locked" into the final outcome—withdrawal from Lebanon—and ascribed no importance to the way it was done. In all his public statements, even before his election as prime minister, he spoke solely of the result, not one word about the process, which, as far as he was concerned, was a marginal, logistic problem that could be solved as in a commando operation—a speedy action in the dead of night—and maybe no one would notice. But the Middle East noticed, and how.

The State of Israel, which has many achievements in new developments and inventions in technology, medicine, and agriculture, introduced to the Middle East a new method of action in political science: "unilateral steps."

What is involved here is not a military surprise attack or a declaration of war, but unilateral withdrawals in which Israel relinquishes assets in its possession for various reasons (mainly internal political reasons), and at the same time tries to persuade itself that in taking such steps—without any coordination or significant protection of its interests after completion of the withdrawal—the country is demonstrating power. After the United States became bogged down in Vietnam, it was said that Henry Kissinger suggested to President Nixon, "Let's say we won and run."[1] In the Middle East, that kind of thinking is not only naïve but also arrogant; nor do we really have any place to run to since the enemy is on our border and not thousands of kilometers away.

A striking element in Barak's call to get out of Lebanon was its resemblance to the words uttered by Yitzhak Rabin six years earlier: "to take Gaza out of Bat Yam."[2] And after all, during his campaign, Barak presented himself as Rabin's heir, following in his footsteps.

I do not underestimate the significant thought process of the different organizations in the defense establishment, particularly in the IDF's research and strategy system, where the leading idea was that an Israeli withdrawal from south Lebanon would pull the ground out from under the feet of the Hezbollah, forcing it to put down its weapons and abandon its terror activities, since it would lose the legitimacy to fight an enemy that does not exist. I have several arguments in this regard, but I will merely refer readers to the first chapter of this book, where I describe the ability to adapt to the existing situation that characterizes the culture in this region. Utilizing this ability, Hezbollah succeeded, despite the withdrawal, to keep its weapons and the enemy it so badly needs, as well as to gain a foothold in Lebanese politics and, in recent years, to control Lebanese politics as well.

IN THE DEAD OF THE NIGHT, UNDER FIRE FROM HEZBOLLAH

The Israeli withdrawal from Lebanon caught me completely by surprise, as it did the overwhelming majority of Israeli citizens. At the time, I was head of the Israeli delegation in Qatar. In the nine months that had passed since I began that post, I had, to my satisfaction, managed to establish good contacts with people in high positions in the emirates and with key figures in the tribal fabric of Qatari society. On May 24, at 6:00 a.m., a colleague, a U.S. diplomat also serving in Qatar, called me, and, without wasting any words, simply said, "Turn on Al-Jazeera." I did. I will never forget the sights and voices I saw and heard on the screen that morning.

The screen was split into two halves. One showed an IDF armor column leaving through the border point with Lebanon and entering Israel; the other half, a vast traffic jam of vehicles.

"The soldiers of the South Lebanon Army [SLA] are running for their lives, begging to be allowed into Israel," the network's correspondents, their voices choked with tears and emotion, reported on the withdrawal—or (in a more faithful translation of the original) the flight of the Zionist army from the resistance forces of Hezbollah, on the day of the greatest victory of the Arab world in the modern age.

Then there was another phone call, this time from the security officer of the delegation, Nissim Palomo, to update me on the developments and to ask when I wanted to get to the office. I said very soon, because according to the set procedure, I had to check out the reactions to a significant event of this kind in the country where I was serving.

In the months that passed since Barak's government had taken office, it was clear to everyone that the Israeli government was serious about its intent to withdraw from southern Lebanon, and it was certainly clear to me and to all employees of the foreign ministry who read the cables on the subject. Nonetheless, it came as a complete surprise. It never occurred to me, not even for a moment, that the withdrawal would be carried out like that: in the dead of night, without an agreement, without guarantees, abandoning the area to Hezbollah, and destroying Israel's deterrent force, which is based on a history of military victories.

In those hours, the hardest of my life, I was torn. I was glad our soldiers were out of Lebanon, and my heart went out to the men of the SLA, people I had fought alongside during my service in Lebanon, and who now were forced to flee in such a humiliating and thankless manner. Reading the subtitles in English and Arabic that appeared with growing frequency on all the networks—stating that Israel was preventing SLA men from entering its territory—I was flooded with anger and shame. I could not bear to see them converging with their families and belongings at the border crossing and begging the Israelis to let them in, as they fled for their lives from the men of Hezbollah and the Lebanese supporters of the organization, who wanted to lynch them. The bitter memory of those pictures surfaced again later, each time I heard Yossi Beilin define the men of the SLA as a moral hump on Israel's back.

Having served in intelligence units and handled agents in the Arab world, I felt my stomach churn with a sense of betrayal as I watched those people who had totally believed, just as I had, that at the moment of truth the State of Israel would remember them and their families and provide them with all the necessary help. Anyone engaged in handling sources and agents knows there is no more important value in this complex, fickle game than the trust the two sides place in each other. As I watched the column of cars of SLA men near the border fence, I saw how, with a single blow, Israel's human intelligence system ("Humint," in professional jargon) was fatally damaged in the Arab world in general and in Lebanon in particular.

Every first-year student of Middle East studies learns about an Arab's cycles of loyalty. He is committed first and foremost to his family, then to his tribe, and afterward to his people and, finally, to his co-religionists. The members of the SLA, who introduced us into their cycle of loyalty, were kicked out of ours as soon as they became a burden. You might say that, eleven years later, the United States did the same when it turned away from its friend in the Middle East, Hosni Mubarak, and went even further when it publicly humiliated him time after time, until the continual public pressure defeated him and caused him to step down. It was an act of betrayal that the United States naively thought would gain the appreciation of the leaders of the demonstrators at Tahrir Square. But I was not surprised that, when Hillary Clinton arrived in Egypt on March 16, 2011, those leaders refused to meet with her. I will discuss that later. But the Saudis and the other Arab countries that were regarded as friends of the United States arrived at this enlightened conclusion from its behavior. And the outcome is the unreserved support of Saudi Arabia, Kuwait, and Abu Dhabi for Egypt and Abdel Fattah el-Sisi, including the payment of aid funds in place of the United States.

On the morning of the withdrawal from Lebanon, my brain, eyes, and ears concentrated on the reports that began streaming into the foreign ministry, and from there to all the Israeli delegations in the world. Although the Western governments supported Israel's withdrawal, I knew then, and certainly know even more today, that the way the withdrawal was carried out was disastrous for the State of Israel. It shuffled the cards in our region and changed the perception that Israel is an undefeatable country.

The reactions of the moderate Arab governments, with which we maintained a dialogue, show that not a single one of them doubted that Israel had been driven back and had not withdrawn from a position of power. The hasty, overnight withdrawal, under Hezbollah's fire, was seen by the Arab world as a real flight. Even more important: for the first time since its establishment, the State of Israel was viewed by the Arab world as a country that withdraws from a territory it conquered without having a preliminary agreement to protect itself and its interests. This rushed withdrawal taught the Arab world in general, and the terrorist organizations in particular, that by pressure and attrition it can push the IDF back and even defeat it.

This immediate impression seriously damaged Israel's standing in the negotiations with the Palestinians. While the Palestinian public watched with frustration and insult how its leadership failed, time and again, in its attempts to gain achievements through negotiations, Hezbollah showed them how on one fine day, as the result of a lengthy, consistent, and violent struggle, it was forcing Israel to withdraw unconditionally from Lebanon. The message was loud and clear. Overnight, key figures in the Palestinian leadership and the Palestinian Authority, as well as journalists identified with the Palestine Liberation Organization (PLO), were openly calling for adoption of Hezbollah's mode of action.

"The Lebanese have given the entire world an example of how to stand firm and have taught everyone the strategy of blow after blow until the enemy succumbs."[3] In an article published shortly after the withdrawal in *Al-Ayyam*, the Palestinian daily published in Ramallah, with the second largest circulation in the Palestinian Authority, the then Palestinian minister of finance, Muhammad Zuhdi al-Nashashibi, wrote, "What happened in Lebanon is a lesson for anyone who wants to win in Palestine."[4]

"This victory has restored our hope that we can liberate our land by force," Dawood al Shirian, a columnist for *Al-Hayat*[5] (a newspaper published in London and regarded as the leading international Arabic paper), wrote the day after the withdrawal. He went on: "It is an important lesson for the Palestinian resistance . . . there is no point in going into the history of the struggle, but we need to be convinced that Israel understands only force, even if that means only a kid throwing a stone in the street. The Palestinian Authority should know that the Lebanese government's support for the resistance was an important element in its victory. Will the Authority internalize that lesson?"[6]

Not everyone was equally anxious for battle, but even the moderates in the Palestinian camp—our potential partners in the complex, sisyphean peace process—read the map exactly the same way and understood the implications of the withdrawal better than Barak did. Later Foreign Minister Shlomo Ben Ami described how disturbed Arafat was by the Israeli withdrawal from Lebanon: "Why did you leave southern Lebanon?" he repeatedly asked his Israeli interlocutors. Ben Ami called that, somewhat derisively, "The new obsession of the Authority Chairman."[7]

But there is no room for derision in the face of the true predicament in which the Palestinian leadership found itself following the unilateral withdrawal that took place in the very midst of the negotiations with it. The author of an editorial printed in the Palestinian Authority's daily, *Al-Hayat al-Jadida*, on the day the IDF spokesman announced the completion of the withdrawal, wrote that the Israeli withdrawal from southern Lebanon "had been carried out solely under the pressure of mortars and Katyushas."[8]

"What is the message that Israel wants to convey with this withdrawal?" the author of the editorial asked with unconcealed bitterness. "Does she want to say to the Arabs: we won't give you your rights, unless you act in this way? If Israel wants to say that, she is dooming the peace process to failure . . . if Israel insists on duplicating her behavior in Lebanon vis-à-vis the other sides, the result will be a duplication of the Hezbollah's behavior."[9]

This was, just to remind readers, in May 2000, more than five years before Israel's next unilateral step—the disengagement, following which Hamas gained control over the Palestinian Authority. On the Israeli side, there was no one to read things properly and extract the lessons. The approach was then and still is "let the Arabs talk."

THE LESSON UNLEARNED FROM THE
EVACUATION OF THE JEZIN ENCLAVE

Prior to the withdrawal from Lebanon, Israel had more than one reason not to carry it out unilaterally, but only within the framework of an agreement under international auspices. Even more frustrating, we also had quite a few opportunities to promote such an agreement, and quite a few potential brokers, some rather surprising, who would have been glad to help. Two years before the withdrawal, on April 2, 1998, a meeting took place in New York between the Qatari foreign minister and heads of the American Jewish Committee. The Qatari minister was accompanied by the Qatari ambassador in Washington. When the possibility that Israel would want to withdraw from Lebanon was raised, the Qatari minister said that it was encouraging news, and no less important, that Lebanon and Syria would guarantee that Israel would not be attacked from southern Lebanon. In other words, two years before the withdrawal it was absolutely clear to the Qatari foreign minister that, before withdrawing, Israel would insist that it would get guarantees, not only from Lebanon but also from Syria. Although the Qatari minister knew his words would be pleasing to the ears of his Jewish listeners, I am certain that he never imagined that two years later Israel would withdraw from Lebanon in the manner it did.

In the meantime, a tiny trial balloon clarified the dangerous implications of a unilateral withdrawal. On May 31, 1999, a year before the withdrawal, the commander of the SLA, Antoine Lahad, convened a press conference at which he announced the withdrawal of his army from the Jezin enclave. This began the erosion of Israel's position. Lahad's requests of the Lebanese government to take responsibility of the enclave failed to elicit a response. The SLA withdrawal came after a long period of pressures by Hezbollah and heavy casualties that the Shi'ite organization caused the SLA. Immediately after his announcement to the media, Lahad ordered his forces to withdraw.

The SLA's withdrawal from the Jezin enclave into the security zone was completed on June 2, 1999, while Hezbollah was increasing its pressure on the SLA forces to create a picture of defeat and flight. Improvised explosive devices were laid that day, and fire was opened at the withdrawing forces. Two SLA soldiers were killed and one wounded.

The withdrawal from Jezin was the greatest gift that Syria and Hezbollah received from Israel. Although Israel stated repeatedly that the SLA and not Israel had been responsible for the enclave, in the eyes of the entire Arab world the unconditional withdrawal from Jezin was seen as no less than a victory over Israel.

On June 2, 1999, Alex Fishman, the military commentator of *Yedioth Ahronoth*, published an article titled "That's What a Unilateral Withdrawal Looks Like."

"Anyone who wants to imagine how a unilateral withdrawal from Lebanon will look, received a precise and embarrassing picture of SLA's withdrawal from the city of Jezin yesterday," Fishman wrote. "The SLA forces withdraw under fire. That's what a withdrawal without an agreement, without understandings and without a minimum of IDF deterrence, looks like."[10]

Fishman also pointed out that all the experts on Lebanese affairs failed in their assessment, according to which the Lebanese government would take responsibility for the city of Jezin, because it is in Lebanon's interest to ensure calm in the area.

On June 3, 1999 (a day after the withdrawal), a cable sent to all the foreign ministry delegations described the situation of the withdrawal and General Lahad's press conference. One of the paragraphs in the cable, which bore the heading "our position on the evacuation of the enclave," stated, "Israeli policy continues to reject any withdrawal from the security zone which is not accompanied by an arrangement."[11]

So the writing was already on the wall in June 1999, about eleven months before the IDF left Lebanon, and was even realistically and soberly interpreted in Israel. But within a very short time, the lesson was forgotten. Maybe it was convenient for us to think that, after all, it was the SLA then, and with the IDF it would be different. This assessment suffered the same fate as most of the others; it fell apart after we carried out the same move, in the same way, and got exactly the same result.

HOW WE FAILED IN THE
DIPLOMATIC ARENA, TOO

The SLA's evacuation of the Jezin enclave was only the first of a series of such acts. It later left several other posts in southern Lebanon in order to take a more effective defensive line against Hezbollah. On January 14, 2000, an official in Washington told my colleagues at the Israeli embassy that officials from the Lebanese embassy in the United States were wondering whether the SLA's evacuation of the posts in southern Lebanon indicated Israel's intent to unilaterally withdraw from southern Lebanon in the future.

Barak's declarations about his intention to pull the IDF out of Lebanon within a year evoked statements by several European countries about their desire to be involved in the process. In early February 2000, France said it would participate in a multinational force to be deployed along the Israel-Lebanon border after the withdrawal. During discussions at the United Nations (UN), representatives of France stressed that they would prefer an Israeli withdrawal carried out in the framework of an arrangement, and again expressed their willingness to send forces to maintain peace in the area.

About a month later, on March 5, 2000, the Israeli government decided on the withdrawal from Lebanon and reiterated its commitment to do so by the middle of the year. That same day, the U.S. State Department published its reaction, in which it supported Israel's decision to withdraw from southern Lebanon as part of the negotiations with Syria and Lebanon, and stated that it was taking steps to bring the parties back to bilateral talks. The problem was that these statements were made a bit too late. The Syrians already understood that they would gain the withdrawal without an agreement, with Hezbollah right on the tail of the IDF, while the Lebanese government, headed by Salim El-Hoss, needed Syrian approval for every move it made. About a month earlier, El-Hoss had said in a press interview that Lebanon and Syria coordinated their actions, and no progress would be made in separate talks.

On March 11, 2000, six days after the Israeli government's decision, the Arab League convened in Lebanon to show its solidarity with the Lebanese people and its support for the country against "Israeli aggression." The Arab League, under Egypt's leadership, instead of serving as a broker in an agreement of understandings with international guarantees, supported Hezbollah's call to escalate military resistance against Israel. While Israel was concentrating on the tactical aspects of the withdrawal and basking in the support of the Western countries, Israel lost control over the move as a whole. Hezbollah, with Syria's support, maneuvered the Israeli government, headed by Barak, into a withdrawal without an agreement, without an honorable exit, without securing the situation in southern Lebanon after the withdrawal, and without any guarantees that Israel's northern border would remain calm afterward.

It would be unfair to place the responsibility for the withdrawal and the way it was carried out solely on Barak's shoulders. In the months prior to the withdrawal, Barak received strong backing from people in the foreign ministry, who believed not only that a unilateral withdrawal without an agreement would cause no great harm, but also that it might even have some advantages for Israel. A position paper written by senior officials in the foreign ministry on March 23, 2000, exactly two months before the withdrawal, said:

> In the event that the withdrawal from Lebanon is not carried out with an agreement, Israel has a cardinal interest in withdrawing within the framework of resolution 425 of the Security Council[12] . . . a withdrawal of that kind will wipe out any pretext by Syria, Lebanon and Hezbollah to continue the fighting.[13]

In this situation, the position paper explains:

> Syria will be placed in a diplomatic bind: she demands that Israel withdraw to the June 4 border in accordance with the UN resolutions, and at the same time objects to Israeli withdrawal from Lebanon in accordance with a more binding resolution of the Security Council . . . Hezbollah too will be forced to act

outside the consensus and international legitimacy, if it decides to launch attacks inside Israel after the withdrawal. [14]

The authors of the paper believed that a unilateral withdrawal in the framework of Security Council resolution 425 would have "additional positive implications":

1. It will, for example, make it easier for us to turn to countries such as the United States, France and Britain [permanent members of the Security Council who voted in favor of this resolution] and argue that it is essential to ensure the safety of the SLA soldiers, and demand that they take some of those that are at high risk.
2. It will expedite a demand on our part (if we should so decide) for a UN or international force to be stationed in southern Lebanon or our suggestion of another security means. [15]

The authors conclude by recommending that the terminology around the withdrawal be changed: "It would be best from the outset not to use the expression 'unilateral withdrawal' but rather 'withdrawal on the basis of 425' or 'withdrawal in accordance with the UN resolutions.'" [16]

On March 29, 2000, two months before the withdrawal, Danny Yatom, then head of the political-security headquarters in the Prime Minister's Office, was interviewed on Arie Golan's radio program. He said that the failure of the Geneva summit between Hafez al-Assad and Bill Clinton would lead to the IDF's withdrawal from Lebanon without an agreement. [17] The amazing fact is that the abortive Geneva summit, which lasted forty-five minutes and related to a peace agreement between Israel and Syria, did not deal at all with Lebanon or an Israeli withdrawal from it. Hafez al-Assad was ill and no longer had the strength to carry on with the peace process; he was totally focused on ensuring the succession of his son and control over Syria by his family, party, and ethnic group after his death.

In the same interview, when asked about the SLA men, Yatom said it was up to them to choose whether to move to Israel, stay in Lebanon, or go to another country. In actual fact, that was not what happened on the night of May 23–24, 2000, when thousands of SLA soldiers and their families were forced to beg to be allowed into Israel.

On April 16, 2000, the Israeli foreign minister sent an official notification to the secretary-general of the UN, informing him that it was Israel's intention to withdraw from southern Lebanon by July 2000. The following day—motivated by Qatar's desire to be part of the solution leading to the withdrawal—the director-general of the Qatari foreign office, Abdul Rahman al-Attiyah, left for Beirut for a series of political meetings. At this point, Qatar still thought that Israel was going to withdraw with an internationally backed agreement of understandings. Shortly after the withdrawal, Qatar changed its mind, so it would not seem that Qatar was defending Israel's honor and saving Israel from humiliation.

The Qatari government publicly demonstrated that it was going along with the view that Hezbollah had defeated and driven out Israel. A day after the withdrawal, on May 25, 2000, the council of ministers of the Qatari government officially announced its satisfaction with the IDF withdrawal from Lebanon and the end of the Israeli occupation of Lebanon, and, on that occasion, extended its greetings to the Lebanese government and the Lebanese people. It was a moderate, diplomatic statement, almost de rigueur, which did not contain even one word about Hezbollah, its victory, or Israel's defeat. But five months later, on October 24, 2000, the emir of Qatar opened the meeting of people's council with these words: "I commend Hezbollah on its victory in Lebanon, on having caused Israel to withdraw. The case of Lebanon has proven that the most modern army is incapable of vanquishing a people that defends its land."

These words unmistakably showed that Qatar was indeed toeing the all-Arab line, which saw Hezbollah as the victor, the one that had driven out the most modern, well-equipped army and caused its defeat. If Qatar, moderate (at that time), pragmatic, and ready to mediate, cheers Hezbollah's victory, then we have probably done something wrong.

That was also the case for Egypt, which stood aside and let us eat the bitter fruit we had grown on our own. Before the withdrawal, we could have turned to Egypt and asked its government to lead a move in the Arab League, to persuade it to call on Israel to withdraw from Lebanon, on the one hand, and on the other, to accept responsibility for the rehabilitation of southern Lebanon and the deployment of the Lebanese army on the border. Egypt would have received credit for the move, Israel would have profited from it, and Lebanon would have benefited as well.

The problem was that we were holding discussions with the United States. It may be more convenient to do business with Americans, but they cannot always do the work for us. Therefore, into the void left by the reverberating unilaterality of our move, which surprised friends and foes, Hezbollah entered.

Immediately after the withdrawal, it was not yet clear whether the Lebanese army would fill the vacuum left by Israel and the SLA, or would leave the border area to Hezbollah, so Israel still enjoyed the benefit of doubt. Very quickly, it became clear how things were moving. On June 2, while I was still in Qatar, I saw a report from the Israeli delegation to the UN saying that at a meeting of the countries contributing to the United Nations Interim Force in Lebanon (UNIFIL), the Lebanese government was refusing to commit itself to a date for sending the Lebanese army to southern Lebanon.

Five days later, a controversy on the issue arose between France and the United States. The French demanded that the entry of UNIFIL be made conditional on the entry of the Lebanese army into the south of the country. In fact, the French were the first ones to anticipate the problem that was just around the corner.

Apart from them, all the other states still believed that the Lebanese army would, in fact, be deployed in the south. It was amazing to see how convinced the majority of the international community was that the Lebanese army would be allowed or able to move to the south, while, in fact, Syria had no intention of permitting it to do so. Syria preferred to allow Hezbollah to control south Lebanon and to continue harassing Israel from the international border.

"A withdrawal like this one will abolish any justification for Syria, Lebanon and Hezbollah to continue the fighting," a foreign ministry document stated, but the logic of the Middle East led to different conclusions: from Syria's point of view, as long as Israel has not withdrawn from the Golan Heights, Israel ought not to enjoy one moment of respite.[18]

On June 10, 2000, Syrian president Hafez al-Assad died, and all international contacts immediately ceased. With the death of the "Syrian lion" (Assad means "lion" in Arabic), Hezbollah stopped waiting for guidance from Damascus and began to exploit the freedom of action it had while the young president, Bashar al-Assad, was busy establishing his rule. At the time, everyone, including Israel, understood there was no longer any hope that the Lebanese army would move southward, and Israel awoke to a reality in which Hezbollah was standing on the fences of its northern border, and no one was giving it any contrary orders. Even worse—after the withdrawal, Iran significantly increased its support of Hezbollah with money and weapons, in order to make Hezbollah the strongest organization in Lebanon.

Several months before the withdrawal, sources in the IDF estimated that Hezbollah had between six hundred and eight hundred men actively fighting against Israel. After the withdrawal, Hezbollah began to strengthen its forces, and today it has many thousands of fighters, and is stronger than the army of the state in which it exists. Early in 2011, information was published stating that Iran transferred a huge sum of $1.2 billion to Hezbollah in 2010 alone.

On June 16, 2000, at 1300h, Kofi Anan, the UN secretary-general at that time, announced at a press conference he convened at UN headquarters that Israel had finally completed its withdrawal from Lebanon. A week later, on June 23, 2000, a presidential declaration of the Security Council confirmed the secretary-general's announcement about the Israeli withdrawal. In the fourth paragraph, the Security Council called on the Lebanese government to maximize its presence in south Lebanon and urged it to undertake powers of law and order. This point also alerted me to the retreat that had taken place in the positions and involvement of the international community. The secretary-general's declaration did not demand that Lebanon send its army southward, but only called on the country to maximize its presence in south Lebanon.

The picture was growing even clearer, and it was bad.

On June 28, 2000, I came to my office, as I did every morning, and pulled the Qatari paper *Al Watan* from the pile of newspapers on my desk. I read it and I was stunned. One of the items in the paper said that the chairman of the Lebanese parliament, Nabih Berri, had stated that Hezbollah should play a role in the Lebanese government and that Amal (Berri's organization) and Hezbollah were cooperating in preparation for the coming elections.

This news really made my blood run cold. Hezbollah, which had begun as a small terror organization with Iranian support, had now become a legitimate element in Lebanese politics. Even Amal, a long-standing organization, had agreed to grant Hezbollah seniority. Amal, founded by Musa Sadr, as the representative of the Shi'ites in Lebanon, had become, over time, an auxiliary organization of Hezbollah, which was guided, supported, and activated by Iran. This statement by Nabih Berri, the leader of Amal, showed that, in fact, the Shi'ites in Lebanon had lost their political independence and were now simply serving Iranian interests. Although Berri also said that 6,600 soldiers of the Lebanese army would be deployed in the south in the coming weeks, that deployment, after Hezbollah had already reached the fence and its soldiers were controlling the posts vacated by the IDF and the SLA, was too late and altogether pointless.

Eleven years later, Hezbollah became the dominant force in Lebanon, causing the downfall of Saad al-Hariri's government and the establishment of a new government, under its influence on January 25, 2011, headed by Najib Mikati.

A CHESS PLAYER AT THE POKER TABLE

In November 2003, Ehud Barak participated in a conference held at the Tel Aviv University Center for Strategic Research, under the heading "Civil-Military Relations in Israel: Influences and Restraints." In his lecture, Barak tried to respond to all of his critics who claimed that the unilateral withdrawal from Lebanon was a colossal failure, that not only did it not profit Israel but, in fact, caused it enormous, long-term damage:

> As Prime Minister, I acted out a deep conviction that the balance of risks and opportunities leaned towards a withdrawal from Lebanon. We were in Lebanon for nearly 18 years with nearly one thousand men killed. It was clear that there was nothing to be gained from staying there. Moreover, it turned out that if the negotiations with the Syrians were unsuccessful and an agreement was not achieved, Israel would have to get out of Lebanon. Once the negotiation with the Syrians in Geneva, in March 2000, ended without a political arrange-

ment, it was clear we had to leave Lebanon within three months and no later, in order to prevent any Hezbollah activity that would drag us into an escalation and compel the IDF to react with a military operation while leaving. We needed to leave while our departure still had the element of surprise. We might have begun planning the unilateral withdrawal at too late a stage, but that was because the military echelon wanted to wait and see whether there might still be a political breakthrough, that would make a unilateral withdrawal unnecessary.[19]

This, then, was a classic example of a multistage plan, in which if one stage fails, you jump straight to the final outcome, without giving it any more thought. Barak's words clearly reveal that Israel's original intention was that an agreement with Syria would precede an Israeli withdrawal from south Lebanon.

Like a clever chess player, Barak retrospectively claims that he foresaw several moves ahead, and the "advance declaration about the intention to leave Lebanon within a year if no agreement with Syria is achieved was meant to deny Hezbollah the possibility to exert pressure that would induce Israel to leave Lebanon."[20]

But in my view, Barak's early declaration to Israel and the entire world that, if elected, he would take the IDF out of Lebanon within a year shows more than anything else that despite his rich military experience, the medal-bedecked officer and former chief of staff totally failed to understand the mind-set of the Middle East. In the Middle East, people do not play chess; they play poker. You do not publicly threaten Assad, saying that if he does not arrive at a peace settlement with Israel, "Israel will show him what's what" and withdraw from Lebanon. Such a public pledge amounts to giving up your trump card in advance, without getting anything in return.

This supposedly sophisticated notion was not understood at all by Arab leaders at the time of the withdrawal, and no one in the Arab world credited Barak for having kept his commitment to the Israeli public and the international community; rather, the Arab world without exception saw only a panicky flight from Nasrallah's vast armies. The claim that "we didn't run away, we just stuck to our commitment," may have "worked" on the Israeli public (although it did not save Barak from losing in the elections following the second Intifada, which the withdrawal encouraged and accelerated), but it did not "work" on anyone on the other side.

The rapid transition from focusing on the Syrian negotiations as our exit ticket from Lebanon, to the decision to withdraw unilaterally, without any attempt to obtain guarantees for Israel's security through a joint international effort, in retrospect looks rash, if not defeatist. I do not deny that Syria wielded a great deal of influence on Lebanon, but it was most likely possible to make different moves in cooperation with the moderate Arab states and several European countries that wanted to be part of the solution, such as

France, to prepare the ground for an orderly withdrawal including certain guarantees for Israel.

In the same lecture, Barak responded dismissively to criticism about the hasty and, to all appearances, humiliating manner in which the withdrawal was carried out and imprinted on the world's mind: "Why didn't the IDF leave in an orderly manner? Why didn't the IDF leave with their head held high? The answer is that from the moment we'd inform the SLA of the date, that information would reach Hezbollah, which would have accompanied our withdrawal with fighting, and the scenario would repeat itself again: Israel would have been forced to react and in the end to withdraw as well."[21]

Once again the tactical perspective of a commander who wants to break off contact and maintain field security blinds the eyes of the statesman and strategist, who ought to have realized how the pictures of the IDF sneaking off in the dark would boost morale in Hezbollah.

Today, more than a decade after that withdrawal, we can safely say that Barak's assessments on the eve of the withdrawal, as well as his replies to the criticism leveled at him afterward, were fundamentally wrong. Although it is impossible to say that the withdrawal from Lebanon was the major cause of the Al Aqsa Intifada, anyone familiar with the Middle East and reads its newspapers, knows that the withdrawal from Lebanon, particularly the way it was carried out, had a profound psychological influence on the Palestinians, who tried to emulate Hezbollah's enormous success.

In this context, it is worth recalling the testimony given by General Amos Malka, the head of military intelligence, to the Winograd Commission established in 2006 to inquire into the events of military engagement in Lebanon. According to him, the withdrawal encouraged the second Intifada and the IDF was only three months off in predicting the exact date.[22]

NASRALLAH CASHES IN

If we had learned from the United States, things might have looked different. Before its withdrawal from Iraq in the first Gulf War (1991), the United States doubled its military strength in the region, so its withdrawal would be an honorable one. The country had learned from bitter experience during its withdrawal from Vietnam. When the United States hastily packed up, South Vietnamese soldiers and their families were forced to knock at the gates of U.S. bases pleading to be taken along. Dozens—if not hundreds—of films dealt with that period, and the United States learned its lesson. What holds for the United States applies even more strongly to Israel, since the United States' enemy is not lurking on its doorstep. In Israel's case, its enemy is doing just that.

Immediately after the withdrawal, Hezbollah did its utmost to humiliate Israel. The Arab world feasted on the news showing the soldiers of their most feared enemy standing helpless in the face of Hezbollah men making it their daily ritual to humiliate the Israeli army: throwing stones, cursing, and yelling insults. In the eyes of the Arab people, not a single Arab soldier—even one from the weakest Arab country—would have agreed to be subjected to such a degrading onslaught. The message engraved in their minds was that Israel was not as frightening as they had thought, that Israel was the one who was afraid. Our solders' discipline and avoidance of provocations was translated as Israeli fear of military confrontation. They believed that because the strength of Israeli society had declined, Israel had withdrawn its vast army out of fear of only six hundred to eight hundred fighters armed with only light weapons. In those days, the Arab world was sure it had discovered the way to defeat the Zionist war machine.

Hassan Nasrallah milked the momentum for all it was worth. Right after the withdrawal, on May 26, 2000, during the victory celebrations of Hezbollah in the town of Bint Jbeil, the secretary-general of Hezbollah delivered his famous speech, which came to be known as "the spiderweb speech." Since the Arab world craved victors, especially those vanquishing Israel, overnight Nasrallah became a hero borne on everyone's shoulders, even those who, until then, had been among the Shi'a's most avowed opponents. Nasrallah's speech was basically Shi'ite, since he stressed Shi'ite elements and the role of the Shi'ite community in the victory, but the Sunni majority overlooked those nuances and crowned Nasrallah as hero of the day.

Anyone who thinks it is natural and self-evident for the Sunni Arab public to support Nasrallah does not understand the depth of the feelings of hostility and suspicion of the entire Sunni community toward the Shi'a. Nor does he understand how strongly Israel's rash withdrawal undermined this most stable tradition in the Middle East. Oddly enough, the man who identified the danger was Yusuf al-Qaradawi, scarcely a fan of Israel, whom I shall discuss later. Al-Qaradawi defines himself as the pupil and follower of Hassan al-Banna, the founder of the Muslim Brotherhood movement.[23] He is regarded as the proponent of the approach that encourages the solution of political differences within Islam through dialogue, but he has never concealed his intolerance for those who question the superiority of the Sunnah as the "correct" stream of Islam.

Like the great majority of the Arab world, al-Qaradawi cheered Nasrallah for having chased Israel out of Lebanon in May 2000, but six years later, he also understood that Nasrallah is a creature likely to rise up against his maker. Nasrallah's popularity following the withdrawal led many Sunnis, including members of the Muslim Brotherhood in Egypt, to convert to Shi'a. The number of Shi'ites in Egypt increased at a significant rate and in 2006 was estimated to be about two million.

On August 31, 2006, two weeks after the end of the second war in Lebanon, when the Arab world was embracing Nasrallah and Hezbollah as the ones who had restored honor to the Islamic nation through their war against Israel, al-Qaradawi chose to caution against the infiltration of the Shi'a into Egypt on the waves of that popularity. In a meeting with the Egyptian journalists' association in Cairo, he warned that the spread of Shi'a in Egypt would lead to a bloody civil war, like the one raging in Iraq:

> My brethren, I support closer ties between Shi'ites and Sunnis and I am in favor of Hezbollah's resistance, but under no circumstances will I allow this support to serve as a justification for a Shi'ite penetration into Sunni countries. That would lead to a civil conflict and ignite a conflagration that will burn everything. . . . The fighting now raging in Iraq, the daily massacre by Sunnis and Shi'ites . . . the same thing can happen in Egypt if this goes on. If the Shi'ite school of Islam is preaching widely, the others will be opposed to that. Then there will be a civil struggle and an endless massacre. Therefore, I say we must be on guard.[24]

I am not certain that Barak, when he proceeded to keep his election promise, took these implications into account in making his decisions and deciding how they would be implemented. But, to my regret, the State of Israel has quite a few "founder's shares" in strengthening Hezbollah and turning it from a tiny militia into the strongest organization in the country in which it operates and practically has ruled from 2011.

The shock waves do not stop in Lebanon, as we have seen. The way in which the withdrawal was perceived in the moderate Arab countries, with which we did not even bother to talk before its implementation, has made Hezbollah the vanguard in the spread of Shi'a, not only in Lebanon but also throughout the Sunni world. The second Lebanon war, which was intended to boost Israel's deterrent power, only partially achieved its aim, with much bloodshed and at a very painful price.

ISRAEL DID NOT LEARN THE
LESSONS OF LEBANON; HAMAS DID

The next unilateral step taken by Israel, about five years after the withdrawal from Lebanon, was the disengagement from the Gaza Strip. There were very significant differences between the two withdrawals: first, the evacuation of the settlements in the area took a very human and social toll and led to a rift in Israeli society. Second, the illusion of tranquility only lasted momentarily.

Although in the disengagement we supposedly did not leave behind a vacuum, but rather handed the Strip like a hot potato to the Palestinian Authority, this time, too, our insistence on resolutely evacuating ourselves—

without talking to the other side and without creating a supportive political envelope—had serious implications.

It was an additional act derived from that same callous, insular approach we developed in 2000. This time, too, the advocates of this unilateral method continued to interpret reality in the way most convenient to them. They stated that "the Palestinians understand that the case of Lebanon is not the case of Gaza." So there is no choice but to once again tell those advocates: the Palestinians do not understand what we want them to understand. The Palestinians understand what they want to understand.

All of our logical, rational explanations did not prevent Hamas from appropriating the disengagement and taking credit for the fact that Israel left the Gaza Strip. Since Israel left without any agreement or guarantees, even its threatening statements that Israel would react with outstanding aggression to every Qassam rocket launched after its withdrawal went unnoticed. Hamas heard the threats and went on launching the Qassams with impunity.

We may not have internalized the lessons of Lebanon, but Hamas certainly did; Hamas did what Hezbollah had done in Lebanon—namely, creating that same pretense that the IDF had withdrawn from the Strip owing to the heavy losses it had suffered. Our withdrawal from Gaza, on September 11, 2005, began the countdown: the poor timing of the withdrawal—three months before the elections in the Palestinian Authority—contributed to Hamas's political strength and its victory at the polls. Arafat may have known how to neutralize the vast administrative machine that Hamas had established, but Abu Mazen did not.

On January 25, 2006, elections were held in the Palestinian Authority, and for the first time, Hamas won a majority of the seats in the Palestinian parliament, contrary to all the estimates of the Israeli intelligence establishment. On June 12–14, while sitting in the unity government with Fatah, Hamas began its military takeover of the Gaza Strip and completed it after killing many Fatah men in the Strip. The disengagement ushered in a process similar to that begun by the withdrawal from Lebanon, which ended when Israel woke up to find Gaza controlled by the Hamas movement, functioning like an Islamic emirate according to the Sharia law. Six months after winning the Palestinian elections, a Hamas force attacked Israeli soldiers on Israeli territory, killed two of them, and took the third, Gilad Shalit, as a prisoner. This incident led to an Israeli military operation in the Gaza Strip. Two years later, on November 27, 2008, after rockets were fired on Israeli cities, Israel launched another operation. In November 2012, another conflict, the last until the writing of these lines, broke out on July 7, 2014, after Hamas fired rockets on Israeli towns and cities. This was after the new Egyptian government stepped up its activity of closing smuggling tunnels from Egypt. Hamas, unable to pay salaries to its people, decided to heat up the area by firing rockets at Israel. Israel's reaction was to launch a large-scale military operation, during which it discovered that Hamas had dug hundreds of assault tunnels from the Gaza Strip into Israeli territory, built dozens of meters underground and reinforced with the concrete provided to Gaza for civilian construction.

Prime Minister Ariel Sharon wanted to establish facts on the ground, and those are the facts that we were left with.

THE NEXT UNILATERAL STEP?

Did we finally learn the lesson? Evidently not. Before Ehud Olmert's rise to power, he sent up a trial balloon with his realignment plan: back to the model of the unilateral disengagement, but this time in Judah and Samaria. Even during the first days of the second Lebanon war, he had a hard time giving up the idea. Later there was the Molten Lead operation, the legal heir of the disengagement from Gaza, but none of that seems to have sufficed.

On June 29, 2010, at a conference marking the tenth anniversary of the withdrawal from Lebanon, Minister of Defense Ehud Barak declared, "Maybe in Finland and Holland there won't be any need for unilateral steps, but in Israel I can promise you that we will still need to make such moves in the future."[25] In relation to "his" withdrawal, Barak said, "I am proud of the withdrawal from Lebanon. What did people want, for us to stay there another eighteen years?"

No one, I believe, wanted us to stay in Lebanon another eighteen years; nor did I. But as I keep arguing in this book, the State of Israel conducts itself in the Middle Eastern arena between black and white: either we get to Beirut in the first Lebanon war, and forcefully influence the election of the Lebanese president, or we withdraw in the dark under fire, abandoning people and equipment, leaving the permanent impression on the Arab world that we were running for our lives when we left Lebanon. Barak only stated two options: to stay in Lebanon another eighteen years, or to leave in the shameful, destructive manner that we did. But that is not the case. It was possible to leave in a different way, and we should have taken that route. It would probably have been more complicated and more difficult, but not impossible—and we would have maintained our deterrence.

One of the main problems of the State of Israel since its establishment has been that it sees the other side, mainly the Palestinians, through gunsights, in a narrow military view, rather than a political, regional, or broad view. I suspect that was the view that led Barak to decide on the IDF's unilateral withdrawal from Lebanon in the summer of 2000. Until a significant change takes place in the thinking of Israeli leadership, we can expect to see additional unilateral steps, just as Barak openly declared we would. By now, we should have understood their cost and implications. Our neighbors understand them very well, and the worst of them will be glad to explain these implications to us again.

We ought to have left Lebanon with an agreement, with guarantees, and in particular with a deterrent force and with our honor—yes, with our honor. It is important to realize that honor is a very significant factor in the region in which we live. This region, its people and its leaders, respect only those who respect themselves. Anyone who flees under cover of darkness from several hundred fighters cannot expect anyone to think well of him, to understand that he is strong and acting responsibly; nor can he expect anyone to remember that he, in fact, announced his withdrawal in advance, so that it is actually only the fulfillment of a promise and not a flight.

So we have to face it: No one understood, no one understands, and there is no chance that anyone will understand moves of that kind in the future. The Middle East is not forgiving to the weak, not even to someone only perceived as being weak. The unilateral loss of assets, without agreements or guarantees, is tantamount to suicide.

Chapter Three

A Demon Called Normalization

Nothing frightens the Arab street more than normalization, except, perhaps, Shimon Peres. Why don't they want our embrace?

It is amazing to discover that in most languages in the world the term "normalization" almost always has a positive connotation, while Arabic is the only language that I know in which the term has a negative connotation. It is less surprising that in Arabic it is nearly always ascribed to Israel: Tatbi'e al-'alaqat maa' Isra'il *(normalization of relations with Israel).*

Of all the levers that serve the organizations in the Arab world that are opposed to the peace process, it seems the objection to normalization is the most popular for provoking hatred of and intensifying fear of Israel—both among the Arab states that have open relations and among those who maintain secret relations with the country. The struggle against normalization makes life very difficult for inhabitants of the Middle East who maintain any sort of relations with Israel, whether economic, academic, or cultural.

Naturally, one of the obstacles in the way of normalization is that in most cases it follows a long period of conflict and war—during which the enemy is systematically demonized. However, the process of demonization carries on even after peace agreements are signed, this time under the leadership of movements of resistance and opposition of those states. What they seem to be saying is this: Even if our governments, in their weakness, have signed political agreements with you, out of strategic considerations, genuine Arab patriots, or, alternatively, believing Muslims, will never be a party to warming up or tightening relations with Israel, nor will they ever forgive Israel's crimes against our people.

In the face of this attitude in the Arab countries, the peace agreements led the Israeli public to adopt an approach that was given the name "brutal pragmatism."[1] This approach undervalues cultural worldviews in the Middle East, as well as the long tradition of opposition to normal relations with Israel. According to it, peace is based on common interests, and those should be strengthened through economic projects and the improved living conditions of the inhabitants of the region—whether they want that or are put off by Israel's involvement in their country: in other words, a "new Middle East."

THE PERCEPTION OF
NORMALIZATION IN ISRAEL

It's a recurring ritual. Every time our ambassador to Egypt ends his tenure, he is interviewed by the Israeli media and, with a deep sigh, recounts the litany of all the restrictions the Egyptian government places in the way of any sign of normalization with Israel, of the problems that beset all Egyptian citizens who have any contact with the embassy, and of the demonstrative absence of any high-ranking Egyptian official at the Independence Day reception held by the embassy in Egypt. In marked contrast, they recall how the Egyptian ambassador in Israel is warmly received on that day and top-ranking Israelis attend every reception he holds, and even the president himself comes on Egypt's Independence Day.

After the interview, interest in normalization rapidly dies down, and flares up again only when an especially virulent caricature appears in one of the Arab countries with which we have a peace agreement, or when the song at the top of the hit parade is like the one written in Egypt: "I hate Israel, I love Amr Moussa."

But while in the Arab world normalization is a fundamental, explosive issue, in Israel it has only symbolic importance. The Israeli economy has managed, and can go on managing in the future, even without broad cooperation with the other economies of the region. Academic institutions in Israel also exist and flourish without cooperating with universities in Arab countries. But cooperation could prove that the approach in Arab countries toward Israel has changed from one of struggle to one of acceptance. For Israel normalization is, therefore, a sign that the country has integrated into the Middle Eastern space and has become a natural and accepted legitimate part of it. But with all honesty, it must be said that the issue is not on the top of the list for our leaders.

The roots of our perception of normalization with our Arab neighbors were already evident in the nineteenth century. The Zionist movement then advocated developing the Jewish entity in Palestine while establishing good neighborly relations with the Arabs in that country, and not engaging in a struggle with them. This attempt failed, and in fact, the development of the Jewish-Zionist entity was attended by conflict with the Arabs of Palestine and the region, which reached its peak in the War of Independence in 1948.[2]

Israel's position relating to the normalization of relations with Arab states was first expressed at the end of the Yom Kippur war, in a speech delivered by Abba Eban at the Geneva peace conference (December 21, 1973):

> It will be necessary for political and intellectual leaders in the Arab world to reject the fallacy that Israel is alien to the Middle East. Israel is not alien to the Middle East; it is an organic part of its texture and memory. . . . Above all, a durable peace must create a new human reality. . . . Let us all atone for 25 years of separation by working toward a co-operative relationship similar to that which European States created after centuries of conflict and war.[3]

This was, as I noted, the first time that Israel officially related to the need for normalization with Arab states as an integral, inseparable part of any peace agreement signed between Israel and its neighbors.

Throughout the years, the most enthusiastic promoter of normalization was none other than the ninth president of the State of Israel, Shimon Peres. He is regarded by the entire world, and rightly so, as one of the most influential leaders in Israeli history in particular and in the history of the Middle East in general, as a man motivated by the belief that "everything is possible," a leader who aspires to change reality in keeping with his worldview and refuses to allow reality to determine his actions. During my diplomatic service, I met with Peres on several occasions and saw how his words are devoured by the audience that comes to hear him, wherever he is.

However, very few in the Israeli public are aware of how Shimon Peres, the man and his vision, repels journalists and opinion shapers in the Arab world. Nothing alarms them more than the expression he coined: "the new Middle East."

When Peres spoke about economic cooperation and the establishment of a common Middle Eastern market like the European common market, his words were interpreted as an Israeli attempt to take over the economy of the Middle East. When he spoke about educational cooperation and the linking of the schools in the region into one educational Internet network, this was regarded in the Arab media as an attempt by Israel to control the minds of the children of the Arab world.

As I noted earlier, in 1992, Peres was accused in an editorial in the Egyptian daily *Al-Ahram* of having "replaced the strategy of territorial conquest with a strategy of economic conquest."[4] What did Arab journalists find so frightening in a man regarded by the Israeli public as a genuine dove, a later recipient of the Nobel Peace Prize (along with Yitzhak Rabin and Yasser Arafat) for his role in the Oslo agreements?

To understand, we ought to look into a book he published back in 1993 with the obvious title *The New Middle East.*[5] In it, Peres presents his view, according to which normalization is the second and decisive phase in the peace process. Its role is to preserve the peace and ensure its continuity, while resting on two legs: economy and culture.[6] The emphasis is on economy, based on the model of the European Economic Community (EEC), which later became the European Union (EU).[7]

"The establishment of peace," he writes, "will gradually and when the time comes, make possible the emergence of a common regional framework, whose very existence will change the face of the region, first and foremost, the consciousness of the peoples of the Middle East."[8]

Peres links economic prosperity to the democratization of the region and, in doing so, ignores the fact that the Arab governments, even in the moderate states most friendly to Israel, are likely to regard that as a threat to their stability (a fear that was realized in early 2011).

> Economic development and social welfare are the prerequisites for the successful democratization of the Middle East. Sixty percent of the world's oil resources are concentrated here. The Middle East has tremendous market potential; its buildup constitutes a great challenge for the region and for world peace. But for the democratic process to take hold, we must first overcome poverty and ignorance and social distress, for these are the cradle of fundamentalism.[9]

When I read that book for the umpteenth time, on July 17, 2014, twenty-one years after its first publication, I noted that Peres's plan contained no small degree of arrogance and pretension. Consequently, his approach was interpreted by its Arab readers as condescension, as if he were explaining to the "underdeveloped" Arab countries how they ought to behave, how to build their political system and their economy, and in particular what they can learn from the "enlightened" Israelis.

"The Arabs and the Israelis," Peres wrote, "have sunk deeply into the politics and strategy of the conflict, because the fact of its existence overshadows all other considerations. However, Israel is learning more and more the secret of the power of modern economy, both political and military power, while many of her neighbors are in a more difficult situation."[10]

Peres himself was aware of how suspicious his Arab listeners were of his vision, but I am not sure he knew how to placate their suspicion. In his speech at the UN General Assembly on September 28, 1993, he said:

> I know that whenever the idea of a common market in the Middle East is raised that arouses the suspicion that Israel is attempting to win preference or to establish domination. May I say sincerely and loudly that we are not giving

up territorial control to gain economic superiority. The age of domination, political or economic, has ended. The time of cooperation has now begun. [11]

A year later, in his speech at the economic summit of the Middle East and North Africa held in Casablanca on October 30, 1994, Peres noted that the purpose of the summit was not to negotiate peace, but rather to build peace in the Middle East from an economic viewpoint. The sentence that the majority of Arab journalists related to was this: "The dream is to erect a new Middle East. A region with no wars, no front-lines, yielding a missile-free and hunger-free Middle East."

But Peres's dream, which grew out of the heady atmosphere of the time, his understanding of the greatness of the hour, and the potential to resolve the conflict, was perceived by large segments of the Arab world as a nightmare. A years-long tradition has made the Arab peoples suspicious, very suspicious.

THE PERCEPTION OF
NORMALIZATION IN THE ARAB WORLD

On September 28, 1970, the president of Egypt, Gamal Abdel Nasser, the most popular leader in the modern Arab world, died. Nasser's worldview was adopted by the masses, becoming an ideological movement named after him that survives to the present day, more than forty years after his death.

Nasser also played an important role in defining the nature of the Arab world's relations with Israel, particularly in creating the values underpinning the Arab world's abysmal opposition to normalization. As long as he was alive, normal relations with Israel were not even on the agenda, and his attitude toward and definition of Israel still impinge upon the thinking of the bitterest opponents of normalization, and have a considerable influence among those Arab leaders who maintain peaceful relations with the State of Israel.

The writings of Nasser's close friend and the man known as his mouthpiece, Mohamed Hassanein Heikal, the legendary editor of the *Al-Ahram* newspaper, clearly indicate that Nasser was a typical product of Egypt's national struggle for independence against Western colonialism in general and the British in particular. On the back of that struggle, he became the leader of Egypt and unchallenged leader of the entire Arab world. Heikal's writings show that, in Nasser's perception, Israel was an agent of Western imperialism, which he believed had been sending its long, greedy arms into the very heart of the Arab space for centuries. [12]

Heikal claimed that Nasser never was reconciled to the existence of Israel and wanted to encircle and isolate the state until it perished. In one of the most amazing descriptions I read, Heikal quotes Nasser saying that Israel should be treated in the same way as the Egyptian villagers treat a bunion:

> They tear off a hair from a horse's tail, tie it tightly around the bunion until it gets no blood flow, dries up and falls off. [13]

Nasser believed that if Israel were isolated and the Arabs refused to accept the country as a legitimate element in the Middle East, she would perish and disappear from the map of the Middle East. This perception, which was prevalent then, and still is shared today by quite a few in the Middle East, ought to have isolated Israel and prevented it from integrating into and living freely in the Middle Eastern space, until the state withered and died.

According to Heikal, hatred of Israel apparently played an important role in Nasser's efforts to keep the Arab world under his and Egypt's leadership, so that Israel became the glue that unified the opposition movements in the Arab world, although their major wars were not against Israel but against the various regimes in the Arab world.

As we can see, in the riots that began in early 2011 in the Arab world, Israel was almost completely absent, although there were a few anti-Zionist slogans in the demonstrations in Egypt. Yusuf al-Qaradawi, in his speech at Tahrir Square, on February 19, 2011, which lasted twenty-seven minutes, devoted only one and a half minutes to Israel. The presidents of Yemen, Libya, and Syria tried unsuccessfully to blame Israel for the outbreak of the riots, but these exceptional cases proved that it is possible, only possible, that the serious economic crisis that ignited the demonstrations in the Arab world no longer needed unifying glue in the form of hatred of Israel.

* * *

On March 26, 1979, the president of Egypt, Anwar Sadat, signed a peace agreement with Israel—the first peace agreement between an Arab country and the State of Israel. This agreement was based on two major anchors: the return of the Sinai Peninsula to Egypt and the establishment of normal relations (an expression explicitly written in the wording of the agreement) between Egypt and Israel. In the wording of the agreement, the components of normal life between Israel and an Arab state were defined for the first time. The topic of normalization was included in the third annex to the agreement, titled "Protocol Concerning Relations of the Parties." It read as follows:

Article 1: Diplomatic and Consular Relations

The Parties agree to establish diplomatic and consular relations and to exchange ambassadors upon completion of the interim withdrawal.

Article 2: Economic and Trade Relations

The Parties agree to remove all discriminatory barriers to normal economic relations and to terminate economic boycotts of each other upon completion of the interim withdrawal.

As soon as possible, and not later than six months after the completion of the interim withdrawal, the Parties will enter negotiations with a view to concluding an agreement on trade and commerce for the purpose of promoting beneficial economic relations.

Article 3: Cultural Relations

The Parties agree to establish normal cultural relations following completion of the interim withdrawal.

They agree on the desirability of cultural exchanges in all fields, and shall, as soon as possible and not later than six months after completion of the interim withdrawal, enter into negotiations with a view to concluding a cultural agreement for this purpose.

Article 4: Freedom of Movement

Upon completion of the interim withdrawal, each Party will permit the free movement of the nationals and vehicles of the other into and within its territory according to the general rules applicable to nationals and vehicles of other states. Neither Party will impose discriminatory restrictions on the free movement of persons and vehicles from its territory to the territory of the other.

Mutual unimpeded access to places of religious and historical significance will be provided on a non-discriminatory basis.

Article 5: Cooperation for Development and Good Neighborly Relations

The Parties recognize a mutuality of interest in good neighborly relations and agree to consider means to promote such relations.

The Parties will cooperate in promoting peace, stability and development in their region. Each agrees to consider proposals the other may wish to make to this end.

The Parties shall seek to foster mutual understanding and tolerance and will, accordingly, abstain from hostile propaganda against each other.

Article 6: Transportation and Telecommunications

The Parties recognize as applicable to each other the rights, privileges and obligations provided for by the aviation agreements to which they are both party, particularly by the Convention on International Civil Aviation, 1944 ("The Chicago Convention") and the International Air Services Transit Agreement, 1944.

Upon completion of the interim withdrawal any declaration of national emergency by a party under Article 89 of the Chicago Convention will not be applied to the other party on a discriminatory basis.

Egypt agrees that the use of airfields left by Israel near El-Arish, Rafah, Ras El-Nagb and Sharm El-Sheikh shall be for civilian purposes only, including possible commercial use by all nations.

As soon as possible and not later than six months after the completion of the interim withdrawal, the Parties shall enter into negotiations for the purpose of concluding a civil aviation agreement.

The Parties will reopen and maintain roads and railways between their countries and will consider further road and rail links. The Parties further agree that a highway will be constructed and maintained between Egypt, Israel and Jordan near Eilat with guaranteed free and peaceful passage of persons, vehicles and goods between Egypt and Jordan, without prejudice to their sovereignty over that part of the highway which falls within their respective territory.

Upon completion of the interim withdrawal, normal postal, telephone, telex, data facsimile, wireless and cable communications and television relay services by cable, radio and satellite shall be established between the two Parties in accordance with all relevant international conventions and regulations.

Upon completion of the interim withdrawal, each Party shall grant normal access to its ports for vessels and cargoes of the other, as well as vessels and cargoes destined for or coming from the other. Such access will be granted on the same conditions generally applicable to vessels and cargoes of other nations. Article 5 of the Treaty of Peace will be implemented upon the exchange of instruments of ratification of the aforementioned treaty.

Article 7: Enjoyment of Human Rights

The Parties affirm their commitment to respect and observe human rights and fundamental freedoms for all, and they will promote these rights and freedoms in accordance with the United Nations Charter.

Article 8: Territorial Seas

Without prejudice to the provisions of Article 5 of the Treaty of Peace each Party recognizes the right of the vessels of the other Party to innocent passage through its territorial sea in accordance with the rules of international law. [14]

* * *

As we can see from the "Protocol Concerning Relations of the Parties," a fair number of the relations was left rather vague in the initial stage, to be formulated in future negotiations, at the end of one or another stage of the Israeli withdrawal from Sinai. In actual fact, the Protocol was never fully implemented. The Egyptians attributed the dawdling implementation of several articles to the outbreak of the first Lebanon war, the crisis about sovereignty over Taba, and the deadlock in the Palestinian autonomy talks. Israel accused Egypt of never having intended to fulfill the Protocol, and stated that Egypt's pretexts amounted to later stipulations that were never part of the agreement or its conditions. In any case, until this very day, a large part of the actions left for the future have not been carried out. That is why the peace with Egypt is always termed "a cold peace."

Sadat, Nasser's successor, was concerned about normalization even before signing the peace agreement with Israel. An article published in *Al-Ahram* on July 3, 1975, quoted from a speech delivered by Sadat before a delegation of U.S. lecturers on a visit to Egypt: "Don't ask me to establish normal relations with Israel. I am prepared to sign a peace agreement and to be committed to it, but it is only natural after a 26-year-long conflict, marked by hatred and bloodshed, that normal relations cannot be established within a moment. We will leave to the coming generations the freedom to act as they see fit." [15]

We will see later on that this worldview, which distinguishes between the signing of a peace treaty and honoring it, on the one hand, and establishing full normal relations, on the other, is shared by many Arab leaders, who also postpone full normalization, or, in another definition, the end of the Arab-Israeli conflict, to the coming generations. This perception, however, is not the final word. It often gives way to more pragmatic considerations. Governments in Arab states, particularly the Egyptian government during Hosni Mubarak's term in office, often used normalization as a stick (or, alternately, as a carrot) vis-à-vis Israel. For example, immediately after Yitzhak Rabin won the elections in Israel and was sworn in as prime minister on July 13, 1992, the Egyptian government decided to take several steps to normalize relations. Less than a year later, in May 1993, the agricultural exhibition, Agritech, was held in Israel. An Egyptian delegation, composed of about seventy members and headed by the director-general of the Egyptian ministry of agriculture, attended the exhibition. It was one of the largest delegations to come from abroad, and throughout the convention, its heads demonstrated their interest in developing cooperative ventures in a wide variety of fields.

The successful visit of the Egyptian delegation, which I escorted as an employee of the foreign ministry, was a direct result of the Egyptian government's decision, but the dedicated work of the late Buma Goldstein contributed greatly. He was an employee of the ministry of agriculture who knew most of the members of that delegation, since he had made endless trips to provide instruction and receive Egyptians coming to Israel for courses. As time went by, I became increasingly appreciative of his enormous contribution to the connection created between the two countries, and realized that true normalization is built not only by courageous government decisions but also by an infrastructure of hard work carried out by good, committed people, imbued with a genuine sense of mission.

Several months after this exhibition, I was posted in Philadelphia on my first mission abroad. During my time there, I had the opportunity to attend a lecture by Dr. Hilal Khashan, a professor of political science, originally from Lebanon, on the subject "The Views of Lebanese Professionals on the Issue of Economic Normalization with Israel." He and his staff interviewed more than five hundred Lebanese professionals and members of various religions from the Beirut area. In his research, Khashan found that although the issue of religion played a certain role in the interviewees' attitude toward the economic normalization of Lebanon with Israel, it did not have a decisive influence. His findings did show that Muslims were more opposed to economic normalization with Israel, and also consider it to be contrary to their religion, while Christian interviewees tended to be more positive on the issue. But 70 percent of the Muslim subjects expressed a pragmatic view and supported the possibility of marketing and selling Lebanese products to Israel.

The reason that repeatedly surfaced in the Muslims' objections to normalization with Israel was suspicion. They were suspicious about Israel's intentions toward the Arab world in general and Lebanon in particular. Long years of denigrating Israel in the Lebanese and Arab media had their expected effect, but the main importance of the research was, in my view, a reverse one: it revealed that even the most vociferous opponents stated that if economic normalization between Israel and Lebanon did take place, they would manage "to live with it."

* * *

Normalization between Arab countries and Israel is one of the issues that constantly troubles the Palestinians. They are afraid their problem will be relegated to the sidelines. Even when the peace process with them seems to be really moving ahead, the Palestinians view normalization as a kind of bonus given to Israel, before Israel has given them what they deserve.

Consequently, when the notion of establishing an Israeli delegation in Qatar first came up, the Palestinians were among its fiercest opponents, even though this delegation mainly served the 24,000 Palestinians who were working in Qatar and enjoyed the privilege of obtaining a visa without waiting for hours in Amman. During the second Intifada, the Palestinian Authority was one of the loudest voices pressuring for the closure of Israel's delegations in the various Arab countries, out of a desire to punish Israel and prevent her from enjoying the "fruits of peace."

The book *A Study on the State of Arab-Israeli Normalization*, written in 2003 by Said Yakin and published by the Palestinian Institute for National Guidance, is a well-reasoned argument against normalization.[16] From the dedication at the front of the book, Said's views on the issue of the Israeli-Palestinian conflict are clear: "Dedicated to the Palestinian victims, whose death has enabled us to live in honor until today."[17] But Said's analysis is not trivial, and it constitutes a bitter, alarming mirror image of Shimon Peres's utopian vision of the new Middle East:

> In order to establish her imperious existence after she was founded, Israel entered into a series of wars, in which she achieved swift geo-political victories; her existence as a Jewish state in the Middle East gained international recognition, in particular in the western bloc, and she was accepted as a member of the UN. Nonetheless, she did not succeed for a lengthy period in achieving the recognition of her legitimate existence in the Arab cultural circle. Nor did she succeed in fulfilling the vision of the safe homeland for Jewish immigrants. Until this very day, the largest number of Jews anywhere in the world have been killed within her boundaries. In addition, she has not succeeded until today in gathering all the Jews and liquidating the diaspora, and the proportion of Jews living in Israel does not exceed 35% of world Jewry after more than 53 years of her existence.[18]

Said argues that since the conferences at Camp David and Madrid, normalization has become Israel's strategic aim, as the country makes use of the "divide and conquer" tactic, which characterized Israel's actions as far back as 1949, when the Israeli government insisted on signing separate armistice agreements with each Arab state after the War of Independence. "One can argue," he stresses, "that from Israel's standpoint, normalization is more important than Arab and Palestinian recognition of a safe Israel, since it encompasses Israel's security in any case."[19]

In the concluding chapter of his book, Said sums up his opinion:

Normalization, as an Israeli view and political project, constitutes the practical, crowning glory of Zionist success in achieving the safety, legitimacy and stability of Israel in the Arab region, which she has exhausted and whose progress she has halted, and within the people to whom she has denied the right of self-determination by destroying its production forces and dispersing its sons to the four corners of the earth.

As a strategic approach, normalization aspires to enable Israel to break out of her economic isolation and enable her citizens to eliminate the tension underlying the identity of the state and its split along ethnic lines. Normalization is Israel's defense plan against the hostility that permeates the hearts of sons of the Palestinian and Arab victims. It is the appropriate modern mechanism for instilling defeat into the collective Arab and Palestinian conscience, so that Israel can live in peace. According to the Israeli view, normalization means causing the Arabs to accept Israel as a legitimate state in the region, like all the other states in the Middle East, and to maintain economic and cultural links with her, as if she were a legitimate historical part of the region and not a foreign element that does not belong to it. Israel has presented the functioning mechanism: to advance the normalization program by means of the Middle Eastern plan that ensures that the Arab identity will be uprooted from the region, in order to ensure that Israel is integrated into the Middle Eastern family.[20]

We can disagree with Said's basic ideological and historical positions, and certainly with the negative motivation that he attributes to Israel's aspirations to integrate as a legitimate state into the region. In his mouth, the yearned-for peace sounds more like a curse on all the nations, rather than a blessing. But we should not ignore his insight in regard to the meanings and implications of normalization.

This sensitivity of the Arabs to the symbolic charge of normalization and their unwillingness to advance on this path without a genuine political breakthrough (and sometimes, as I suspect in the case of Said, even after all possible breakthroughs) are factors we need to take into account before we rush forward.

Normalization can help mitigate our demonization in the Arab countries. It can also be a human bridge for gradually building confidence and creating common interests. But it must not become—through glib, arrogant, and grandiose statements about a "new Middle East"—the supposed proof of Israel's imperialist intentions that the opponents of the peace process are looking for. We are walking on eggshells, so please, let us move slowly and carefully. And how can we do that? I will try to explain by describing one of my own experiences during my diplomatic service in Qatar.

QATAR 1999–2001:
EVALUATING RELATIONS

In September 1999, about four weeks after I arrived in Qatar, I decided to take the initiative and approach a financial company to try to promote economic cooperation. One morning I decided not to wait for Muhammad to come to the mountain. I turned to my wife Ornit, then the commercial attaché of Israel's ministry of commerce and trade in Qatar and Oman, and asked her for the name of a company with whom we might like to establish economic cooperation. She recommended a local company that exported minerals to eastern markets. A local friend gave me the owner's phone number.

Before I called him, I was uncertain about what language to speak. Since I speak Arabic with an Egyptian accent, it's hard to tell that I am an Israeli. I did not mean to surprise or embarrass the guy, but I finally decided to hold the conversation in Arabic, and according to the accepted cultural codes in phone conversations in the Arab world, I began:

I: *al-Salam alaikum.*

He: *Alaikum al-salam.*

I: Mr. Doe?

He: Yes, this is Mr. Doe speaking, please, how can I help you?

I: I hope, sir, that I am not disturbing you.

He: No, no, you are not disturbing me, my brother, please go on.

I: I thank you for your courtesy, but if the time is not convenient, please do not hesitate to tell me and I will call later at a more convenient time.

He: Why do you think it is not convenient? The time is convenient and I am at your service. We are brothers; how can I help you?

I: (talking at top speed without stopping for commas or periods) My name is Eli Avidar and I am the head of the Israeli delegation in Qatar and I wanted to meet with you to discuss the product your company sells to China since I believe there is a chance that Israeli companies will want to purchase that product.

Silence on the other end of the line. After a long time, the owner of the company said:

He: I am sorry. I do not want to work with Israel.

He hung up.

I was not offended or hurt. I reminded myself that it was not personal. Then I smiled to myself and said, "Eli Avidar, welcome to the Arab world."

I came to Qatar knowing full well where I was going. I learned that by following events in the Arab world for years, during which I also became aware of the depth of Arab hostility toward Israel. After years of working in the Arab world as part of the Israeli intelligence community, I had now come to live officially and openly in an Arab country.

During my service in Qatar and my work with economic factors in the Emirates, I am glad to say that often the people I contacted reacted positively to my invitation. In quite a few cases, the Qataris asked that the meetings take place not with them, but with their business managers, most of them foreign residents, from India or Europe. Those company owners did not want a direct contact, so they could always back off if the connection became widely known. On several occasions, certain companies denied the contact with us when it was exposed, and those same company owners were forced to "rebuke" their Indian or European business managers for having entered into those contacts.

Qatar is an especially interesting country for a test of normalization with Israel, since it is one of twelve states that are members of the Arab League that have no significant Jewish history or a direct conflict with Israel. Others in this group include the Gulf states, Mauretania, Somalia, Djibouti, and Comoro Islands.

It is interesting to compare, for example, Egypt and Qatar insofar as normalization is concerned. Relations between Israel and Qatar were established about twenty years after the signing of the peace treaty with Egypt, but when it came to normalization, the wealthy emirate was free of most of the shackles that constrain Egypt.[21] Throughout the entire time of my service in Qatar, I never heard any Qatari official utter the term "internal constraints," which the Egyptian government frequently uses as an excuse for the deadlock in normalization with Israel.

In Egypt, the opposition to normalization is led by various opposition movements, such as the Nasserist el-Amal party, whose leader declared that the State of Israel was founded for the purpose of dividing Egypt from the rest of the Arab world, and that Israel is a forward post for the United States in the Arab world.[22] In Qatar, in contrast, the front for opposition to relations with Israel is led by conservative elements from among the people in power, along with high-ranking religious leaders in the Arab world. These opponents never exerted much influence on the policies of Emir Hamad bin Khalifa Al Thani, the former ruler of Qatar. It is generally accepted by everyone that criticism of Israel is permitted as long as it does not contain even one word denouncing Qatari-Israeli relations at the time. As a matter of fact, this agreement applies not only in Qatar but also to the other Arab countries that are relatively friendly toward Israel.[23]

But Qatar also underwent a process of change, and during the military operation in December 2008, Qatar decided to break off relations with Israel. This was at a stage in Qatar's relations with the United States when it felt confident enough to take that step in view of the growing U.S. interest in the emirate. Qatar's support for Hamas, which began in 2006, became overt and significant after the severance of relations with Israel until it turned out in 2014 that Qatar was financing all of Hamas's military actions. And both Hamas and Qatar were openly supporting the Muslim Brotherhood in Egypt, during the riots against Mubarak and especially after Mohamed Morsi was ousted from power. The Qatari Al-Jazeera channel, in addition to its massive coverage in its broadcasts, has established a special channel for Egypt, which throughout all hours of the day reports on the activities of the Muslim Brotherhood against Abdel Fattah el-Sisi. A year into the reign of the new emir, Tamim bin Hamad Al Thani, the supposed even-handed policy of his father disappeared. The new emir is an ardent supporter of the most extreme Islamic movements in the Middle East.

Moreover, the freedom of organization, which existed in Egypt before Mubarak was ousted, and obviously afterward, does not exist in Qatar. In Egypt that freedom caused the government a serious headache. The various trade unions in Egypt are controlled by two major opposition groups: the Muslim Brotherhood and the Nasserist left-wing movements. In Qatar, on the other hand, no workers are organized on a professional basis, since most of the professionals are foreign residents working in Qatar under a work permit that can be canceled at any given moment.

In Egypt, all of the movements, organizations, parties, and people opposed to the Egyptian government, as well as to normalization with Israel, enjoy almost total freedom of expression and express their views incessantly in all the media and at every public forum. In Qatar, however, it is impossible to freely conduct a serious intellectual discourse. The newspapers can only print the words of clergy on current affairs and religious rules, along with advice based on the laws of the Muslim Sharia.

But make no mistake: Among the Qataris past and present, normalization with Israel is perceived as a bonus given to Israel, not as a mutual step intended to draw two friendly countries closer together. From the inception of relations with Qatar, the widely accepted approach is that Israel should not be allowed to enjoy the fruits of normalization, until the Palestinian issue is resolved and the other conflicts between Israel and its Arab neighbors end.

Not surprisingly, it was Saudi Arabia that pressured Qatar on the issue of normalization with Israel. Saudi Arabia did not look favorably upon that tiny emirate's attempt to independently promote a move of this sort that has regional implications, without first obtaining the agreement of the large kingdom. Some rather serious pressure also came from Syria, which felt that the warming up of relations between Qatar and Israel might weaken Arab pressure on Israel. But most surprising of all, the country that tried consistently to put sticks in the wheels of normalization between Qatar and Israel was none other than Egypt, the first country in the Arab camp to sign a peace treaty with Israel.

In the early 1990s, when Egypt managed to get out of the isolation enforced on it for having signed a peace treaty with Israel, Egypt returned to its natural position of leadership in the Arab world. As part of that comeback, Egypt wanted to be the one to control and supervise the pace of normalization of relations between Israel and the Arab world, at times aggressively. Amr Moussa, the Egyptian foreign minister, labeled the states that established relations with Israel following the Oslo agreements with the disparaging term *harwala* (those who rush to sign an agreement with Israel). This was during the Middle East and North Africa (MENA) economic summit held in Amman in October 1995—the conference during which the agreement of relations between Qatar and Israel was signed.

The Egyptian government, fearing it would lose control over the pace of the process, instructed its ambassadors in the various Arab states to closely follow the progress of the relations between Israel and the states in which they were serving.

Shortly after I landed in Qatar, I was invited to a pleasant courtesy visit with the Egyptian ambassador in the emirate. I was received by a junior member of the embassy staff who led me to the ambassador's office. As soon as I entered, I was greeted by one of the most important figures in the Egyptian culture of hospitality—the waiter. That young Egyptian wore a white shirt, black trousers, and a black bow tie. I felt as if I were in an Egyptian film, the kind screened in Israel every Friday afternoon that my family and I watched religiously.

"Tishrab al ahwa ezay ya basha? Teila, mazbuta aw khafifa?" (How would you like your coffee, sir? Strong, precise, or weak?), the waiter asked. Those well versed in Egyptian culture and Egyptian cuisine know that *mazbuta* is brewed Turkish coffee, made up of an equal number of teaspoons of black coffee and sugar.

When he noticed the expression of satisfaction on my face at the sight of the waiter, the ambassador smiled and said he would not be able to manage without his staff that traveled with him to all of his diplomatic posts. All during my visit, the Egyptian ambassador took pains to treat me politely and amicably, so that I began to think (wrongly, of course) that this reflected his attitude toward Israel. After exchanging a few more words of courtesy and hearing that I was born in Egypt, the ambassador showed a great deal of interest in my Egyptian biography. Afterward he focused solely on the nature of the relations between Qatar and Israel. It did not take long before I realized that despite his attempt to make our conversation seem like an amiable dialogue between diplomats, it was actually more in the nature of an interrogation, so that he could later reply to questions posed to him by his superiors in the Egyptian foreign ministry.

As for me, I was mainly interested in learning about the strengthening of the relations between Egypt and Qatar, in view of the tension then prevailing between the two states, especially since the ousting of the previous emir of Qatar, Khalifa bin Hamad Al Thani, who had been favored by Egypt. These relations reached their lowest point in 1996, the year in which the Israeli delegation in Qatar was opened. In keeping with the finest Arab tradition, each side enlisted its official media to disparage the other side. Caricatures appeared in the Egyptian press depicting the new emir of Qatar speaking while hiding behind the podium a milk bottle in his hand—in order to mock him for his young age and inexperience. The Qatari press, for its part, got back at Egypt by defining the country as "the old lady whose heyday is over." But the conflict did not end with these derisive exchanges. Qatar expelled many Egyptians who were working in Qatar, and Egypt reacted by canceling the exemption for an entrance visa that Qataris wanting to visit Egypt had enjoyed until then, and placed many obstacles in the way of Qatari residents applying for such visas.

In November 1997, the tension peaked when Egypt refused to participate in the MENA conference that convened in Doha. The absence was interpreted by the Qataris, rightly so, as an insult, and from then on Qatar took advantage of every opportunity to taunt Egypt. You might say that Al-Jazeera's critical coverage of events in Egypt over the years was a sort of Qatari revenge for Egypt's derisive, arrogant attitude toward Qatar. This criticism reached its height with the outbreak of the riots in Egypt in early 2011 that ended with Mubarak's ouster.

This, then, was the background to the amicable courtesy talk between the Egyptian ambassador and me, but none of this was mentioned explicitly, as the two of us sipped our aromatic black coffee. The visit ended with a warm handshake and an agreement to stay in touch.

In November 1999, I was invited, together with my wife, to attend an official event held at the Doha Sheraton hotel. Like the other heads of diplomatic delegations in Qatar, I waited in line to shake hands with our host, right behind the Egyptian ambassador and his wife. When they turned around and noticed us, I could see at once from the expression on his wife's face what the ambassador really thought of me and what he had told her about me. As she turned her head away without saying a word, the ambassador asked me in a friendly tone what I was doing at that affair. He probably meant to say he was surprised to see me at an event for ambassadors, since the relations between Israel and Qatar were not on a full diplomatic level, and I was there as the head of a delegation, not as an ambassador.

I asked His Excellency the Ambassador in exactly the same friendly tone, "*Ala, huma mastasharush saa'dtak able ma'azamuni?*" (What? Didn't they [the Qataris] consult with you before inviting me?)

He paled and replied, "*La, la, la, enta fehemteni ghalat.*" (No, no, no, you misunderstood me.)

I placed my hand on his shoulder and, while smiling, said, "Never mind; have a pleasant evening."

I found out later that before all future official events, the Egyptian ambassador would check in advance to see if I had been invited by the Qatari foreign ministry. He was also one of the organizers of a petition signed by several Arab embassies complaining to the Qatari foreign ministry that our delegation was being given the status of an embassy, contrary to what Qatar had stated.

My first lesson from this story was that normalization with Israel was often likely to serve Arab states as a bargaining chip or an affront in quarrels that really have nothing to do with us. No matter how hard we try, as long as normalization—or, more precisely, its absence—is regarded as an ultimate test of all-Arab loyalty in which each nation watches over its friend/rival, it will be very difficult to promote it at the pace we would like. The second lesson, the more important one, was that we should not despair, not be deterred, and especially, as I noted earlier, not take offense.

THE QATARI CIRCLES OF POWER:
TO FALL BETWEEN THE CRACKS AND
GET UP SMILING

As for offenses, there was no shortage of those. The beginning of my service in Qatar, on August 19, 1999, was far from calm. I arrived at the emirate at the end of a serious, widely covered legal battle around the building that housed the Israeli delegation. It is a very telling example of the way in which Israel often falls victim to quarrels that do not relate to the country itself.

To sum up the events: In 1996, with the opening of the Israeli delegation in Qatar, no local individual or company agreed to rent it a property. Fawaz al-Attiyah, the media adviser of the Qatari foreign minister, Hamad bin Jassim, who was also in charge of the relations with Israel, rented a property in his name from a member of the Al Thani family, the most important family in Qatar, and then sublet it to the Israeli delegation, all of this with the knowledge and consent of the foreign minister. The owner of the property was only told that the building would be used for the needs of the Qatari foreign ministry. When he discovered that the property was meant for the Israeli delegation, he applied to the court, claiming he was deceived. Rumor had it that the link with Israel angered him far less than the fact that the price the delegation paid to Fawaz was four times the price he was getting from him.

At first, the legal proceedings were kept relatively quiet. We were certain we had no part in this hornet's nest and that the diplomatic immunity we enjoyed by virtue of the agreement with Qatar would protect us from the court. But as soon as the local media were in the picture, Israel was dragged into the affair as the party that had supposedly deceived the property owner and was unprepared to vacate the premises. For about a year and a half, Israel was exposed to a media barrage on a daily basis. This served the Qatari government, which, among other things, wanted to show that the relations between the emirate and Israel during Netanyahu's term in office were not the same as they had been during the governments of Rabin and Peres.

Fawaz al-Attiyah later was removed from his post and went to London to study. He had very significantly influenced the building of relations between Israel and Qatar, and after he left, no one was appointed in the Qatari foreign ministry to deal with the subject of Israel. Some say that Fawaz had fallen out of favor not because he rented the property to the Israelis, but rather because of the suspicion that he was beginning to overshadow the foreign minister in the public's eyes. In the Qatari foreign ministry, as in every other office and organization in the Arab world, there is no room for an overly dominant number two next to the boss. The irony is that the present foreign minister of Qatar, Khalid al-Attiyah, is Fawaz's cousin and represented him at the delegation trial in 1999. I met with him after I came to Qatar, at his request, and he seemed to be a moderate person. Today he is the foreign minister, the one who justifies Qatari policy vis-à-vis the international community and Hamas. But let us go back to the period in question.

On May 31, 1999, an article was printed in the *A-Sharq* newspaper reporting that a Qatari citizen had managed to oust the Israeli delegation from his house, and that the Israelis were once again searching for a home for their delegation. This was the background and the atmosphere when I arrived in Qatar. If I thought the atmosphere would warm up as a result of the changes in government in Israel and Ehud Barak's election as prime minister, I was soon proven wrong.

If there was an expectation in Israel that, with the change of government, relations between the two states would be raised to ambassadorial level, the Qataris had different intentions. One of the first requests I submitted to the local government immediately after my arrival was to meet the Qatari foreign minister. The reply I got was that the minister was "busy." I knew that until I met with the foreign minister, my status as head of the Israeli delegation would be merely symbolic, with the Qataris doing the bare minimum required. So I persisted.

In October 1999, the General Assembly of the United Nations (UN) was going to meet in New York, where the Israeli foreign minister, David Levy, would meet with his Qatari counterpart. In preparation for that meeting, I sent a cable to the senior deputy director-general of the foreign ministry, requesting that, in his meeting with the Qatari foreign minister, Levy raise the need for a meeting between us, as part of the efforts to improve relations between the two states. He replied that the issue was already on Levy's agenda and he would indeed bring it up at the meeting.

After the meeting between the two foreign ministers, the senior deputy director-general reported that the Qatari foreign minister asked that I call his office to make an appointment since he was interested in reviving the relations between the two states. I also learned that the initiative did not come from Levy, but actually from his Qatari counterpart. In fact, Levy never raised the issue about a meeting with me. I knew that the message the Qataris had received was that the Israeli foreign minister had no problem with Qatar's cool attitude toward the Israeli delegation there. I was gratified by the Qatari minister's request, but I soon learned that my gratification was premature.

After the foreign ministers' meeting, I met with the head of the office of the Qatari emir. I knew him through a mutual friend, a man who represented one of the largest economic groups in Israel. At the start of our meeting, I told him that despite what had been agreed in the meeting among the foreign ministers, all of my requests for an appointment with the foreign minister had gone unanswered. Four weeks later, when we met again, he surprised me by asking whether my meeting with the foreign minister went well. When I replied that such a meeting never occurred, he placed a call in my presence to the head of the foreign minister's office, Muhammad Jiham Qa'wari, who told him that the foreign minister did really want to meet with me, but there was a delay because of more urgent matters, and the meeting would take place soon.

"You see?" the head of the emir's office said after hanging up. "Everything is fine, all you have to do is be more patient. The minister is busy, but as you just heard, they will contact you soon to set a date for the meeting."

Two weeks later, I met him again, this time on another urgent matter. "Well," he asked at the beginning of our meeting, "did you meet with the foreign minister?"

"I didn't want to talk about that because I didn't want to upset you," I replied, "but if you really want to know, I still haven't met him and my requests are still being ignored."

His face grew red with anger. "If you think this meeting is a whim of mine, or is at the discretion of the foreign minister, you're wrong. The instruction to hold a meeting came from the emir himself."

Again he picked up the phone and again called the head of the foreign minister's office, and this time summoned him to a personal meeting at the emir's palace, the following day at ten in the morning.

At 10:15 a.m. the next morning, the head of the emir's office called me, and before I could utter a word, he began berating me: "Eli, you simply are impatient. The foreign minister is interested in meeting you, but his schedule is very tight, and he can't stop everything just to meet with you."

This time, too, our conversation ended with the statement "The minister will contact you soon." I had no doubt that he was making this call in the presence of the head of the foreign minister's office, and that, after admonishing him, he had not wanted to appear to be too pro-Israeli. So he had to even things out by backing up the foreign minister and rebuking me while Qa'wari was listening.

Bottom line: Everything remained the same. About two weeks after that phone call, I still had no appointment with the foreign minister. Nor did I get a call about that from his office. Only later did I learn that when the Qatari foreign minister heard that the head of the emir's office had intervened in the matter, he decided to flex his muscles and show him who was more senior. Consequently, he deliberately put off arranging a meeting with me.

When I understood that no good would come of the intervention of the head of the emir's office (and I certainly did not want to be at the focus of a power struggle between Qatari officials), I decided to change my tactic. On November 18, 1999, I received a briefing cable from the foreign ministry in Jerusalem about the peace process. It requested all Israeli ambassadors and representatives throughout the world to initiate talks in the local foreign ministries in order to explain Israel's positions.

At nine thirty in the morning, about an hour after I received the cable, I made a direct call to the Qatari foreign minister's cell phone. I had obtained the number a week before while smoking a nargila with a group of Qatari friends.

"*Al-Salam alaikum*," I said to the voice that answered on the other end of the line (I knew it was the minister's personal bodyguard).

"*Alaikum al-salam*," he replied.

"I would like to speak to the foreign minister," I said.

"Who is speaking, sir?" he asked.

After I introduced myself, he asked whether the matter was urgent and could not be delayed, and I replied laconically that I wanted to speak to the minister.

"I'll check your request and get back to you," the bodyguard replied and hung up. A few seconds later, my phone rang. The head of the emir's office was on the other end: "What happened, Eli? Why did you call the minister's private mobile? Has anything serious happened?"

I replied in the negative and went on in a casual tone, "I called the foreign minister because I was asked to convey a briefing from the Israeli foreign minister, David Levy."

When he understood that my call did not involve an urgent security matter, he said he would deal with the matter. A few minutes later my phone rang again. This time the head of the emir's office was speaking in an angry tone: "The foreign minister is furious with you. They thought there was a security warning. He was about to leave for Pakistan but following your call they stopped the plane from taking off because they thought something urgent was going on. I told him he can take off and that everything is okay, but you should know our foreign minister is very annoyed with you."

Three days after that conversation, on the morning of November 21, 1999, the phone in my home rang. I was asked to come to the foreign minister's office within an hour, for a meeting with him. When I arrived at the site of the emir's palace, where it is located, I was ushered into the minister's office. He looked angry.

The foreign minister of Qatar, Hamad bin Jassim (or by his nickname HBJ), is known for his acumen and creativity, which on more than one occasion has annoyed Arab, Western, and other governments. He is an impressive man, sophisticated and shrewd, who played a key role in the quiet coup in which the former emir took over power from his father. According to the rumors, the former emir appreciated his abilities, and perhaps that is why he had to leave Qatar when the emir was also abroad. Today bin Jassim does not hold any position in Qatar after the former emir handed control over to his son Tamim.

He was seated on an armchair in the sitting area to my right, and the head of his office sat beside him. The minister's hands were crossed on his chest, and, contrary to the usual custom, he did not greet his guest, but waited for me to speak first.

"Good morning, Your Excellency," I opened in Arabic. "I thank you for devoting time to this meeting and appreciate it very much. I understand you just returned from a difficult visit to Pakistan and I am grateful for this gesture."

"No problem," the minister replied curtly in an impatient tone.

At this point, I decided to take off my diplomatic hat and dispense with the manners I'd been taught at the foreign ministry. I looked straight at the minister and asked in spoken Arabic, *"Enta zaa'lan meni?"* (Are you angry with me?). The minister looked at me as if he did not understand my words.

I went on: "Are you angry with me, sir? If you are for some reason, I have no idea why, and if I angered you, it certainly was not intentional."

The foreign minister straightened up in his chair and began to speak, gesturing with his hands: "I am not angry with you at all, but you ought to know that you are playing a dangerous game. In regard to external affairs, you conferred with people who are not involved in such matters, and I really do not like that."

"Sir, I called your office dozens of times. My foreign minister sent me a cable stating that you had asked for a meeting, but still nothing happened, and all of my requests were totally ignored. I did not want an unnecessary crisis to develop here."

"Listen carefully," the minister said, placing his right hand on his chest to demonstrate his sincerity. "I want to give you a piece of advice like a big brother. Don't play inside the circle of powers in Qatar. I am at your disposal and so is the head of my office."

The office head's jaw nearly fell open upon hearing his boss's statement, all the more because of the thought that from now on he would have to maintain contact with me.

"Sir, the chief of protocol maintains close contact with . . ." the head of the minister's office said. Before he could continue, however, the minister waved his right hand, signaling to him to be quiet.

"I repeat, I am at your disposal and the head of my office is at your disposal, and do not turn to anyone else."

To underscore the seriousness of his intentions, the minister said, "The former head of your delegation did not want to leave the offices in accordance with the court's ruling. We informed the Americans that if you did not vacate the building, the head of your delegation would be declared persona non grata. And why is that? Because the political adviser of your prime minister came to a meeting with the emir in 1998 and you did not want me to know, but I finally found out and participated in the meeting."

It was Dore Gold, the political adviser of the then prime minister, whose visit to Qatar was coordinated by the Mossad and infuriated the Qatari foreign minister.

I was amazed and said, "Sir, do you really believe that this matter concerned the foreign ministry or the previous head of our delegation in Qatar? Do you really think that if we had known about it, we would have allowed such a thing to happen? We were not connected to that."

"In our region, everything is connected to everything," the minister replied and ended the discussion on that subject. After that cloud had been dispelled, the meeting moved on to more practical matters; we discussed promoting bilateral relations, raising the level of diplomatic relations, the entry of Israelis into Qatar, the import of Israeli goods to Qatar, the Qatari press, a political dialogue between the states, and similar issues.

But someone once said that nothing is free in the Arab world; only the Jews like to give things for free. Consequently, the very next morning I was summoned to a meeting with the head of the minister's office, who told me, "As a sign of the warmer relations between the states, the foreign minister asks you to permit Nayef Hawatmeh, the head of the Democratic Front for the Liberation of Palestine, to enter the area of the Palestinian Authority."

I replied with a smile that such a request is more appropriate to "very warm relations," not to the kind that have just begun to warm up, but I would look into it and get back to him soon. A few days later, I gave him the official reply of the Israeli government, worded in keeping with the finest diplomatic tradition: "The Israeli government cannot, at this stage, allow Nayef Hawatmeh to enter the area of the Palestinian Authority. Nonetheless, we have taken note of Qatar's request, and if it should become possible in the future, we will be sure to coordinate his entry through you."

THE QATARI MEDIA:
HOW TO WIN A FIXED GAME

The Qatari government often used the local media to promote negative reporting and deplore normalization with Israel. A good example is the case of the evacuation of our delegation's premises. But not only that, on August 11, 1999, the newspaper *al-Rayah* printed an article titled "The Bombs of Normalization," following Mauretania's decision to violate the Arab League's order and establish full diplomatic relations with Israel. The article concluded by saying, "Undoubtedly Israel aspires to promote her aims, and the bombs of normalization now look more threatening than Israel's atomic bombs."[24]

On October 28, 1999, that same newspaper printed another article that warned:

> [I]t appears that all Arab and Islamic states are fated to finally fall into Israel's net. The United States is constantly pressuring the Arab states to normalize their relations with Israel, and this without waiting for the achievement of Palestinian rights. I am not saying that the Arab states should fight against Israel, the era of the military struggle has ended, but the conflict has not ended and there is no reason why we should give in. If so, then why do the Arab states fall, one after the other, into Israel's net? Is the only reason America's pressure, or perhaps there is also something tempting about normalization with Israel?
>
> My conclusion is that in these times, interests talk. Relations between states are no longer a function of religious, linguistic, historical or geographical affinity. On the basis of the benefit to be gained, Israel has more to offer Muslim states than the Arab states do. It seems that the Arab countries never bothered to find anything in common with Islamic countries other than an expression of feelings of brotherhood.[25]

On more than one occasion, I was helped by Jewish organizations in the United States in my attempts to restrain the rancorous tone of the Qatari media. Early in 2000, a delegation of twenty-one members of the board of the American Jewish Congress, headed by its president, Jack Rosen, came to

Qatar. I asked to talk with them before they met with representatives of the government. They came to our offices, and I showed them the caricatures of Prime Minister Barak in a Nazi uniform. Rosen asked for a copy and received one. I learned afterward that at the meeting with the emir, Rosen raised the problem, and the emir replied that it was an untrue rumor. When Rosen pulled out a photocopy of the caricature, the emir blushed and said he would deal with the matter. He was obviously surprised by the fact that Rosen had the copy.

It is important to understand that all of the Qatari newspapers, and certainly the Al-Jazeera TV channel, are controlled by the Qatar government and guided by its interests. The game is fixed, but it's not always lost in advance. On April 4, 2000, Ayelet Yehiav, the spokesperson of our embassy in Cairo, called to tell me that an Egyptian acquaintance, Said Galal, a member of the Egyptian peace movement, was coming to Qatar to participate in a popular Al-Jazeera show, titled *The Opposite Direction*, hosted by Dr. Faisal al-Qassem. Al-Qassem is a Syrian Druze, a provocative figure known for his pan-Arab views. He is a graduate of the drama department at Hull University in England, and his acting skills help him create drama in the studio. His show caused worsened relations between Qatar and many Arab states that were offended by what he said, and particularly by the fact that he provided a forum for oppositional elements.

"Eli, are you prepared to call Galal and perhaps invite him for a coffee so he won't feel lonely there?" Ayelet asked.

I called the hotel where he was staying and suggested we meet so he could pass the time pleasantly. When he agreed, I sent a car to pick him up at the hotel, and he arrived at my office at two o'clock. After a brief chat, I was impressed by his amiability and especially by his courage. I knew how hard it could be for a man like that in a country like Egypt, where the government and the opposition movements join forces against open normalization with Israel, and certainly against an organization called "The Egyptian Peace Movement."

After about half an hour, I asked if he knew what he was getting into on the show that night, and what his strategy would be. "I plan to arrive dressed informally, probably wearing a polo shirt, and the method I am going to follow is that of the philosopher. After every question they ask me, I'll look up at the ceiling, think a bit, and after a few seconds, I'll reply," he said.

I felt myself break into a cold sweat. That man was going to one of the most aggressive studios in the Arab world, and Faisal al-Qassem, the host of the show, would eat him alive. It was no wonder that al-Qassem had invited him, I thought to myself. He wants to make the approach of calling for peace with Israel a ridiculous delusion, and turn the members of that movement into a joke in the eyes of the tens of millions who watch the show.

"Listen, my friend," I said to Galal. "I don't want to offend you, but I don't think you understand what type of a show you've been invited to and what you're going to go through on it. I think I can help you prepare properly, but first of all, you need to want me to do that and you'll have to devote at least two hours."

He replied that he would be glad to hear my advice, and so we began preparing for his appearance on the show. At that point, in my heart I thanked Naomi Benzur, the media adviser for the cadet course I took at the foreign ministry. She taught me how to sit in a studio, how to behave, how to hold the interviewer's attention, and—most important of all—what not to do. I also was grateful then to an American Jew named Beck Buchwald, owner of one of the largest, most important media consultant firms in the United States, who, in 1994, gave the group of Israeli diplomats serving in the United States (myself included) a media workshop in conjunction with the American Jewish Congress.

I'll never forget how, at the opening of the workshop, Beck invited one of the veteran consul-generals to participate in a simulation of a TV interview. Beck, playing the role of the interviewer, asked the diplomat a question, and the reply the diplomat gave took three and a half minutes. Afterward, Beck asked all those present what they thought about the reply. They all answered politely that they thought it was a good, informative reply, which included all the important elements.

"What do you think?" Beck asked the diplomat, who hadn't realized he was the first victim in the workshop. He replied that he thought his answer was fine. Then Beck said, "I think it was a piece of shit! What the fuck are you doing? Get to the point; repeat your message. Short, short, short . . ." As he spoke the last three words he gestured with his right hand as if he were striking his left palm with an ax.

And last but not least, I was thankful to the late Joseph (Tommy) Lapid for his loud outbursts on the Israeli panel show titled *Popolitika* and the way he took over the cameras even when he hadn't been given permission to speak.

I explained to Said Galal how the TV studio is built, how the man in the control room has to move the camera in his direction as soon as he opens his mouth and speaks loudly enough even if it isn't his turn to speak, because the viewer at home will feel uncomfortable hearing the voice of someone he cannot see. I told him what a sound bite is, so the message gets across within only six to nine seconds. I taught him how to express the same idea in different words and to repeat the message again and again. I explained that the show lasts an hour and a half, and that he has to use the time allotted him to convey the message and, when necessary, to interrupt the other guy by using several relatively simple tricks.

The most important thing, I told him, was not to be offended. I explained that he simply should not take offense or take personally anything the other interviewee or the host says, "When you interrupt the other interviewee, he will turn to you and ask you to be civilized and not interrupt him just as he doesn't interrupt you, and to respect the codes of Arab manners. Let him waste his time on manners and politeness and go on with what you want to get across. Change the wording of the message and do not get flustered by the host or by the invective."

It was right after the failure of the Geneva summit between Bill Clinton and Hafez al-Assad in 2000, following which the U.S. government blamed Assad for having rejected its generous solution. The wording of the message I suggested to Galal was this: "Syria has wasted twenty-three precious years since Assad turned down President Sadat's offer to join him in the peace process."

In addition, we worded different versions of the same message:

"I do not understand what has changed in the last twenty-three years."

"Can you explain why Assad has wasted twenty-three years?"

"What has Syria gained from twenty-three years of refusing peace?"

And many other versions, all repeating the words "twenty-three years."

When the show started as planned, I sat in my living room in Doha, Qatar, and muttered to myself that if Said Galal followed 20 percent of my suggestions, he would get through the show in one piece. At the studio, Syria was represented by no less a personage than Abdullah al-Ahmed, the deputy director-general of the Ba'ath movement and one of its most eloquent spokesmen.

I was wrong about Galal. From the first moment, the show turned into a volcano. Said Galal accepted all of my suggestions, perfected them, and doled them out at a much, much higher dosage than I had advised. He took total control of the studio; interrupted the Syrian participant throughout the show; succeeded in silencing the host, al-Qassem, when he exaggerated; and—most important of all—was not offended, and did not fold when the Syrian urged him to stop interrupting.

Midway through, the show stopped for a news broadcast. When it returned, Galal launched into a tirade, stating that al-Ahmed had threatened him during the break and said to him, "May God return you to your children in peace." Galal accused the Syrian of having threatened him in keeping with the tradition of totalitarian Syria. The studio was in total chaos.

When the host got everyone calmed down, he asked Galal a question on a different subject, and Galal replied, "I understand your question, but I think it is important to focus on the issue of why the Syrians waited twenty-three years until Geneva."

At this stage, Faisal al-Qassem lost his temper and began shouting, "You've repeated that twenty-three million times and you are not answering my questions!" He turned at once to Abdullah al-Ahmed and yelled, "Answer him already; give him an answer and stop yammering about his interruptions."

Listeners who contacted the studio were mostly members of the opposition in Egypt. One was Mustafa Bakri, editor of the opposition weekly *al-Usbu*, who screamed and cursed Said Galal on the live broadcast. It wasn't a show—it was complete chaos, and it seemed that the host, who was used to commanding the show, was at a total loss. He looked miserable, as if he were praying for the show to be over and end his suffering.

Two days later, I met an acquaintance who happened to be at the Al-Jazeera studio after the end of the show and saw Faisal al-Qassem and his assistants standing around in the corridor. He told me that al-Qassem looked "done in," and was yelling at his assistants: "I was humiliated tonight, I was humiliated as I never have been before in my life, and that Abdullah al-Ahmed was incapable of giving him a simple answer."

My acquaintance went over to al-Qassem and asked him, "Who suggested that you invite that Said Galal?"

Al-Qassem replied, "That al-Ahmed pressured me. He wanted me to hold the show at any cost after the failure of the Geneva summit, and said, 'You can even bring Yitzhak Shamir to confront me.'"

The show is broadcast live on Al-Jazeera, and usually afterward there are two reruns at different times, to allow viewers from far-away continents and different time zones to watch it. But not this time. The show was never broadcast again after that first live broadcast.

I was glad that I had been able to help Said Galal successfully cope on that show, which was meant to be a fatal trap for him and the approach he represents—a movement of Arab citizens who advocate peace with Israel. Later, when I founded the Forum for a Smart Middle East, I tried more than once to get on al-Qassem's show. I was told that it was not possible, because he does not invite Israeli Jews to participate on his show. I can only assume that if he should read these lines, I'll have even less of a chance of getting on the show.

If we thought that the media in general and Al-Jazeera in particular are important, the riots and revolts of 2011 came along and magnified their impact. Al-Jazeera can not only report on riots but also maintain them, intensify them, and even quell them. Al-Jazeera had founders' shares in the coup in Tunisia. It followed the events and gave enormous support to the demonstrators from the moment a resident set fire to himself after his vegetable stand was destroyed until the flight of Tunisia's president to exile in Saudi Arabia.

Egypt was a similar case. Al-Jazeera reported continually on the riots there in general and at Tahrir Square in particular. Even when the channel's activity was prohibited in the first weeks, it managed to broadcast photographs smuggled out of the country. The prohibition failed and was a significant factor in the fall of Hosni Mubarak's government, something that was unthinkable before the outbreak of the riots.

Al-Jazeera also has another type of influence: the channel's decision not to report massively on the riots in Bahrain in February 2011—even when, in the largest demonstration, one hundred thousand inhabitants took to the streets (out of a total population of eight hundred thousand in the entire country)—led to the cessation of the demonstrations.

The channel's lack of coverage also dictated the agenda of the international networks. When troops from Saudi Arabia and the United Arab Emirates entered Bahrain on March 14, 2011, to help the kingdom suppress the riots, it reported that event merely as an action arising from the regional cooperative agreement.

In the Middle East today, unlike the situation in the past, governments rise and fall by force of the media. As I said, this is an arena that Israel cannot afford to abandon, no matter how difficult and hostile it is.

ECONOMIC NORMALIZATION IN QATAR: BUSINESS AS USUAL?

The Qatari business sector is the group that, for a long time, had the most positive orientation vis-à-vis normalization with Israel. Often, however, the conditions and offers made by businessmen from the principalities do not meet any logical economic criterion. They are motivated by the feeling that they are paying a high price in advance for economic cooperation with Israel, and hence the Israeli companies have to knuckle under and agree to imaginary profit margins.

Qatar's Chambers of Commerce Association, which in the early years of our relations was an organization that maintained a favorable connection with us, changed its attitude over the years, and almost completely cut off all ties during the second Intifada. The burden was then placed on local businessmen, who receive no government support or encouragement.

I do not underestimate the price that businessmen in the Arab world interested in economic ties with Israel have paid and are still paying. In Qatar these businessmen represented a thin layer of the population, and the interest that motivated them was not shared—either ideologically or economically—by any others. In the large financial concerns, the owners and the chairmen of the corporations are Qataris, and under them, I quite often came across managers of Arab origin—Palestinians, Algerians, Egyptians, or Lebanese—who were far less committed to this cooperation than the owners. In quite a few cases, those managers were successful in persuading the company owners to pull out of the joint ventures.

Qatari businessmen were apprehensive about public criticism, and the lower their position and family status, the more fearful they became. Their nightmare was to wake up one morning to find themselves accused of conducting normal relations with Israel, without any government backing.

Although at the time, Qatar canceled the restrictions of the Arab boycott on the importation of goods from Israel, the Qatari companies were compelled to resort to creative maneuvers to carry out such imports without public knowledge of their actions. They had to do this to avoid becoming hostages of some clerk who might publicize the fact that they were importing goods from Israel. Qatar is a small, tribal state. The men meet every evening in *majles* (a living room located in the homes of wealthy men in the Emirates, isolated from the rest of the home where the owner receives his male guests). The slightest of rumors, certainly one connected to Israel, would find its way to all the *majalis* in the principality within a few hours.

Qatari businessmen went to great lengths to avoid that outcome. They brought various fruits into the emirate with certificates of origin from countries that never heard of that fruit. A Qatari businessman, who imported high-tech products from Israel, would receive the goods through a European country, regularly declare he had lost the certificate of origin, and pay a negligible fine of several hundred dollars. He added with a smile that his employees would haggle with the custom officials over the unjustified fine, and that distraction always worked.

Economic interests do not always win out over the hostile atmosphere. In 1998, my wife Ornit completed the cadet course of the ministry of industry and commerce and waited to be posted abroad. The challenge was to find a place where we would both have professional work, and Qatar definitely fit the bill. I was concerned because I knew she would be facing a difficult professional period—not only because she was an Israeli but also because she was a woman in a conservative Arab state. But Ornit was not perturbed, and I was pleased when she was appointed Israel's commercial attaché to Qatar and Oman (with which we had similar relations at the time). Several months after we arrived, she decided to look into the possibility of Israeli companies purchasing by-products of the Qatari petroleum industry instead of importing them from Europe. So, one morning she found herself at a meeting with two managers of a Qatari government company, both of Palestinian origin. The meeting was held in a very professional manner, and it ended with the agreement that the parties would check into the possibility and meet again within a few days.

The follow-up meeting never took place. Instead, the following day the meeting was reported on the front page of the popular morning newspaper *A-Sharq*, under the heading "Israel Uses Beautiful Woman to Persuade Qatari Businessmen to Trade with Her." The item quoted the two managers—their names and the names of the company remained anonymous—who said that a (female) commercial representative from the Israeli delegation in Qatar had come to their office to convince them to conduct business with Israel and that they had stuck to their refusal although she had done her utmost to persuade them.

"Beautiful Israeli women who seduce Arabs"—that is the accepted phrase in written Arab culture, in relation to the work methods of the Mossad in Arab countries, and now it turned out that it had sunk roots in the economic sphere as well.

In those moments, I felt guilty about having dragged my wife into the Qatari adventure, but she did not blink an eyelash, and continued to work tirelessly to promote business between Israeli and local companies. Apparently, it took her no time to internalize the commandment: do not take offense.

THE QATARI ACADEMIA AND NORMALIZATION

When I first took my position in Qatar, one of my main aims was to try to develop Israeli-Qatari relations in the academic sphere. I asked for a meeting with the president of Qatar University, Dr. Abdullah Bin Saleh Al-Khuleifi. The reception was warm and courteous, but when I asked if he would agree to consider academic cooperation with Israeli universities, he replied that local public opinion would not allow that. "Nonetheless," he added, "we would be glad to host well-known Israeli experts who have foreign passports." From his body language, I understood that his suggestion would also never see the light of day.

Later a mutual friend told me that Fawaz al-Attiyah, the patron of relations with Israel, had come to Qatar on a visit from London, where he had been "exiled" for the purpose of his "studies" following the affair of the delegation's building. I had heard about him and his involvement in furthering connections and negotiations with Israel, and I was pleased when my friend suggested he introduce us. Al-Attiyah came to the meeting with our mutual friend, wearing a red *kefiya*. He looked as if he were afraid to be seen in my company and, throughout our conversation, made sure that the *kefiya* covered part of his face. After about an hour, when the atmosphere had warmed up, I said to him, "I wanted to ask you about something that's been troubling me, and I can't seem to find a solution. I recently met with the president of Qatar University, and we spoke about academic cooperation, lecturers from Israel coming to give lectures at the university in Doha, and Qatari academics giving lectures in Israel."

Just to be clear: al-Attiyah had racked up the highest number of hours of meetings with Israelis, and had even been the one sent to sign the agreement of relations at the conference in Amman in October 1995. Nevertheless, he glared at me and fired off the following reply: "That's how you are, you Israelis. You begin by sending lecturers to universities, and at the next stage you want to influence the minds of our next generation."

He answered in spoken Arabic, without any preparation or forethought. I looked at him impassively and said in a calm voice, "You know what amazes me? That an answer like that comes from someone like you, a man of the world, educated in the West, who has met with Israelis and whom Israelis regard as a true friend, and from you of all people, I get this kind of an answer? The truth is that I'm angry at myself, not at you. It makes me angry to think that I'm disturbed when I see the demonstrations in the Arab world, instigated by inflamed, uneducated masses. And why should I be angry at the demonstrators, if you, someone who knows us, thinks the way you do?"

In Arabic my reply was harsh, very harsh. Al-Attiyah launched into an explanation of why I did not understand his intention. I replied that the conversation had taken place in Arabic, and I do understand Arabic. He apologized. We concluded the meeting. He returned to London, and I was left with a bad feeling. The very people whom I thought were the lever to peace with the Arab world also harbored prejudices they could not rid themselves of.

Perhaps the pressure of the very existence of the meeting, his sensitive situation in Qatar, and the fear that the foreign minister who had ousted him from his position would learn about the meeting all had an adverse effect on his ability to hold his tongue. In March 2010, the press reported that Fawaz al-Attiyah had been arrested by the Qatari authorities, after publishing a book in which he interpreted historical events of the al-Attiyah tribe contrary to the official state-imposed version.

And yet I believe that generations of gradual confidence building will pass until the basic conspiratorial approach toward Israel gives way to a mature, realistic, more genuine approach. In the meantime, the Israeli point of departure should be that even the best of our friends in the Arab world scrutinize even our most beneficial and innocent moves with very suspicious eyes, and their commitment to cooperation with us is fragile and limited.

RELATIONS WITH QATAR AT THE OUTBREAK OF THE SECOND INTIFADA—AN ALTERNATIVE WAY TO MANAGE A CRISIS

A little more than a year after I arrived in Qatar, the Middle East was embroiled in one of the gravest crises in its history. The promising peace process led by the Israeli government, which pressed for a comprehensive peace with the Palestinians, and a U.S. president more committed to the process than at any time in the past, ended in a flare-up that culminated in the outbreak of the second Intifada, on September 28, 2000.

As anticipated, the Intifada produced negative public opinion toward Israel throughout the Arab world. This provoked demonstrations and militant declarations by the various opposition groups that called on their governments not to remain indifferent, to support their Palestinian brethren and to cease all steps toward normalization with Israel. Until that stage, there were three Israeli embassies in the Arab world—in Egypt, Jordan, and Maureta- nia—and four Israeli delegations of partial status—in Morocco, Tunisia, Oman, and Qatar.

With the outbreak of the uprising, the Arab League convened for an emergency meeting in Cairo in October, and decided to lower the level of the relations. Egypt and Jordan recalled their ambassadors and left temporary appointees in Israel.[26] The four Arab states in which there were Israeli dele- gations at a lower level were asked to sever relations with Israel. Later in the month, the Israeli delegations in Oman, Tunisia, and Morocco were, in fact, closed down.

In Oman, the head of the Israeli delegation was summoned to a meeting at the Omani foreign ministry in October 2000 and asked to leave the country for a two- to three-week vacation until things calmed down. In the correspon- dence between the head of the delegation and the responsible officials in Jerusalem, he was instructed to tell the Omanis that he had no intention of going on vacation, and that they had to decide whether they wanted the delegation in Oman. Very soon the Omanis replied that he had to leave Oman within seven days with his entire staff and close down the delegation.

In Tunisia, two demonstrators were apparently killed[27] during a demon- stration against Israel, and the head of the delegation was asked to leave the country within only forty-eight hours. Since, from the very outset, the dele- gation's work in Tunisia was difficult and replete with obstacles, no one was surprised by the brutal decision.

In Morocco, everyone was taken by surprise, given the historical warm (albeit generally unofficial) relations between the two countries. Along with the Arab League's decision, the significant element that tipped the scales was a demonstration organized by the Moroccan government in support of the Palestinians. Contrary to the Moroccan government's assessment, about a million and a half people participated in the demonstration. In view of how high emotions were running, the Moroccan government was compelled to take an immediate decision, and the head of the Israeli delegation was in- formed that he had to vacate the delegation within thirty days.

Qatar obviously should have been the next in line, particularly in view of the poor relations that prevailed between the two states between 1998 and 1999. I estimated that the second Intifada would not end within a short time,[28] and that the Qataris would have a hard time resisting the local and inter-Arab pressure to close down the Israeli delegation. Consequently, there was a need for some counter-pressure.

I began by mapping the trips of Qatari leaders to official meetings outside the country and the planned official visits of foreign groups and organizations to the emirate, in order to find people who could help, and indeed I did. The Israeli deputy chief of mission in our embassy in Washington made sure to raise the subject with the U.S. secretary of defense, William Cohen, before he left on his trip to Qatar. In parallel, he sent messages to the U.S. embassy in Qatar to bolster Israel's case and to ensure the ambassador's active involvement in the crisis.[29]

The Israeli ambassador in Germany was asked to brief the chancellor before his planned visit to Qatar at the end of October 2000. Indeed, during the chancellor's meeting with the emir in Doha, the subject of the Israeli delegation was the first major point to be raised.[30] At the same time, the embassy in London made sure to brief Tony Blair's adviser on the peace process, Sir Michael Levy, who also raised the subject in his talks with the emir. The three received the same answer: Qatar would not give in to the pressures and would retain its relations with Israel. There were some additional political moves, but for now, it is better to keep them secret.

More pressure, unexpected by the Qataris, was brought to bear by Cornell University, which had been invited by Qatar to open an extension of its medical school in Doha. The project was led by Sheikha Mozah bint Nasser Al Missned, the emir's wife (he has three additional wives, but Mozah Al Missned is his preferred wife and she fills many official functions in the emirate). The president of the university's board of governors at the time was Harold Tanner, an American Jew, who was also president of the American Jewish Committee.

Tanner came to Qatar, and during talks with the emir said that he could not recommend the establishment of a Cornell extension in a state that would discriminate against lecturers and students from Cornell (the reference was to lecturers of Israeli origin, of course). The emir replied that he intended to maintain relations with Israel, and Tanner informed him that if so he would support the establishment of the Cornell extension in Qatar.[31] Consequently, on April 10, 2001, the agreement between Cornell and Qatar was signed.

For about a month and half after the outbreak of the Intifada, the Israeli delegation in Qatar initiated thirteen international contacts with the Qatari government for the purpose of creating pressure to ensure that relations between the two states would be maintained. Qatar had no difficulty resisting the domestic pressure to sever the ties. On October 30, 2000, the Qatari newspaper *al-Rayah* printed the following short report: "Recently various attempts have been made to set up a committee to fight normalization, because of the situation, but these attempts have failed because they are illegal."[32]

Qatar's main problem was the pressures from the other Arab states. The timing was extremely sensitive: the eve of the tri-annual meeting of the Organization of the Islamic Conference (OIC), during which Qatar was supposed to be declared president of the organization and symbolically, president of the Muslim world.

To prepare for the conference, the Qatari government invested huge sums of money in improving the country's image before the visit of all the heads of Islamic states, most of whom would be visiting the principality for the first time since the former emir had taken power.[33] About two weeks before the summit convened, on November 1, 2000, Syria sent Hassan Nasrallah to object to Qatar's presidency of the Islamic Conference. After him, several figures from Syria, as well as Salim El-Hoss, former prime minister of Lebanon, issued similar statements.

On November 5, Qatari newspapers wrote that Iran, the present president of the OIC, had announced it would boycott the meeting in Doha. It was clear to me that in that situation, Qatar would not be able to resist the pressure, and that Iran would be joined by Saudi Arabia, Bahrain, Libya, and Yemen. These together would create a critical mass that would lead to the cancellation of the meeting in Doha and torpedo Qatar's appointment as the organization's president.

At lunchtime on that day, I sent a cable to the foreign ministry headquarters, suggesting that we close down the delegation of our own volition from November 7 until the end of the conference on the 14th, to relieve some of the pressure on the Qataris. My intention was for us to keep a low profile at a time when hundreds of journalists from all parts of the Arab world would be descending on Qatar, and especially with the arrival of the foreign ministers, who were expected to land in Qatar on November 7 for a preliminary meeting. That same day, the director-general of the foreign ministry, Dr. Alon Liel, called to find out what was behind the idea of closing down the delegation. I told him that so far the Qataris were withstanding the pressure very well, but they would not jettison efforts that had taken three years to build the legitimacy of the present ruler, as well as an investment of billions of dollars, only to keep our delegation in their country. I added that the United States would understand them and would not provoke a crisis following such a step, since it has important economic interests in Qatar. I ended by requesting that he approve my suggestion to close down, since at a time like that we had to act wisely.

"Go ahead," Liel said and ended the conversation. About a half hour later, I had a call from the foreign minister's office, asking if such a step wouldn't make it easy for the Qataris to sever relations. I replied that they could cut off relations without any problem right then and there, but they did not want to, and we should help them get through the days of the conference. I received the foreign minister's consent as well, and we closed down the delegation as planned.

In the afternoon hours of November 8, 2000, Saudi Arabia announced that it would boycott the summit at Doha. About two hours later, I was urgently summoned to the office of the U.S. ambassador in Qatar, Elizabeth McKune. At our meeting, Elizabeth said, "I've just come from a meeting with the foreign minister of Qatar, who asked me to convey to you his request that you all go on a two-week vacation, until the summit is over and the pressure on Qatar subsides."

I smiled and said, "Please inform the Qatari foreign minister that the Israeli delegation has been closed since yesterday morning, and he can issue any statement he likes. Our families are in Israel now in any case, and the two emissaries who are here with me in Qatar have moved in with me. No one will see us or hear us until the summit is over."

THE DISAPPEARANCE OF THE FAMILIES

Now I will try to explain why our families were in Israel at the time. On November 7, at ten in the evening—about a week after the beginning of the second Intifada and at the height of the demonstrations throughout the Arab world—I got a phone call from the deputy director-general of the foreign ministry, Nissim Ben-Sheetrit. It was not our first conversation that week. We had had several in which Ben-Sheetrit checked out the situation in Qatar, in order to decide whether to evacuate the families of the emissaries until the situation calmed down. In all of the previous conversations, I had said, "The situation here is not simple, but I am asking you not to consider any evacuation. My family should remain here, and I take the responsibility."

Nissim opened that conversation by saying, "I request that you put the families of the emissaries on the first plane to Israel." As I did in the previous conversations, I argued and said I was taking responsibility; I asked that my family remain and I would allow the others to decide about their families. Ben-Sheetrit listened to me and then said immediately, "Eli, I'm not calling to check or to ask your opinion. I am instructing you to evacuate the families at once. The instructions to your security officer as to the security procedures are already on their way." Now that I understood there was something more here than just concern about fiery demonstrations in Qatar, I did as I was told.

It turned out that the decision to evacuate the families had been taken on the basis of intelligence received by security agencies in Israel—that a squad of terrorists had arrived in Qatar. They were planning to carry out an act of terror against the delegation, specifically an attack on me, the head of the delegation. Abruptly, at around two in the very early morning, we woke our three young children and took them out of their beds and moved them to the airport and from there to Israel.

As I said, during that period, the emissaries had moved in with me to make it easier for the delegation's security officer to protect the employees. But the story did not end there. On November 12, the Arab media in Qatar reported the arrest of four Kuwaiti citizens linked to Osama bin Laden's organization, who had been planning to carry out acts of terror in Kuwait and Qatar. It also reported on the arrest in Qatar of another member of the group of North African origin, after he crossed the border with a fake Saudi passport.

Details of the attempt to carry out an attack in Qatar were only reported in the Kuwaiti media on July 5, 2001, after they were revealed in the verdict against the Kuwaiti al-Qaeda terrorist Muhammad al-Dusari, who had formerly volunteered in Afghanistan in the war against communism and since then had been recruiting foreign soldiers and civilians in Kuwait and Qatar to carry out attacks. In the conspiracy, which extended over Pakistan, Kuwait, and Qatar, officers and soldiers in the Kuwaiti army and others from Kuwait and Qatar participated.

We learned that the Qatari authorities had received information about a squad that had arrived in Qatar to make preparations to assassinate me. The zero hour was set for the first day of the Islamic Conference in Doha—November 12, 2000—in order to create a worldwide media effect due to the presence of the leaders of the Islamic states in the city. The squad was arrested in good time in Qatar. In cooperation with the Kuwaiti security organization, the commander of the squad was arrested in Kuwait and about 150 kilograms of explosives intended to send me sky-high were found.

That was in 2000, when al-Qaeda was far less known but far more effective, when it was operating freely inside Afghanistan under Taliban rule. And in May 2011 (a day before the Hebrew version of this book went to press), President Barack Obama delivered a speech to the nation and announced that U.S. forces had killed Osama bin Laden in Pakistan. I thought that was an event that marked an important victory against one of the most murderous symbols of terror that has ever arisen. I could not help smiling at one sentence in the U.S. president's address: "We must also reaffirm that the United States is not—and never will be—at war with Islam." Even at that moment, he took care to draw a distinction between Osama bin Laden and the Muslim world. A wise sentence!

THE DAY THE DELEGATION VANISHED

Let's go back to the U.S. embassy. As I said earlier, the ambassador asked me, on behalf of the Qatari foreign minister, to send the delegation on vacation, and she heard that I had already done so the day before on my own initiative. She was surprised by my reply, and happily responded with one word: "Great!"

"I will talk to the Qatari foreign minister," she added, "and will update you later." About an hour and a half after our meeting, the ambassador called to tell me that the foreign minister had sounded relieved, requesting only that we cut off all contact with the media until the end of the Islamic Conference and refrain from reacting to any published statement. I informed the headquarters of the Israeli foreign ministry of this request by telephone.

That same day, an unofficial rumor originated from the Qatari foreign minister that Qatar had decided to freeze its relations with Israel. The following day, on November 9, 2000, the subject was covered widely in the local and international media. When they learned about the freezing of relations, Saudi Arabia and Iran announced that they would be coming to the conference, which opened as planned on November 11, 2000. Five hundred journalists, who arrived in Qatar to cover the conference, turned the delegation building into an attraction, and photographs of the locked delegation were broadcast throughout the Arab world, against the background of the report about the frozen relations with Israel.

On November 10, *Yedioth Ahronoth*[34] reported that Qatar had surrendered to the pressure brought to bear on the country, and that relations with Israel had been severed. Two days later, the staff of the newspaper began to sense that something fishy was going on, and printed a new item[35] stating that, despite the notification that relations had been severed, the Israeli diplomats were in Qatar and had not been asked to leave. That same day, a gag order was issued forbidding the publication of anything about the Israeli delegation in Qatar, a measure that ensured secrecy throughout the days of the summit.

At the opening session of the summit, most of the Arab leaders at the conference commended the emir of Qatar, Hamad bin Khalifa Al Thani, on his courageous step in severing relations with Israel. The staff of the Israeli delegation in Qatar watched these speeches broadcast live on the Qatari national television channel, from the living room of my home in Doha.

About a week after the conference, on November 18, 2000, the U.S. secretary of defense, William Cohen, visited Qatar. At a press conference at the conclusion of his visit, he was asked if he had discussed the reopening of the Israeli delegation with Qatari officials, and what the U.S. position was on this issue.

"I would hope that the Qatari government will reopen the Israeli delegation as soon as possible," he replied. "I believe that in times like these, it is more important than ever before to leave the lines of communication open between all the parties involved. But that is a decision that only the Qatari government can take. Qatar was one of the first states to open such a delegation, and I hope the situation will enable them to reopen the delegation at an early date, as soon as they feel it is possible to do so."[36] The U.S. secretary of defense knew we were in Qatar, since he had been briefed by the embassy in Washington before leaving for the Gulf. He kept the move secret from the media that was covering his visit.

About a month after the Islamic Conference, the delegation in Doha resumed full operation, and relations actually improved insofar as coordination with the Qatari government was concerned. On November 23, the families also returned to Qatar, after spending about six weeks in Israel. Afterward, when I visited Israel and met with various officials in the ministry's headquarters, I was asked several times questions such as "Tell us, how can they tell the world that they won't close our delegation and then, three days before the Islamic Conference convenes, announce to the whole world that they are closing down the delegation, and, in actual fact, you were in Qatar during the summit, and afterward the delegation went back to business as usual?"

I tried to explain that the Middle East is not a region of straight lines and straight angles, but rather of round, winding lines that allow a large measure of flexibility. I explained that if we had acted according to Western codes during the crisis, the delegation in Qatar would have closed down as the one in Oman did, because we would have had no other choice. I tried to explain that, in a crisis of this kind, Western behavior, which sanctifies the accuracy and absoluteness of every statement or every move, would not have worked. I could see on the faces of those who queried me that they did not understand.

Sometime later, I came across the writings of the ninth-century Muslim author and scholar Abu Muhammad Abdullah Ibn Muslim Ibn Qutaybah al-Dinawari, who explained this kind of conduct in the most coherent manner. In his book *A Collection of Stories* (*Uyun al-Akhbar* in Arabic), he wrote:

> Abu al-Khataab told us and said: Muhammad bin Sawar told us and said: Hisham bin Hassan told us and said: Al-Hassan (the Prophet's grandson) would tell us today about the Hadith (a tradition about the Prophet that is handed down orally) of the Prophet and repeat it the next day, and added to the story and deleted from the story, but the meaning was the same meaning.
>
> Abu al-Khataab told me and said: Maimon told us and said: Jafer bin Muhammad told us from his father's mouth, and said: Khudeifa bin Al-Yaman said: We are Arabs! We change the day of the occurrence forward and backward, we add and we delete details, but we do that without the intention of lying.[37]

The Iranians and the Saudis had backed the Qataris to the wall, forcing Qatar to come up with a creative solution in order to emerge from the crisis with as many gains as possible. The Qatari government wanted the meeting of the Organization of the Islamic Conference to take place in Doha, so that

Qatar would be declared its president. They also wanted to keep the Israeli delegation in Doha, to situate itself as a unique, politically independent state unafraid of coming out against the conventions that prevail in the Arab and the Muslim world. Qatar succeeded on both counts, and I was privileged to play a part in this fascinating game.

During the military "Cast Lead" Operation, on January 16, 2009, Qatar announced that it was severing relations with Israel and expelling the Israeli diplomats from Doha. I am not familiar with the details of the moves carried out during that period, but this time the relations really were severed.

The unreserved support of Hamas led the Qataris to behave suspiciously in early 2010, when they offered to renew diplomatic relations with Israel in exchange for Israel's consent to allow construction materials to be brought into Gaza. The Israeli government refused both offers, since it understood that the construction material would be used for military—not civilian—purposes. This suspicion was confirmed by the discovery in July 2014 of the large-scale system of terrorist tunnels from the Gaza Strip into Israeli territory, built by Hamas.

AND FINALLY:
DESPITE EVERYTHING—A BRIDGE

The question of normalization between Israel and the Arab world has been part of our lives since the establishment of the state, and even before that. The picture that arises from an examination of the situation is one of a yawning abyss that separates the two sides on this issue.

The State of Israel aspires to normal relations with the Arab world, which are expressed not only in a signed peace agreement and in the fulfillment of its security obligations, but also in economic and cultural content in all spheres of life. We perceive normalization as an indication of the sincerity of the other side's peaceful intentions, that a true peace had been achieved, not a temporary cease-fire. Hence we attribute to normalization a strategic, almost a security, significance, far beyond its economic and sentimental value.

Israel's willingness to make concessions over the years is based on the expectation that her political concessions will be met with acts of normalization by the Arab states and by a cessation of the psychological, intellectual, media, and economic warfare, not only by a cessation of combat on the battlefield. Full normalization with the State of Israel in the Middle East will make it clear to us and to the whole world that the state of war between Israel and its neighbors has come to an end. That is the "end of the conflict" that we all yearn for.

The moderate Arab governments, on the other hand, view normalization as a means of defining the level of relations with Israel. Normalization is also regarded as a "prize" given to Israel in exchange for its progress in the peace process with the Arabs, and as a lever to dictate policy in Israeli-Arab relations. The various Arab states know how to identify the areas of interest that are important to them, and they know how to maintain close relations in those areas. Usually, these cooperative activities are discussed in intelligence and political situation rooms, far from the public eye. Those states are wary about exposing their close relations in public expressions of economic, cultural, or other forms of normalization. They are also attentive to the position of the refusal organizations in the Arab world—both on the left and in the circles of extreme Islam. These view normalization as an Israeli strategy aimed at strengthening its status in the region and, at the end of the process, gaining control over the Middle East and its economic resources. Years of instilling the hatred of Israel have made anti-normalization propaganda a very effective tool in the attempts of the opposition movements to incite the masses against the government, which in the meantime has changed its tune and is trying to arrive at a compromise with Israel—a Frankenstein monster that has risen up against its maker. At this point, the leaders are compelled to retreat in the face of the masses, and events in Morocco in 2000 are a good example.

The solution is to remain resolute, patient, and—no less important—to be modest in the proposals we make and to gradually promote the moves we initiate. I think that Israel ought not to play into the hands of the enemies of normalization by making sweeping, bombastic proposals, such as the perception of the new Middle East that was presented in 1993. Unquestionably that perception was premature, and, at the same time, it delayed the introduction of normalization because it provided too many justifications for the opposition movements in the Arab world, which cried out that it was an Israeli conspiracy to take control of the Middle East.

This perception also angered all the leaders of the Arab world, including the friendliest among them, whose impression of Shimon Peres's vision was that the State of Israel was calling for all the regimes in the Middle East to be replaced by democratic governments. I believe that more modest and less pretentious proposals could have delivered far better results.

Normalization in the economic sphere should be carried out far from the eyes of the camera, unattended by public statements of our leaders. Every such statement is cheap and effective kindling in the hands of those lighting fires in the refusal movements. We can see how the "Egyptian gas deal" between Israel and Egypt became the focus in a corruption investigation of the Mubarak family and the Egyptian businessman Hussein Salem, and how convenient it was for the former government of Mohamed Morsi to fix public attention on it.

Economy has no limits, and it can exist and be creatively built for the good of both sides that desire it. But the economy has to remain outside politics, and certainly should not be contingent on the progress or lack of progress in the peace process. In the final analysis, businessmen in the Arab world want to earn money and to find opportunities for their companies to be more profitable. They differ fundamentally from those extremist religious scholars who live off contributions and have never worked a day in their lives. These businessmen also differ from the leaders of trade unions in the various Arab states, who gain control over those unions not in order to improve the status of the engineer or the doctor, but rather to disseminate the fanatical message, which holds that the will of God is that the workers ought to die the death of martyrs fulfilling his word.

The Israeli government has a role to play here: it can ease economic transactions with Arab states and remove bureaucratic restrictions that are burdensome to Israeli businessmen operating in Arab countries. These businessmen have to engage in sophisticated, grueling activity in order to cope with the opponents of normalization in the Arab world, and the Israeli government should at least make things easier for them domestically.

In the academic field, a quiet dialogue is being conducted among Israeli academic institutions and those of the Arab world. Those cooperative activities are conducted privately by academics on both sides and are not attended by public memoranda of understanding among universities, which would stoke the ire of the extremists among the Arab academic staff and students. I had quite a few meetings with lecturers from the Arab world during my diplomatic service abroad, but to ensure their personal safety I refrain from mentioning their names.

In the communications field, I see a real breakthrough in normalization with the Arab world. For many years, the Arab population in the Middle East acquired its perceptions and images of Israel through that controlled, tendentious media of Arab governments. The situation in 2015 is totally different. There are means of communication that move across borders, and we have to do our best to enable them to freely report from Israel and about Israel. The Israeli government ought to invest far more in training capable spokesmen for the Arab media, since the generation that speaks the language, understands the culture, and can speak in a frequency comprehensible to the inhabitants of the Middle East is vanishing. Instead of being impressed by those spokesmen who accurately translate Hebrew press releases into Arabic, we should give the stage to those capable of conveying the message in Arabic in a manner understood by both viewers and listeners.

The case of Qatar is, in my view, a test case that represents a potential for normalization with an important group in the Arab world. My service there proved to me without a doubt that, despite all the difficulties and the obstacles, when the two sides had a common interest, the move succeeded. The combination of resolve and an understanding of the local cultural codes led to the success of many ventures, most of which I have not referred to here.

To my regret, Qatari interests have changed, and today Qatar invests its resources to gain support in the West, by acquiring soccer teams, hosting the World Cup, and purchasing fashion houses in Europe. At the same time, Qatar invests huge sums in support of extremist Islamic movements in the Middle East, which somehow go unnoticed. At present, Israel is not a player in the set of Qatari interests, but that could change at any time in the future.

Another important difference between us and our potential partners in the process lies in our sensitivity to the subject. While normalization is on the agenda of Middle Eastern governments, of trade unions, of the opposition movement, and of the mass media in the region, in Israel we still relate to it as something incidental and devote hardly any thought to it, with the exception of idealists possessed of a sweeping vision, like Shimon Peres.

We should define normalization as normal life with the Middle Eastern states, not as a vehicle for change, change in their perceptions, their form of government, their mode of study, their social structure. The Middle East is a geographical region populated by ancient peoples, cultures, and worldviews. We need to respect that, and we should not radically interpret the notion of the chosen people and turn ourselves into the instructing people, the explaining people, or the people who determine how other peoples should live.

On the other hand, I am categorically opposed to the perception of "full normalization," which would demand that Israel change its identity and adapt to the Arab world, as Boutros Boutros-Ghali suggested in 1976. Statements like the one made by Shimon Peres in 1994—"Unquestionably Israel's next objective is to be accepted as a member of the Arab League"[38]—do not promote the process; on the contrary, they impede it, because they arouse the opponents of the process and give the moderate Arabs vain hopes.

While we seem to be clear about what we demand of Arab states in regard to normalization, we have never devoted enough thought to the question of what is demanded of us. Will our acceptance as an integral part of the Middle East also require us to change the way in which the State of Israel defines itself? Will we be asked to give up part of our identity?

Normalization with the Arab states certainly does not justify a change in the definition of the State of Israel as the state of the Jewish people—a state comprising seventy cultures of communities that have returned to join together. We are not talking here about the name of a street that the municipality decides to change; we are talking about an identity, a culture, and an age-old dream that was realized sixty-six years ago, and it is important not to dismiss it because of our desire to integrate into the region out of that same "brutal pragmatism," which also defines the most significant things as "unimportant."

Normalization with the various Arab states will come, but not as we expect, rapidly, in the flash of an eye. It will result from a smart, resolute policy that is sensitive to the culture of the region and respects the history of its peoples. The accumulation of the activities in this spirit will, over the years, lead to a state of peace and cooperation in our region. Patience, modesty, resolve, and optimism are the elements that will make possible progress toward this goal.

And to all those who say the Arab world will never accept us, and that true normalization is impossible, I will only say that I never dreamed that forty-seven years after I was expelled with my family from Egypt, my voice would be broadcast on an Egyptian TV satellite channel, and my words as a son of this people and a son of this country would be heard on prime time on Arab satellite channels.

The bridge over the gaping abyss between our approach and that of the Arab world should be built wisely and cautiously, but by no means should its construction be left for the coming generations, as Sadat suggested. We have to conduct ourselves wisely, cautiously, and respectfully so that the coming generations of the Middle East will have a strong, stable bridge, until no one remembers that there was once a gaping abyss here.

Chapter Four

Economic Sanctions

Economic sanctions did not work in Cuba, did not work in Iraq, and hardly ever worked anywhere. So why are we the only ones who are convinced we will bring Gaza to its knees?

On January 25, 2006, the Middle East awoke to a new political reality. After four decades of unchallenged rule over Palestinian politics, Fatah, Yasser Arafat's organization, lost power to an organization that had come into existence two decades after it. Hamas's victory in the elections for the Palestinian Authority was seen by Israel and by the other regional and international players as no less than an earthquake.

The election campaign that was supposed to end, as most of the experts predicted, with a Fatah victory—and, as a result, the stabilization of the violent internal Palestinian dynamics, finally bringing the sides back to the negotiating table—became, within twenty-four hours, the worst nightmare not only of Israel but also of many Western countries, as well as of the moderate Arab states. An extremist Islamist terror organization had taken power in one of the most explosive regions in the world, not in a violent coup but in a democratic process. Against the 41 percent of votes gained by Fatah, which gave it 36 percent of the seats in the Palestinian legislative council, Hamas won 44 percent of the votes and 56 percent of the seats, becoming the new head of the Palestinian Authority.

"If the *rais* were alive, such a thing would never have happened," I was told by one of Arafat's closest advisers, at lunch in December 2009. "If it had happened during the time of Abu Amar, the elections would have been decided even before they took place. The ballot boxes would have been closed, sent to the counting center, counted in the fastest way possible, and

Hamas would never have won." The election results may have reflected the will of the Palestinian voters, but the immediate implications in no way eased their already difficult lives. The publication of the results led to an immediate escalation in the level of inter-Palestinian violence throughout the Gaza Strip, and despite the joint efforts of Hamas and Fatah to defuse the situation in the streets, there was real fear that it might lead not only to a flare-up of civil war but also to an all-out war with Israel. On the other side, in Israel, the earth shook, too, although not in the streets, but in the corridors of power. While hurling mutual accusations about who was responsible for the intelligence failure, for not having anticipated Hamas's victory at the polls, the Israeli government and the heads of the defense establishment began feverish discussions on how to cope with the situation and how to overturn it. The Israeli government decided to create a situation in which the Palestinian people in Gaza would realize their mistake and topple Hamas from power. The method it chose was economic sanctions.

In this chapter, I try to examine whether the use of economic sanctions against more than one million inhabitants of one of the most crowded, poverty-stricken areas in the world was the right action for Israel to take. I will also discuss Israel's insistence on continuing to manage this crisis according to the same basic patterns that had guided Israel until then, although the very surprise of the Hamas victory ought to have made clear to all of us that the rules of the game had changed. Already at this stage, I want to stress that, in my view, everyone felt overly self-confident and arrogant, adopting an approach of "we'll bring them to their knees." If the leaders of the country had examined past experience, they would have discovered that in most cases in history when economic sanctions had been used to achieve political aims, without resorting to additional means, the move had failed dismally, and in the end the damage was far, far greater than the gain.

THE DAY THE AMERICANS
HAD TO CUT THEIR OWN CIGARS

Economic sanctions are generally defined as

> coercive economic measures taken against one or more countries to force a change in policies, or at least to demonstrate a country's opinion about the other's policies. Economic sanctions typically include measures such as trade embargoes; restrictions on particular exports or imports; denial of foreign assistance, loans, and investments; or control of foreign assets and economic transactions.[1]

Early testimonies about the use of economic sanctions can be found as far back as 433–432 BC. Pericles, an Athenian politician, decided to punish the inhabitants of the city of Megara, claiming they had cultivated a plot of land belonging to one of the goddesses. The real motive for this measure was a political one; after Pericles learned that the Megarians had joined Corinth and Sparta in an alliance against Athens, he decided to punish them by means of economic sanctions, with the aim of deterring anyone who might think of acting against Athens in the future.[2] In the second half of the twentieth century, particularly since the end of the Cold War, economic sanctions have become the major tool in managing international disputes. Since it does not require the physical involvement of the states employing it, and the price tag that goes with the sanctions is relatively low compared to direct military intervention, they have become increasingly popular. The imposition of economic sanctions on a state is generally carried out in one of two ways: by the United Nations charter (Article 16 of its charter grants the organization a mandate to deploy economic sanctions in cases of threat of aggression or breach of peace) or by a specific state by its own initiative.

The first case in the twentieth century of the organized use of economic sanctions took place in 1935, following Mussolini's invasion of Ethiopia, which was a member of the League of Nations. The organization reacted by declaring Italy an aggressor and imposing economic sanctions on the country. In fact, this step was completely ineffective, and it had no influence on Mussolini. While France and Britain expressed their objection to Mussolini's aggressive moves vis-à-vis Ethiopia, they were reluctant to take any steps that might anger the Italian dictator and push him closer to Hitler. In the end, not only did the sanctions fail to have any effect on Italy, but they also led to worsened relations between Britain and France.

Between 1945 and 1990, the UN Security Council deployed economic sanctions in only two cases, but since 1990 that number has increased to eleven. During this period, sanctions were taken against the former Yugoslavia, Libya, Somalia, Liberia, and others. Of all the countries that have used this tool, the United States heads the list. "A nation that is boycotted is a nation in sight of surrender," the U.S. president, Woodrow Wilson, said in 1919.[3] "Apply this economic, peaceful, silent, deadly remedy and there will be no need for force. It is a terrible remedy. It does not cost a life outside the nation boycotted, but it brings a pressure upon the nation which, in my judgment, no modern nation could resist."[4] Since 1945, the United States has imposed economic sanctions against more than forty states—either on its own or jointly with other states.[5]

Economic sanctions are supposed to obviate the need to undertake military action, and at the same time to achieve three main aims (or some of them): to demonstrate dissatisfaction with the target nation's policy, to demonstrate the resolve of the punishing nation to its allies, and to clarify to its public at home that it will act resolutely to safeguard its national interests.[6]

In nearly all the cases in which economic sanctions have been deployed, the sender states (the ones imposing them) are larger and richer than the target countries.[7] But to make the sanctions effective, the sender country's GNP has to be ten times larger than that of the target country. If the aim is to destabilize the other country, the GNP has to be at least *one hundred* times as large.[8] This is, then, one of the difficulties in effectively imposing economic sanctions.

Economic sanctions are usually divided into two types:

1. The prohibition of the importation of goods from the target state to the sender state. This causes the target state a loss of income and markets.
2. The prohibition of the exportation of goods from the sender state to the target state. This step is less frequently used, because in most cases, those states find alternative sources to fill the gap, and the main damage is actually caused to the sender state.[9]

One of the main elements in the deployment of economic sanctions is the freezing of assets and bank accounts of the target state and/or its heads— mainly as a bargaining chip to be used in the stage when the parties try to resolve the crisis.[10] A current example of the use of this measure was Security Council Resolution 1737. On December 23, 2006, following Iran's failure to comply with the demands of the international community to halt its nuclear program, the UN Security Council adopted a resolution allowing the imposition of sanctions on Iran. These sanctions included, among others, a ban on the supply of raw materials, equipment, and technology related to uranium enrichment, nuclear activity, and ballistic missiles; a ban on the exportation of weapons to Iran; a freeze of assets; and restrictions on the movement of Iranian persons.

To implement this resolution, the U.S. Treasury Department acted in a focused, comprehensive manner vis-à-vis governments and private companies, and, at the same time, the United States brought pressure to bear on banks and other financial institutions that worked with Iran—for the purpose of restricting Iran's financial channels and trade links as much as possible.

But economic sanctions have never succeeded unless they were accompanied by complementary means. In most cases, it is necessary to take secret and semi-military measures against the target state at the same time.[11] That is the main conclusion reached by a series of comparative studies that examined the effectiveness of the sanctions. This conclusion is reinforced when the goal of the economic sanctions is to destabilize the government in the target country—the very goal of the State of Israel when it decided to impose sanctions on the Palestinian Authority when Hamas took power.

An excellent example of the failure of economic sanctions, taken from the twentieth century, is the U.S. boycott on Cuba. In 1960, to prevent the spread of Fidel Castro's revolution, the United States tried to overthrow his govern-ment by means of economic sanctions. At first, the United States restricted the quantity of sugar that could be imported from Cuba and, at the height of the crisis, prohibited any trade with Cuba at all. At the same time, the United States brought pressure to bear on its allies in the West to reduce their trade with Cuba and their investments in it. In the final analysis, the U.S. embargo on Cuba did not succeed in toppling Castro; it only strengthened the ties between Cuba and the Soviet Union. Until the fall of the Soviet bloc in the early 1990s, Cuba enjoyed massive Soviet economic aid; the Soviets sup-plied Cuba with oil at a low price and purchased sugar from Cuba at a high price.

The collapse of the Soviet Union sealed off Cuba's main lifeline, and Cuba rapidly declined into a deep economic depression. In 1992, three decades after the economic sanctions began, the United States showed the whole world that it was still determined to achieve its goal, and it tightened its trade embargo with Cuba, a step that further worsened the already low standard of living of the Cubans and threw the country into a crisis. Howev-er, despite the enormous economic hardships Cuba is facing, the United States' attempt to overthrow Castro has totally failed. Although the embargo worsened the situation of Cubans, it did not achieve its political aims, but only provoked the derision of other countries toward the United States. The UN General Assembly adopted many resolutions denouncing the U.S. em-bargo and stating that it hindered the sovereignty of states and free trade. Fidel Castro remained as the unchallenged leader of Cuba for another forty years, even though, in 2015, his brother Raul serves as its president.

The Cuban economy recovered, and the majority of countries in the world did not join the United States' efforts. This case has proven yet again that countries prefer their own financial interests over doing what strong allies want them to do. [12]

Cuba was not the last failed attempt. In the 1970s, the U.S. administration imposed a partial embargo on the sale of grain to the Soviet Union, as a reaction to the Soviet intervention in Afghanistan. At the same time, the United States announced its plans to boycott the 1980 Olympics in Moscow and tried to persuade its allies to do the same. In actual fact, despite the embargo, agricultural produce continued to flow to the Soviet Union, and some countries even increased their exports to it. On the sports level, the U.S. attempt also failed. Although many countries, including Israel, joined in the ban and canceled their participation in the Moscow Olympics, the event was held as planned and 5,217 athletes from eighty countries took part in it.

These examples illustrate the fact that although economic sanctions are a tactic that supposedly does not involve high risks for the country applying them, it turns out that they actually do cause the sanction-sending country damage. Quite a few examples show that it is actually the sanction-sending country that pays the highest price. Its exporters lose markets, and if the sanctions involve imports, the prices of various products rise, adversely affecting the citizens of that country (one example is the shortage of Cuban cigars in the United States).

In the case of Iraq, the United States thought that economic sanctions would cause Saddam Hussein to reveal his plans to develop weapons of mass destruction. That did not work, and in the end, the United States invaded Iraq and overthrew Saddam's regime. The Iraqi case is a good example of a situation in which economic sanctions did not undermine the central government, but actually unified the citizens of Iraq, inducing them to support their leader and avoid any attempt to topple him despite his ruthless rule. [13]

By their very nature, economic sanctions cannot provide an immediate result. In order to produce the desired outcome, precise planning and full cooperation by other factors are needed, but also, and perhaps primarily, patience and forbearance. Sometimes that isn't enough either, and the example of Iran attests to that. In that case, the experts assess that what led to the failure of the sanctions was not the element of time, but rather the absence of resolve. If the government in Iran had felt that the world really was very resolute in its decision not to allow it to develop its nuclear program, the sanctions might have achieved their purpose and the Iranian government would have reconsidered its policy. [14] But the Iranians understood the lack of international determination, and the rise to power of Hassan Rouhani, who was regarded as a moderate Iranian president, led the United States to persuade Europe to join in a common effort to resolve the issue of the Iranian nuclear program, which involved canceling some of the sanctions and continuing the negotiations about ending them. Today it is clear that Iran will not give up its nuclear program, and the negotiations being conducted with the country are only about the levels of enrichment and their scope.

If those are the results, or, to be more precise, the lack of results, in so many cases, we should ask two questions. First, what causes this option to fail time after time? And second, but no less important, in view of the ongoing failure of sanctions, why do countries not only fail to stop using them but actually use them more often? Moreover, in March 2014, the United States and Europe imposed economic sanctions against Russia after Vladimir Putin ordered the annexation of Crimea to Russia using military force, which seems to have had hardly any effect once again.

The main reason economic sanctions fail is because the declared aims of the sending country are not compatible with the types of sanctions it is using. [15] The more modest the aims are, the higher the chance of achieving them by means of economic sanctions. [16] Moreover, it is very difficult for one country to cause significant economic damage to another and to enlist partners in the effort. I have already mentioned the large gaps in the size required in order to impose an effective economic boycott. Even if the sanctions are effective, that does not mean they will achieve their goal. The reason is the boomerang effect: in most cases, the economic sanctions provoke unrest, frustration, and anger among the inhabitants of the country being punished against the punishing country, and not against their own government—the original target of the sanctions. That is exactly how the Palestinians reacted when Israel imposed sanctions after the Hamas victory at the polls. In such cases, the sanctions cause the people in the target country to close ranks and to do nothing to undermine their government.

The main explanation for the fact that this ineffective tool is becoming more popular is its relatively low price in human life, on both sides. In addition, sanctions have a high visibility; if the entire world is talking about them, then it seems we have done something after all. Economic sanctions have become the refuge of countries frustrated in the face of a situation that underscores their helplessness, or their unwillingness to engage in military or political action. However, as we have seen, sanctions also have a price: they harm the economy of the country that applies them and they foment hatred toward it among the citizens of the target country—a hatred that often achieves the opposite result.

So how and when it is possible, nevertheless, to use economic sanctions as an effective tool? Only when it complements military or semi-military action, just as today some Arab countries and some Western countries are doing in their war against terror. In this situation, those countries combine intelligence and military action, along with economic measures such as freezing the assets of terrorist organizations and disrupting the flow of money to finance their operations. The main aim of such sanctions is specific and limited, and they are not directed against an entire country or an entire public, but against an underground organization that has only a partial foothold in the public, if at all.

With these examples and conclusions in the background, it's time to check out the Israeli-Arab arena.

FROM THE ARAB BOYCOTT
TO THE ISRAELI BOYCOTT

In the history of the Israeli-Arab conflict, it was the Arabs who first used the economic weapon. In 1951, the Arab League adopted a resolution intended to destroy Israel monetarily, after the attempt to bring it down militarily failed in the War of Independence (1948–1949). Every Arab country was forbidden to maintain economic relations with the new, young player in the area that had been forced upon them by the UN three years earlier. To plug up as far as possible any "holes in the sieve," and to maximize the damage to Israel, the

League stated in its resolution that there would be three aspects to the boycott:

1. A prohibition on all Arab countries to import goods manufactured in Israel or exported from Israel.
2. The boycott of companies doing business with Israel.
3. The boycott of companies doing business with companies that are doing business with Israel.

At the height of the Arab boycott, Arab countries boycotted 8,500 companies throughout the world, including the automotive giant, Ford, and the largest beverage company in the world—Coca-Cola. In certain cases, the boycott was successful. For example, Japan, which is totally dependent on Arab oil, almost totally abstained from any commercial ties with Israel until the beginning of the 1990s. But the bottom line is that the chances of the Arab countries to ruin Israel by means of economic sanctions were better than Israel's chances of overthrowing Hamas by means of such a measure, about fifty-five years later.

DON'T TAKE THE PLASTIC
COVERS OFF THE ARMCHAIRS

The years 2006 and 2007 were not simple ones for Israel, the Palestinians, or, in fact, the entire Middle East. On January 4, 2006, three weeks before the Palestinian Authority elections, the prime minister of Israel, Ariel Sharon, suffered a stroke and was replaced by Ehud Olmert on January 18, 2006. Israel still clung to the concept that Hamas was going to lose in the elections. Tzipi Livni was appointed foreign minister, and Acting Prime Minister Olmert (Sharon, unconscious, was still officially considered prime minister) also appointed her the head of the team negotiating with the Palestinians. As soon as she took office, Livni began a round of talks with foreign ministers throughout the world, including the U.S. secretary of state, Condoleezza Rice; Javier Solana, the person responsible for the foreign policy of the European Union (EU); and many others. In these talks, she made clear that Israel was determined to stick to its position that Hamas was not a partner.

Throughout the eighteen months that passed from the rise of Hamas to power in the Palestinian Authority, in January 2006, until the Hamas government was fired by Abu Mazen because Hamas forcibly took control of the Gaza Strip, Israeli policy has been based on three major decisions relating to the imposition of economic sanctions on the Hamas government and, in certain contexts, on the entire Palestinian Authority. [17]

On January 29, 2006, four days after the results of the elections in the Authority were known, the government headed by Olmert convened to discuss the new situation. After the meeting, the government secretary, Israel Maimon, released a statement to the press, in which he quoted the words of the acting prime minister:

> Once we knew the results of the elections in the Palestinian Authority and Hamas' victory, I consulted with various persons in order to analyze the new situation. At the end of the consultations, we announced that the State of Israel would not conduct any negotiations with a Palestinian administration, if any part of it were an armed terrorist organization that called for the liquidation of the State of Israel. This position has resonated throughout Israel as well as in the whole world—and as far as I can judge, it also gained broad agreement as well as nearly frontal [thus, in the original] understanding of all the international agencies.
>
> In parallel we stated that Israel will continue to act against terror everywhere and at all times, in every context when such actions are called for. In other words, there is no intention to compromise in this regard. . . . We have decided that the Foreign Minister and I will hold contacts with the international community . . . in order to transmit Israeli messages and to consolidate a unified political front. Over the weekend, I spoke with the president of Egypt, the King of Jordan, the British Prime Minister, the president of France and the Secretary-General of the UN, and I said that Israel will not conduct any dialogue with Hamas or with the Palestinian Authority before it and its head fulfill the following conditions: the terror organizations disarm and abandon the path of terror, they recognize the existence of the State of Israel and rescind the Hamas charter that calls for her destruction, and recognize all the agreements signed between Israel and the Palestinian Authority and all the understandings reached between them.
>
> The position of the leaders with whom I spoke was identical to ours. They stated that they would continue to maintain no contacts with Hamas in its present composition, or with the Palestinian Authority with Hamas at its head, unless these conditions are fulfilled. We shall continue to conduct a political campaign and to expand understandings with the international community in this spirit. Tonight I am going to meet with the chancellor of Germany, Angela Merkel, who is arriving on a visit to Israel, and I will discuss the issue with her.[18]

At the end of the meeting, Olmert summed up his position and instructed the government to act in accordance with them:

1. The State of Israel adheres to the "road map" and continues to demand that the head of the Palestinian Authority carry out its commitment to disarm all the terrorist organizations and their infrastructures.
2. The State of Israel will not conduct any negotiation with a Palestinian government, if even one part of it is an armed terror organization that calls for the destruction of the State of Israel.

3. Israel will continue to act against terror organizations wherever such action is required.
4. The State of Israel will be in touch with the international community to ensure that it will not conduct a dialogue with Hamas or the Palestinian Authority before it and its head fulfill the following conditions: the terrorist organizations disarm and renounce the path of terror; recognize the existence of the State of Israel and rescind the Hamas charter that calls for its destruction; recognize all agreements signed between Israel and the Palestinian Authority and all the understandings reached between them.
5. In the coming days, I will hold a consultation relating to all the practical issues to be dealt with vis-à-vis the Palestinians now after the results of the elections, such as the transfer of funds, the movement of members of parliament between Gaza and Judah and Samaria and others. After these consultations with the relevant people and agencies, we will formulate a decision according to which we will act. [19]

This statement reflected the prevailing mood in the Israeli government following the results of the elections in the Palestinian Authority; it was, in fact, a kind of warning—if not a threat—of Israel's intention to impose economic sanctions on Hamas and the Authority. The Israeli government wanted to make it clear to all the players involved in the game, on both the local and the global scene, that Israel definitely did not intend to accept the results of the elections, particularly the leadership of the Authority government by Hamas, so long as no significant change took place in the positions of that terror organization toward Israel.

The fact that the transfer of funds is mentioned only at the end of the statement indicates that, at this stage, the government still believed that its resolute position and the support of the international community would produce the desired results without Israel needing to take any real action. The basis for this hope was the supportive reactions received in Prime Minister Olmert's office and that of Foreign Minister Livni from many world leaders. At this point in time, the imposition of economic sanctions was only a secondary option, while the major element—international pressure and a policy of boycotting the Authority—would, so Israel hoped, ensure that a Hamas government would not be established in the Authority.

On February 19, 2006, when all attempts to prevent the establishment of a Hamas government in the Authority had failed—and the day after the new Palestinian parliament, with a majority of Hamas members, convened—the Israeli government adopted resolution 4,705:

> The establishment of a Palestinian parliament (18 February 2006) controlled by a Hamas majority and the anticipated end of the transition government, will

turn the Palestinian Authority into a terrorist authority, unless Hamas, which control the Palestinian Authority, accepts in full the three preconditions decided upon by Israel and confirmed by a decision of the International Quartet:

1. Recognition of the State of Israel and annulment of the Hamas charter.
2. Abandonment of the path of terror and dismantlement of the terror infrastructure.
3. Recognition of the agreements and understandings reached by Israel and the Palestinians.

Accordingly, the Israeli government has decided to immediately take a series of steps, at this stage, vis-à-vis the Palestinian Authority:

1. Since the term of the transition government has drawn to an end, no funds will be transferred from Israel to the Palestinian Authority.
2. Israel will apply to the international community so that, with the termination of the transition government, it will cease giving any financial aid to the Palestinian Authority, other than humanitarian aid given directly to the Palestinian population. For that purpose, Israel will continue to assist the activity of humanitarian organizations engaged in aiding the Palestinian population.
3. The transfer of means and aid to Palestinian security organizations will be prevented. [20]

At the first stage, the Israeli government succeeded in gaining the Quartet's[21] agreement to three of its demands to the Authority: the recognition of Israel, the affirmation of the existing agreements between the Authority and Israel, and the renunciation of violence and the disarmament of Hamas. [22] This was Israel's way of telling Hamas that if it did not fulfill these three demands immediately and fully, its members would do well to save themselves the trouble of removing the plastic covers from the new seats in the government offices. In order to achieve its aims and to make the Palestinian Authority and Hamas understand that there are other ways to cause them damage besides military force, Israel planned to delay or stop the transfer of funds to the Palestinian Authority, to hinder the flow of contributions to it, and to act to undermine its legitimacy within the international community. [23]

The implications of this decision for the inhabitants of the Authority were extreme. Until then, Israel had transferred taxes to the Authority at a rate of $60 million a month, which the Israeli government collected for the Authority at customs points. [24] This amount constituted about one-third of the $165 million that the Authority needed each month for its minimal existence. [25] Israel's plan was simple: once Israel stopped transferring these funds to the

Authority, this loss of revenue would increase the economic pressure on the Palestinian street and on the officials in the public sector, and these two sectors would direct their anger at their government. Employees of the Authority who would not get their salaries would cause chaos in the public system. This would finally lead to the collapse of the Hamas government and perhaps even of the apparatus of the entire Authority, without Israel having to apply any military force.

On paper, this plan seemed to have considerable potential for success, and certainly was a far better option than the military one. But Israel failed to take into account one element that is crucially important when implementing a plan of this kind. The Gaza Strip is one of the poorest, most overcrowded places in the world, and the economic situation of its inhabitants is bad in any case. Worsening this situation by imposing economic sanctions is apt to lead to a humanitarian crisis that can provoke anti-Israel reactions worldwide, and that result, one can assume, would be exploited by Hamas.

And that's exactly what happened.

IS THAT ALL YOU HAVE TO SUGGEST?

In March 2006, the income of the Palestinian Authority was reduced by 60 percent as a result of the economic embargo and Israel's freeze of the Palestinians' tax money. A small amount of the economic oxygen that the Authority needed was sent to it by Arab countries, whose donations went directly to Abu Mazen. He used that money to pay salaries, reducing the pressure on Hamas.[26] But the Arab states were not the only ones to come to the Authority's rescue. That month, it also received $42 million from the World Bank to save it from an economic crisis and from the need to stop providing basic social services to the inhabitants.[27]

On Thursday, March 23, 2006, I was summoned to a meeting with Foreign Minister Livni. Her adviser, Ditta Kohl Roman, was also at the meeting, held in the foreign minister's Tel Aviv office. Livni wasted no time in telling me why I had been called to meet with her.

"I've been told that you can help us regarding the sanctions against the Hamas government. What can you tell me?"

I replied that it would be unprofessional to give her an in-depth answer, but there was no doubt that every means should be used to prevent funds from going to Hamas through the Palestinian Authority, and that one of the main ways of doing that was to place the Authority under the supervision of the FATF, the Financial Action Task Force. I also recommended that the freeze on the transfer of tax monies to the Authority should be continued, despite international pressure, but, at the same time, the Erez crossing should be opened for the supply of humanitarian aid. I explained that preventing the transfer of basic products, fuel, and electricity would lead to international pressure, which would cause us more harm than good.

My brief reply surprised Livni. "That's it? That's all you have to suggest?" I ought to mention that those were her first days as foreign minister.

"Minister, I just hope we can implement these recommendations for a long period, without international pressure forcing the government to change its mind," I said.

At the time, I was at the Middle Eastern economy section in charge of the humanitarian issues vis-à-vis the Palestinian Authority. In practice, I dealt with the sanctions imposed on the Hamas government and was a permanent representative of the foreign ministry on the forum of the Coordinator of Government Activities in the Territories (COGAT), which met once a week and was chaired by General Yosef Mishleb, the coordinator. The members of the forum were representatives of the civilian administration, the research branch of the Israel Defense Forces (IDF), other security officials, and people from the foreign ministry.

At the end of April 2006, a few weeks after this meeting, I was summoned to a discussion in the foreign minister's office in Jerusalem. Participating in the meeting also were the director-general of the foreign ministry, Ron Prosor; the director-general of the ministry of justice, Aharon Abramowitz (later appointed director-general of the foreign ministry on May 21, 2006); the prime minister's political adviser, Shalom Turgeman; the prime minister's military secretary, Gadi Shamni; the economic deputy director-general of the foreign ministry, Yossi Gal; and a few other employees of the foreign ministry.

The subject of the discussion, the mechanism to keep track of Palestinian Authority funds, was set after, in recent weeks, Livni had been contacted by several foreign ministers, especially from Europe, protesting against the embargo. In particular, they complained about Israel's freeze of Palestinian tax money. Every additional phone call like that increased the risk that Israel would not be able to withstand the pressure.

The meeting lasted an hour and a half, nearly all of it devoted to a theoretical discussion led by the foreign minister. The sentence that she repeated several times was this: "I actually like the idea of placing the Palestinian Authority under a receivership." The idea had developed during the discussion of a plan to establish an international supervisory mechanism, which would include, among other things, recruiting hundreds of clerks worldwide to follow and examine the movement of funds to the Palestinian Authority.

Then, out of the blue, when it seemed the discussion had worn down, the foreign minister threw a bomb into the room. "I don't want to collect taxes for them at all," she said. "As far as I'm concerned, we can have the containers dropped off in Gaza and let them deal with it." I looked to the right, I looked to the left, and I saw that none of those present was planning to react. It was one of those times when you know that in another minute you're going to do both the best thing and the worst thing possible. I asked for the floor. At first, Livni ignored me, and when I insisted, she said, "Eli, I know your opinion; it's okay."

"Minister," I replied, "even though you know my opinion, I'd like to state it myself. Hamas needs about $180 million a month to maintain itself in Gaza. If you give it the containers in Gaza, you'll be transferring $60 million to it that it will collect from taxes and you'll be enabling them to use the money for other purposes."

Shalom Turgeman, coming to Livni's aid, said, "Eli, what are you talking about? You know they're so impotent, they'll never manage to collect the taxes themselves."

"Shalom, what are you talking about?" I replied. "You know Hamas is not Fatah. They'll shoot the first man who refuses to pay in the foot, and in the end they'll collect a lot more than $60 million."

At that stage, the foreign minister closed the discussion.

We walked out of the office to the second floor of the building, where the offices of the heads of the foreign ministry were located. I sensed an atmosphere of confusion in the air. Several days later, I learned that the foreign minister had floated the idea to Prime Minister Olmert. It seems Olmert had been briefed in advance about Livni's idea by some of the people who had been at the meeting. His reply was a resounding no.

When the Hamas government was sworn in on March 25, 2006, it became clear to Israel that just as money cannot buy everything, its absence cannot destroy everything. Israel reacted by deciding that what doesn't work with force might work with more force. On April 11, 2006, the government adopted decision 4,780, under the heading "Israel's policy vis-à-vis the Palestinian Authority after the establishment of the Hamas government":

> Following the elections in the Palestinian Authority, and after the swearing in of the Hamas government on March 25, 2006, a government that does not recognize the existence of the State of Israel and the agreements signed with it and does not renounce the path of terror, we have decided:
>
> The Palestinian Authority is a terror authority hostile to Israel. The State of Israel, including all parts of its administration, will not maintain any ties with the Palestinian Authority and its government agencies.
>
> The Palestinian Authority is one authority, and hence we will not relate differently to the chairman of the Palestinian Authority or to the office of the presidency. However, Israel will not personally ban the chairman of the Palestinian Authority.
>
> Foreign donors who visit the region and meet with Hamas officials will not be received, during the same visit, for meetings with Israeli officials.

Israel, together with the international community, will coordinate ways of providing the humanitarian aid to the Palestinian population, not through the government system.

Subject to security considerations, the crossing points from Israel to the Gaza strip will remain open to enable the entry of humanitarian aid into Gaza.[28]

Israel now understood that it may have lost many points when it failed to take into account the danger that a humanitarian crisis would be created in Gaza and that Hamas would exploit it. The development of a large-scale humanitarian crisis in Gaza would not only lead to international pressure and the end of the sanctions but also further damage Israel's image in the world. Hence, in its decision about the crossing points, Israel changed its position from keeping them absolutely closed to opening them for the passage of aid.[29]

The caveat that was added to the clause about the crossing points was not Israel's only retreat from its original position. In contrast to earlier decisions and declarations of the Israeli government—in which the entire Palestinian Authority had been defined as a terror entity and all of whose components had to be banned—a caveat was added to the third clause of the decision. According to it, the ban would not be applied to the chairman of the Authority. This change was a result of pressure applied by the U.S. government, which resolutely refused to break off contacts with Abu Mazen and the members of his staff.

In a report that arrived from Washington dealing with U.S. policy on contacts with the Palestinian Authority, a U.S. official made it clear to his Israeli counterpart that the United States was firm in its decision to continue maintaining direct contact with Abu Mazen: "America cannot permit herself to remain without a party for dialogue on the other side." All of Israel's attempts to persuade its ally, the United States, to freeze all contacts with Abu Mazen—in view of the fact that he had given legitimacy to the Hamas government—were in vain.

Three months after Hamas's rise to power, on April 25, 2006, Stuart Levey, the undersecretary for terror and financial intelligence of the U.S. Treasury Department, arrived for a series of discussions. He met with senior officials of the Mossad, the National Security Council, and the foreign ministry to discuss a plan that the United States had published only a few days before about a "financial attack" on Iran. The talks were also meant to deal with the joint effort to prevent the transfer of funds to the Hamas government.

In preparation for the meeting, I was asked to formulate some recommendations for the foreign minister on the struggle against Hamas. In that memo,[30] I noted that the most effective way to bring pressure to bear on the new Hamas government was by freezing all the tax money that Israel had been transferring to the Authority, and by preventing the transfer of funds to the Authority from abroad. This would make it difficult for the Authority to pay salaries to the government's employees and force it to use the money it was smuggling into Gaza for that purpose. The weak link in the Authority's apparatus is that 80 percent of its annual budget—$1.2 billion out of $1.5 billion—goes to pay salaries. If these are not paid, the public employees will riot, and that will lead to new elections. I also explicitly noted that Israel must not apply pressure to prevent humanitarian aid, since a crisis of that kind would immediately invite heavy international pressure on Israel, leading to greater support for Hamas by the Palestinian public and the rest of the world, too.

At this stage, the European Union and the United States had already announced that they would not provide budgetary aid to the Authority and that they would channel aid funds directly to humanitarian needs. In my paper, I added that Israel should persuade the United States to pressure the Arab donors to act in the same way. I recommended to the foreign minister that she focus international attention on Hamas's intention to fire thousands of workers and to absorb members of Hamas and Hamas institutions into the Palestinian budgetary setup, at the expense of the existing employees and institutions.

I summed up my paper for the foreign minister with a series "dos and don'ts":

- The State of Israel must not prevent humanitarian aid. We should not decide how many glasses of milk a Palestinian child should drink. All aid in the form of food, medical equipment, and clothing should be permitted.
- Debts for water and electricity should be deducted from the tax monies, and a regular supply of fuels should be permitted, after the appropriate reduction. The remaining millions should be transferred to a body such as the World Bank, after reaching an agreement that the funds will be transferred to the territory of the Palestinian Authority in the form of food, medicine, and clothing.
- We should significantly increase the number of medical treatments inside Israel, due to our humanitarian concern for the Palestinian people. The State of Israel is fighting Palestinian terror, not the Palestinian people.
- We must leave the Karni crossing open, since it is a major lifeline for the Strip. When it is closed, the inventory of staple items for Gaza seriously decreases. In keeping it open, we are taking calculated risks, as we have done until today.
- We should immediately enforce the declaration of funds entering through couriers and money changers at the different border crossings. We also

have to deal thoroughly with large sums of money that arrive through the crossings.

- We should ask the United States to initiate a process to make Palestinian humanitarian aid subject to the laws of the FATF. A U.S. statement on the subject will immediately influence the international banks that are operating vis-à-vis the Palestinian Authority, and will later influence the creation of a mechanism to control the funds coming to the Palestinian Authority.
- We should avoid causing any difficulties for the international aid organizations because that will suggest that we are opposed to humanitarian aid to the Palestinian Authority, and will lead to international pressure and put an end to the concerted opposition to Hamas.

In addition to the operative suggestions in my paper, I formulated a series of messages that ought to be transmitted again and again to the international media:

"Israel welcomes all humanitarian aid to the Palestinian people and will assist in this effort. A Palestinian child need not suffer as a result of the historical mistake made at the polls."[31]

Hamas has millions of dollars in its coffers and should use that money to ease the population's suffering. Hamas used donated funds to finance an expensive election campaign in order to gain control of the Palestinian Authority, and now it intends to take over the Palestinian budget and subjugate it to its organizational needs.

Ismail Haniyeh's statement about the "empty money box," besides being untrue, is meant to prepare the ground for the dismissal of thousands of employees of the Palestinian Authority in order to make jobs available for Hamas people. Hamas wants to use the Authority's budget to strengthen its own organization and institutions and is going to place its people and institutions into the Palestinian budgetary system.

"THEY'RE NOT GOING TO GET ANYTHING," THE AMBASSADOR STATED FIRMLY

On May 2, 2006, during his visit to Israel, Stuart Levey, the U.S. undersecretary of the Treasury, held two meetings with Israeli officials. The main meeting with Foreign Minister Livni, in the presence of the U.S. ambassador to Israel, was preceded by a preparatory meeting chaired by Miriam Ziv, deputy director-general for strategic affairs in the foreign ministry, who deals with issues related to preventing the financing of terror. The meeting, at which I was also present, was devoted mainly to the Iranian issue. When the subject of economic sanctions against Hamas also came up, Levey made the

U.S. position clear in one sentence: "Enough; we cannot do more than we have already done until now."

Despite his firm and impatient reply, I turned to Levey and said, "Sir, Hamas's financing comes from funds that are smuggled and transferred from sources whose identity is unknown to us. Is it possible to make the Palestinian Authority subject to the supervision of the Financial Action Task Force?"

After briefly consulting with his assistant who was sitting to his left, Levey replied, "This is something we can do." I had hoped that my request would be implemented, but I had not imagined it would be implemented so quickly.

Shortly after Levey's return to the United States, the Treasury department published a warning that was disseminated to all banks and financial institutions, stating that the Palestinian Authority should be treated as a body acting in violation of the laws prohibiting money laundering. This had immediate repercussions. Afraid of becoming entangled with the FATF, Palestinian banks suddenly refused to accept or transfer funds intended for the Authority, and even stopped transferring salaries to the Authority's employees. U.S. banks acted immediately to avoid exposing themselves to legal claims. International human rights organizations working in Gaza were aware of this situation, and in reports they published during that period they stressed that this measure was making it very difficult for the Authority to function.[32]

At the end of the meeting I just described, Stuart Levey met with Minister Livni's staff, in the presence of the then U.S. ambassador, Richard Jones. At the meeting, Jones, who had the rigid appearance of a military man, put forth a far more extreme line than Israel was suggesting at the time, and certainly more extreme than the one presented by the undersecretary of the Treasury at the previous meeting. At a certain stage, the talk moved on to the question of whether there was, in fact, a humanitarian crisis in the Gaza Strip, or whether it was just a false picture intended to increase international pressure on Israel.

During the discussion on this question, I expressed my opinion that Israel should not transfer funds to the Strip except for food, medication, and clothing. Jones's reaction to my suggestion was, "By no means. They're not going to get anything."

It later turned out that Jones's rigid position was not in keeping with the more compromising position of the United States that was presented by Secretary of State Rice.

IF THERE IS NO BREAD,
LET THEM EAT TOMATOES

On May 21, 2006, Israel had already felt the brunt of the lesson that many states had learned previously when they had imposed economic sanctions in an attempt to change an existing government. In certain cases, the damage caused to the sending country was apt to be greater than that caused to the target country. While Israel was trying to decide what the next step would be, Hamas understood that the best way to divert fire from it and turn it against Israel would be to aggravate the picture of the distress that was broadcast daily from the Palestinian street directly to TV screens worldwide. That worked really well: the worse the situation became, the more international pressure was applied to Israel.

At this juncture, the government of Israel adopted resolution 54, on May 21, 2006:

> Subject of decision: providing humanitarian aid to the Palestinian population in the form of medical aid. Further to the government's decisions no. 4,705 of 19.2.2006 and 4,780 of 11.4.2006, and in order to enable humanitarian aid to the Palestinian population.
>
> To immediately transfer to international aid organizations to be determined by the Minister of Defense, in coordination with the Prime Minister, medications and medical equipment at a value of 50 million shekels, to be financed from the funds that the government formerly decided not to transfer to the Palestinian Authority—this for purpose of transferring the medical equipment and medicines to Palestinian medical institutions. The medicine and equipment will be transferred after coordination with the aforesaid medical institutions, through the selected international aid organizations. [33]

The basic idea was excellent: to show the world that Israel is not indifferent to the suffering of the inhabitants of the Gaza Strip, and is doing everything possible to relieve it. The problem was the caveats that Israel chose to introduce into the decision. First of all, the insistence that the aid would be transferred not through the office of Abu Mazen, but directly through international aid organizations "to be determined by the Minister of Defense," divested it of any content. [34]

On May 24, 2006, at three o'clock, three days after the government decision, I was summoned to a meeting with the COGAT chair, General Yosef Mishleb. Others attending the meeting were a representative of the World Health Organization (WHO) and Lieutenant Colonel Daniel Bodwan, head of the branch for international organizations in COGAT headquarters. Before the meeting began, Bodwan told us that the WHO was going to refuse to accept NIS 50 million from the Israeli government to purchase medicine and transfer it to the Gaza Strip. General Mishleb opened the meeting and said that the Israeli government wanted to transfer medicine to Gaza through the WHO, which has the means for doing so. The representative of the WHO stated categorically that he could not do that and that none of the other international aid organizations active in Gaza would do anything that is not coordinated with the Hamas government. He added that he had spoken to the

Hamas minister of health, who had told him that he refused to accept the medicine, and demanded that the money be transferred in cash to the Hamas government, the only one who would decide how to use it.

The meeting was embarrassing. It was evident that the WHO representative felt uneasy, since he knew that the position he had just put forward was absolutely in opposition to the aims for which his organization had been founded. Finally, after being pressed to do so by General Mishleb, the WHO man agreed to transfer the matter to the decision of the organization's executive board in Brussels. But it transpired that this step had no effect, since the organization refused to change its decision, claiming that it refuses to act in any way that might endanger its people.

The WHO was not the only humanitarian organization that refused to cooperate with Israel in this matter. Even the representatives of USAID (United States Agency for International Development) rejected Israel's suggestion that it transfer medicine to the Strip.

Although the attempt to transfer medicines through international aid organizations failed, it did win some points for Israel in the international arena, especially from the international human rights organizations.[35] To my regret, it was a one-time attempt that was never repeated. In my view, it was essential to find creative ways to transfer different types of humanitarian aid to the population, while clearly declaring that "the Palestinian people are not our enemy."

I do not regard a declaration of that kind as merely a way of explaining Israel's position to the world. I truly believe that the Palestinian people are not our enemy, and the Palestinian child is not our enemy, and we therefore ought to make sure they get humanitarian aid and strictly maintain the separation between the extremist leadership of the Gaza Strip and its inhabitants. It was important to initiate the transfer of humanitarian aid in the form of food, in various ways, to the Strip—especially since it was Palestinian money and not the money of the State of Israel.

Hamas's refusal to enable the transfer of medicine and food from Israel to Gaza through aid organizations proved itself. International pressure was applied to Israel. In June 2006, the United States gave in to the pressure applied by Europe, Russia, and the United Nations, and agreed to establish a temporary international mechanism, which circumvented Hamas, to transfer donations in aid to the Palestinian people. The mechanism was called TIM (Temporary International Mechanism for Assistance to the Palestinian People). The U.S. decision did not surprise Israel, because there had already been signs from Washington that the U.S. government could no longer withstand the pressure. The establishment of TIM was a direct continuation of the Quartet's May 5, 2006, declaration about the necessity of providing for the needs of the Palestinian populations.[36] The mechanism stated that the transfer of donations to the Palestinian Authority would be carried out in three phases.[37] The first, emergency support of services, such as health, education, and social aid, would be implemented by the World Bank; the second, supply of the energy needs of the Palestinian Authority to Judah and Samaria and the Gaza Strip, would be implemented by a donation from the European Representative office; and the third, payment to those in need of relief and pension payments to employees of the Palestinian Authority, would be implemented by donations from Europe and the Arab world.

The Israeli government accepted the first phase; it accepted the second phase with a reservation and was firmly opposed to the third phase. But the United States succumbed in this case to European pressure in order to avoid dismantling the coordinated international activity.

The transfer of donations to the Authority led to lessened pressure on Hamas as well as on Israel, but despite Israel's significant advantage—and the fact that it was the strong player in the game—it was actually Hamas, the weak side, that achieved its aims in this crisis. And that was not the last time.

On June 28, 2006, as part of the military escalation against Hamas in the Gaza Strip, protecting the land from rocket fire, the Israeli air force bombed Palestinian power stations and left 50 percent of the Strip's residents without any electricity. This was meant to harm Hamas, but in actual fact it only stepped up the pressure on Israel from the international community, which feared that as a result of the lack of electricity, the sewage pumping stations in multistory buildings and centers for wastewater treatment would stop functioning and potentially cause an outbreak of epidemics in Gaza.[38]

Israel was facing a problem. Every attempt to increase the economic pressure on the Gaza Strip with the aim of making life difficult for Hamas not only failed to achieve that goal but actually increased the pressure on Israel by the international community. As part of the attempts to come up with a solution that would lead to a quick, effective outcome, various and sundry ideas began to emerge.

In a discussion held in the office of COGAT, which dealt with, among other things, the idea of preventing the entry of flour trucks into Gaza, General Mishleb said that, in a meeting he had attended, he was told that due to the freeze on the export of goods from Gaza to Europe, a huge number of loads of tomatoes had accumulated, and that these were rotting in the hot sun in the Palestinian agricultural areas. He related that one of the men at the meeting had jumped up and suggested, "So then let the Palestinians eat tomatoes instead of bread." Mishleb said he had to explain to that guy that the nutritional value of one pita is equal to that of a crate of tomatoes, and it would be a mistake to allow a shortage of flour in the Strip.

Although Israel had decided at first not to transfer tax money directly to the Authority, and had entrenched itself in that position for a long time, at a certain stage, there was a proliferation of voices calling for a change in it. This was both in order to lessen international pressure and to strengthen the moderate elements in the Authority. On December 23, 2006, Olmert and Abu Mazen met, and the following day, the government adopted resolution 917:[39]

> Following the Prime Minister's meeting with the Chairman of the Palestinian Authority yesterday, Saturday evening, 23.12.2006, and the desire to assist moderate elements in the Palestinian Authority (it was decided) to transfer 100 million dollars of the Palestinian tax money being held in Israel for humanitarian purposes in the Palestinian Authority, through the office of the chairman of the Palestinian Authority and according to his objectives, which he stated at the meeting with the Prime Minister.[40]

About the meeting between Olmert and Abu Mazen on December 22, 2006, which led to this decision, Olmert himself wrote in a chapter of his book published in the *Yedioth Ahronoth* newspaper:

> In my eyes, it was not a case of guile, or even generosity, but rather an attempt to make clear to them [to the Palestinians] that we do not intend to amuse ourselves with negotiation, or to procrastinate, but to lay a foundation for serious dialogue.[41]

Olmert told how stunned Abu Mazen was when he said that Israel was prepared to transfer $100 million to him, and not the 50 million shekels he had asked for. That in itself showed how serious Israel was in the negotiation, and Abu Mazen said to the man sitting next to him, "We are beginning an entirely new period, it is different from everything there was in the past."[42]

In this case, too, it was not a step taken in reaction to a surprising development in the territory, but an act intended to prove Israel's seriousness in the negotiation it wanted to hold with Abu Mazen. Still, we need to bear in mind that the freeze on the transfer of the tax monies was meant to pressure Hamas and to cause its government to fall, but it seems that at that point in time, the Hamas government was already a fait accompli as far as the Israeli government was concerned, and the new move was for the purpose of reaching a peace agreement with the Palestinian Authority headed by Abu Mazen.

Three months after Abu Mazen began receiving the tax money directly, on March 17, 2007, as a result of pressure by the Palestinian public (mainly pressure from the leadership of the Fatah and Hamas prisoners in Israeli prisons), a Palestinian unity government was formed. The following day, the Israeli government adopted resolution 1,407, intended to strengthen Abu Mazen's position, along with an ongoing attempt to undermine Hamas's position:

> In light of the fact that the new Palestinian government, according to the platform formulated and approved by it, does not accept the conditions of the international community, i.e., to recognize the State of Israel's right to exist,

abandon terror, dismantle the terror infrastructures, and to honor and fulfill the agreements signed with Israel, including the road map, Israel cannot work with that government, or any of its ministers.

Israel will continue to work with Abu Mazen and to promote with him security issues and issues related to improvement of the living conditions of the Palestinian population.

The platform of the Palestinian government includes, among other things, the use of terror as a legitimate right, the acceptance of prior agreements with Israel only according to Palestinian interests, and the restrictions the chairman of the Palestinian Authority has placed upon himself (submitting every arrangement with Israel for approval by the new Palestinian national council and approval by the Palestinian diaspora, for example). This platform, in fact, grants Hamas and the terror organizations the right to veto any arrangement reached in future with Israel and limits the possibilities and the range of subjects that Israel can discuss with the chairman of the Palestinian Authority.

Israel will continue to demand that the chairman of the Palestinian Authority fulfill all of his commitments: to bring about the unconditional release of the abducted soldier Gilad Shalit, to stop the firing of Qassam rockets, to dismantle the terror organizations and infrastructure in the Palestinian Authority, and to fully implement the first stage of the road map.

Israel expects the international community to continue the policy it adopted throughout the past year, of isolating the Palestinian government until it complies with the three Quartet conditions. [43]

Israel has not changed its position; the country is in favor of peace with the Palestinians in accordance with the road map. Israel advocates a two-state solution for the two peoples. The Israeli government is prepared to open negotiations with every government in the Palestinian Authority, whatever its composition may be, that will fulfill the conditions of the international community and will be prepared to discuss every issue with it.

This gesture and the empowerment of Abu Mazen may have prepared the ground for continued quiet peace talks between Abu Mazen and Olmert, but they did not achieve the desired pressure on the Hamas government. The Palestinian unity government was formed, but it did not last long, and on June 13, 2007, in a well-organized military operation, Hamas elements took control over the Gaza Strip. Abu Mazen reacted by announcing the dissolution of the unity government and the establishment of an emergency government. In the wake of these developments, and with the aim of strengthening Abu Mazen, on June 24, 2007, the Israeli government decided to continue working with him and the Palestinian emergency government headed by Salam Fayyad, as well as to transfer to the Authority the frozen tax monies plus interest. [44]

Abu Mazen's dismissal of the Hamas government and the establishment of a government in Ramallah headed by Fatah led to the cessation of TIM's activity. From then on, the donations were directly transferred to the Palestinian Authority, as was the case before the rise of Hamas to power.

However, although the sanctions against the Authority had ended, the sanctions imposed on the Gaza Strip under Hamas control continued.

MILLIONS OF DOLLARS IN TUNNELS

In the final analysis, Israel's attempt to change the reality it woke up to on January 25, 2006, by means of economic sanctions was a total failure. At the end of eighteen months of pressure and endless attempts and ploys, Hamas was still adamant in its refusal to recognize Israel, to abandon the path of terror, and to honor the agreements signed in the past by the Palestinian Authority.

In contrast, Israel's image and its power of deterrence took a hard blow, in the eyes of Hamas, the Palestinians in the street, and the entire Arab world. Like the situation created during and after the second Lebanese war against Hezbollah, in this instance, too, Hamas was perceived to be the winner, and Israel—the loser. The three predefined conditions for removing the sanctions were not met.

Israel learned a hard lesson from this episode, which boils down mainly to the need to avoid a lack of focus and defining overambitious aims. In the process of taking the decisions that led to the imposition of economic sanctions, Israel did not define for itself its short-term objective or its long-term aspiration.[45]

While in the initial phase, Israel defined the Palestinian Authority in its entirety as an enemy; several months later, Israel viewed Abu Mazen as the only partner with whom it could conduct a dialogue, as well as an ally in its war against Hamas. Until Israel changed its approach, the country had stuck to its position, refusing to listen to voices coming from the area or the international community. Consequently, precious time, many resources, and advantageous points were wasted.

Another flaw in the policy of economic sanctions was Israel's indifference to the desires of the Palestinian public and to the fact that Hamas was adept at understanding the needs of that public and influencing it. After all, Hamas won in the elections not because the Palestinians were so fond of its leaders or their principles, but because they were fed up with the corruption that had spread throughout the Palestinian Authority and the Fatah leadership.

In voting for Hamas in the elections, the Palestinian public was, in fact, showing that it strongly desired the formation of a Palestinian unity under a firm leadership, which would make it possible to cope with what they regarded as their true enemy—Israel. Israel's imposition of economic sanctions, which was perceived as a collective punishment against all the inhabitants of the Gaza Strip, did not help bring about a change in the attitude of the

Palestinian public. Throughout its entire term in office, the Hamas government continued to enjoy wide popularity among the public until it forcibly took control over the Strip on June 17, 2007, which led to the dismissal of the unity government. As a result of this act, Hamas suffered a 7 percent decline in support among the Palestinian public.[46]

The effectiveness of the sanctions imposed by Israel on the Authority was not impaired only because of Israel's flawed conduct, but also because Hamas exploited the anti-Israel noise created worldwide by the sanctions to smuggle millions of dollars of donations that came from Iran, Qatar, and Islamic charitable organizations, through the crossings from Egypt into the Gaza Strip.

Surveys conducted in the territory of the Authority during the period indicated that the Palestinian public supported Hamas's efforts to smuggle funds into the Strip during the visits of several of its leaders in Iran and Qatar. While the public believed that senior officials in the Fatah administration were siphoning off money for themselves, Hamas was perceived as an organization acting incorruptibly to improve welfare services.

This was not a new area of activity for Hamas. In fact, from the moment Israel disengaged from the Strip in September 2005—when its control over the Philadelphia route, which separates the Strip from Egypt, also ended—until January 2006, Hamas used that route and the tunnels dug under it for smuggling money and weapons into the Strip, while the Palestinian enforcement agencies and the Egyptian authorities turned a blind eye. After the establishment of the Hamas government, the smuggling of money became a routine occurrence. Another channel that Hamas used to move money to the Strip was diplomatic couriers: the Hamas government ministers, who, armed with diplomatic Palestinian passports, traveled to the Gulf states and Iran, brought money from there through Egypt, and in view of their official status, the Egyptian authorities refused to arrest them. When they left the Strip for Egypt and returned, these couriers encountered no special difficulties from the guards at the Rafiah crossing, who belonged to the Palestinian presidential guard that reported to Abu Mazen. Israel was not the only one to suffer because all parties looked the other way; Abu Mazen himself paid a heavy price. While Hamas did not pay salaries to the Authority's employees, certainly not to those belonging to Fatah, it used the funds it smuggled to establish a military intervention force known as *al-kuwah al-khassa* ("the special force"), which numbered about 5,500 soldiers.[47] Using this force, which was equipped with the finest weaponry, Hamas took total control over the Strip in June 2007.

One of the main aims of imposing economic sanctions is to disrupt the daily lives of the public living in the target country, in the hope that pressure from below will be directed toward the ruling echelon, demanding that it solve their distressful situation and change its behavior. But that is generally valid when the population in question is a "regular" one, a definition that does not fit the situation of the inhabitants of the Gaza Strip.

The Gaza Strip has always suffered from economic hardships and the highest rate of poverty and overcrowdedness in the world. For many years, long before the imposition of economic sanctions, most of its inhabitants have depended on benefits and relief aid from the United Nations (UN) and other international aid organizations. Nor was the scope of export from the Strip ever high or significant in comparison to the number of inhabitants; in fact, exports served as a rather marginal element in its shaky economy. It is not clear, then, what led Israel to make things worse in this sphere, which, in the best of times, had almost no effect on the livelihood of most of the Gazans.

How did Israel's allies act in this crisis? Of all of Israel's friends, the United States displayed the greatest determination, but it, too, refused Israel's request to boycott Abu Mazen and the entire Authority. In the end, the United States also folded in face of the demands of the European Union, Russia, and the UN and agreed to the establishment of a donations mechanism that circumvented Hamas. This decision came about despite the fact that, on the eve of the Quartet's meeting, U.S. officials informed Israel, through their Tel Aviv embassy, of their position, which opposed the establishment of the mechanism. The United States was also opposed at first to Israel's sweeping demand that salaries should not be paid to the Authority's employees, and insisted that this prohibition not include employees of health and education facilities.

Paradoxically, after Hamas's victory at the polls, the United States, a country committed to a policy of democratization in the Middle East, was forced to cope with an undesirable democratic outcome and to support economic sanctions against the Authority under Hamas leadership, even though it had been elected in free elections. [48]

Moreover, in early 2011, riots broke out in Arab countries, posing similar challenges to the United States. The rebels in Tunisia were supported by the United States in the cause of democracy and against corruption. In Egypt, the demonstrators gained even greater support, and the United States did not hesitate to publicly offend President Mubarak. But as the riots advanced to the oil-producing countries, this policy drew to a halt, and the United States changed its approach, declaring that it supported governments moving toward reform and not automatically supporting demonstrators calling for full democracy.

The results of the elections in the Palestinian Authority changed the attitude of the extremist Muslim organizations toward democracy. Hamas's success in imposing a totalitarian Islamic rule by democratic means led people like the elderly Egyptian sheikh Yusuf al-Qaradawi to say things that seem to have been translated from statements issued by the White House, when he addressed the crowd at Tahrir Square on February 18, 2011. Hamas—with its victory at the polls and the way it met serious challenges—was a role model for many of the demonstrators in Arab countries that called for democracy.

To go back to the international conduct in relation to the sanctions, the situation with Europe was more complex than the one with the United States. While, at first, the European Union joined in the Quartet's demands of the Palestinian Authority, later it invested all of its efforts in providing humanitarian aid to the Authority, particularly to Gaza, even when that meant strengthening Hamas and weakening the sanctions. The TIM mechanism was supported mainly by the European Union, and it was Europe that led the process of weakening the economic sanctions imposed on the Authority under Hamas's leadership.

Other players involved in this crisis were the UN and Russia, but they were not allies of Israel in this crisis. From the outset, Russia and the various UN agencies led the camp that called for direct talks with Hamas. It was only the Quartet's demand for a unified framework of decision making that kept them from acting independently.

DAHLAN FLEXES HIS MUSCLES

At the beginning of this chapter, I wrote that when economic sanctions are aimed at destabilizing the target country, it is very important at the same time to engage in subversive and intelligence activity defined as "semi-military."[49] Israel had the ability and the possibilities to do that in this crisis, but it chose not to use these means, not to help people like Mohammed Dahlan, who could have been a counterweight to the Hamas government.

On January 7, 2007, the Fatah movement held a mass rally to mark the forty-second anniversary of its establishment. Tens of thousands of Palestinians came to the rally, vilifying the Hamas organization and calling it "Shi'a," alluding to its ties to Iran. This rally could have been a starting point for a challenge to the Hamas government, but Israel chose to stand on the sidelines; from then on, the course of events was inevitable until Hamas gained complete control over the Gaza Strip and Dahlan fled to Ramallah.[50]

After the rally, Hamas began to systematically annihilate the leaders of Fatah in the Strip. Once a week or once in two weeks, a senior Fatah member was killed. For me, that was a red alert. One Wednesday, when I regularly attended a forum chaired by General Mishleb, I invited myself to a meeting with one of the leading officials in the research branch of the Intelligence Corps who dealt with the subject; I tried to apprise him of my view that Hamas was conducting a well-planned campaign to annihilate Fatah's center of power in the Strip, following that rally at which Dahlan and Fatah had flexed their muscles.

"It's a focused liquidation," I told that officer. "Hamas was alarmed by Dahlan's show of power at the rally and is acting to weaken him. We have to help Dahlan." I drew the officer's attention to Hamas's establishment of a special force as a move toward taking total control over Gaza.

"Look," he said dismissively, "in Gaza a war of forces is going on and each side is killing people from the opposing side. We don't see a special situation here that justifies any special attention or intervention."

We all know the end of the story.

The irony is that Dahlan, who then was fighting against Hamas, was interviewed on Al-Jazeera after a press conference at Sharm al-Sheikh on October 5, 2000, after the outbreak of the second Intifada; he said with pride that the Authority had released twelve Hamas and Jihad leaders in Gaza, in reaction to the Israeli military escalation in the Strip. The released men were the ones who had threatened his life seven years later, murdered his people in cold blood, caused him to flee to Ramallah, and took control of the Gaza Strip by force.

GAZA DID NOT COLLAPSE

January 2007 marked a year after Hamas's victory at the polls and the imposition of economic sanctions by Israel. Although it seemed as if the Authority was about to undergo a particularly difficult time economically, the data showed a different picture. From the figures published by the Central Bureau of Statistics of the Palestinian Authority, on December 26, 2006, it turned out that, in the first eight months of 2006, the Authority had received aid in the amount of $500 million, and the total amount forecast until the end of the year was $760 million. During a parallel period in the previous year, 2005, before Hamas rose to power, the Authority had received only $325 million— less than half. Most of this money came from the TIM operated by the Quartet, which, according to the European Union, financed health services, medical equipment, and welfare services for about forty thousand poor families in Gaza.

At the same time, the Authority's Central Bureau of Statistics reported a significant decline in domestic income, from $1.29 billion in 2005 to $370 million a year later. The major reason for this decline was that Israel had stopped transferring the tax money it collected. In December 2006, Israel agreed to release $100 million of that money directly to the chairman of the Authority, Abu Mazen.

Taking into account the aid and tax money that went into the coffers of the Palestinian Authority during Hamas's first year in power, the Authority's income declined at a rate of about 31 percent. Hamas tried to grapple with this sharp decline by cutting the Palestinian government's expenses to a minimum, a measure that did result in a reduction of about 38 percent in the operating expenses of the government ministries. That same year, the Palestinian Authority invested nothing in development, except for constructing two new hospitals—an investment that enabled it to reduce the expense of medical treatments outside its territory.

Moreover, more than 75 percent of the Palestinian Authority's employees, who earned less than $450 a month, received their wages from TIM immediately after the start of the sanctions, or from internal and other aid sources. Abu Mazen's office succeeded in paying salaries from monies that came directly from the Arab League. The 12,500 highest-paid employees of the public sector received their monthly salary in December on time. Shortly afterward, they received the rest of the money owed them as pay in arrears. As a result, the strike by the public sector in the Authority ended after only one month.[51]

In the most severe stages of the sanctions, when employees of the Authority did not receive their wages for about five months, the anticipated angry demonstrations did not occur. The employees continued to come to work so their jobs would not be taken by others. The government remained stable. Gaza did not collapse.

* * *

As Israel learned the hard way, economic sanctions do not achieve their goal. It did not work in the Iraqi case, nor is it working in the Iranian case. In practice, in most cases such sanctions achieve completely opposite results: instead of separating the people from the extremist ruling group, it causes them to unite around the government. It is never a good idea to act out of anger: "They elected Hamas and now we'll show them what a stupid choice that was!" The more brutal and deep-cutting the sanctions are, the greater the distress they cause the civilian population, which leads to worldwide opposition. The final result is that the sanctions are divested of any content. That is what happened in Gaza.

There was a need in the past and there will be in the future, to combine focused, effective sanctions with other measures, especially semi-military ones, such as intelligence and psychological warfare and political subversion. Since it is indisputably clear that the side under sanctions will try to overturn them and to arouse worldwide opposition to them, the sender of the sanctions must intelligently create counter-levers against propaganda that focuses on the humanitarian harm supposedly caused by them. It is important to maintain an uncompromising, resolute policy, but one that is at the same time humanitarian and humane. It is also important for heads of state to make this policy loud and clear. The challenge is to create a separation between the people, who are not our enemy, and the extremist, fanatic leadership that is leading them to disaster.

The State of Israel focused on the final outcome—overthrowing the Hamas government—and forgot to consider the right way to achieve it. When we embarked on our effort to achieve the goal, we enjoyed nearly wall-to-wall international support, and ended with merely the partial support of the United States. We took the wrong path. We based it on evaluations that were not supported by past experience, as well as—and perhaps mainly—on arrogance and exaggerated self-confidence.

Hamas, on the other hand, invested all it had in the effort, in managing the crisis, and very skillfully succeeded in creating levers of international pressure on Israel, in maintaining the stability of its government, in gaining the sympathy of many countries in the world, and legitimation by important countries like Russia. As I write these lines, Hamas maintains stable rule over the Gaza Strip even after the last conflict in the summer of 2014, and despite the ongoing cease-fire negotiations, Hamas continues to meet all the commitments it made when it won the elections: not to recognize the State of Israel, not to abandon the use of terror, and not to honor the agreements signed between Israel and representatives of the Palestinian people before January 2006.

When the Israeli government took the decision to overthrow the Hamas government by means of economic sanctions imposed on the Gaza Strip, many of the decision makers believed that Israel could "bring Hamas to its knees." Today it is clear that the sanctions did not achieve their goal, but rather caused suffering to more than one million people. The picture might have been different if Israel had combined the sanctions with a broader array of means and focused actions against Hamas. Since it failed to do so, we are today witnessing a regional situation that until now had been familiar to us from remote places such as Afghanistan or Sudan—countries ruled by extreme Islamic organizations. The big question is: Will we learn the lesson of Gaza or will we repeat the same pattern of action in the next crisis?

We did not have to wait long for an answer. On April 28, 2011, a memorandum of understanding was signed between Fatah and Hamas in Cairo. It outlined steps toward the establishment of a Palestinian unity government and announced a date for general elections to be held a year later. The statements made by Prime Minister Netanyahu, through his ministers and other members of the Knesset, could have been copied from others made in early 2006, when Hamas won the general elections, or from March 2007, when a Palestinian unity government was declared. On May 1, 2011, Israel already declared it would delay the transfer of tax payments to the Palestinian Authority, and it looked as if the process was about to repeat itself, with all of the same mistakes.

What could have been done differently? A friend from Hong Kong told me once, "You have to stop dropping bombs on Gaza and start dropping cans of sardines. People need to eat." Simple but true. By caring for the everyday needs of the Gazans, we would have pulled the rug out from under Hamas's claims that Israel was starving the people in Gaza and turning it into a large concentration camp. If we had sent food and medicine—yes, even from the air—that would have earned Israel international sympathy and enabled it to focus the sanctions on the Hamas government and not on Gaza's poor inhabitants. And, above all, it would have demonstrated the morality that underlies our policy, since the Palestinian people are certainly not our enemy. The Palestinian people are our neighbors, and we need to act with all the means at our disposal against the extremist factors, but at the same time with humanity and understanding toward the people caught in Gaza. I know it is not simple, but it is possible, it is moral, it is right, and it is the smart thing to do.

Chapter Five

The Shi'a

The Shi'a community in Lebanon could have been our natural ally. Instead, we turned it into one of our bitterest enemies. Is there a way back?

For about 1,400 years, since it was founded and up to the first half of the twentieth century, the Shi'a community was on the margins of Islam. Throughout all of this time, it suffered betrayals, oppression, and humiliation—both by other factions in Islam and by foreign elements, including Israel in recent decades. In the last three decades, particularly since the rise of Ruhollah Khomeini to power in Iran and the growing strength of Hezbollah in Lebanon afterward, a dramatic change has occurred in the status of the Shi'a in the Arab and the Muslim worlds. Today it threatens the centuries-old hegemony of the Sunni faction and the stability of the governments of many of the Arab countries that are considered moderate. Recently, this threat was tangibly expressed in Bahrain. Israel had an excellent opportunity to turn the Shi'ites in Lebanon into allies a quarter century ago, but Israel chose to ignore them and turned them into its worst enemies. Why did we make that mistake? And how is it still possible to rectify the situation?

THE IMAM WHO TAUGHT
ME ABOUT MAIMONIDES

My first baptism of fire in the intelligence community was in Lebanon, a quarter century ago, but I remember it as if it were yesterday. Only two weeks after I completed the intelligence officer course, I was posted as a case officer in the Liaison Unit for Lebanon. At the time, the young officers were usually sent for a training period before going to Lebanon, but because there was a shortage of Humint (human intelligence) officers in the central sector of Lebanon, and owing to my command of Arabic, the process was shortened in my case.

On my first day on the job, after I spent the night in a village in the south Lebanon security belt, the civilian administration officer, a major from the Druze community, said to me, "Come, join me for a tour and learn what no one will teach you anywhere else." I went with him gladly. I sat alongside him in the front seat of a black, dust-covered Mercedes with Lebanese plates. The trip took no more than five minutes, but to me it seemed much longer. I felt like an infant leaving his home for the first time, exposed to a vast variety of sights, faces, sounds, and smells.

We were on our way to a meeting with a Shi'ite Lebanese, about whom I'd been told only that "you ought to get to know him."

Although I'd been told that this was a routine meeting that would take place with the same man every few months and I was not asked to do anything before or during the meeting, I was as excited as if the future of the State of Israel depended on its outcome. My imagination was also working overtime. I envisioned a meeting taking place among olive trees in the midst of a pastoral grove, facing an officer in one of the Shi'a factions in Lebanon, a Kalashnikov rifle hanging over his back, one magazine in it and two others attached to the butt with a rubber band.

But my disappointment was as great as my imagination. The pastoral grove was replaced by a one-story house. It was a *husseiniya* structure—a religious meeting house of the Shi'ite community, where the men gather. We were received by a Shi'ite clergyman, who was wearing a pristine white robe, a black turban on his head, and a big smile on his face. Fate had it that my first encounter with a Lebanese was not with a high-level intelligence official nor with a fighter in one of the military militias active at the time in southern Lebanon, but rather with a Shi'ite religious leader of one of the smallest communities in southern Lebanon—a clergyman who had completed his studies in a Shi'ite *madrassa* (seminary) in Iraq.

The meeting was opened by our host, who, according to the finest Arab tradition, poured Lebanese coffee into small porcelain cups. Alongside these, he placed a tray of the best *kunafeh* I had ever tasted. When our host realized I was new to Lebanon and that my knowledge of the Shi'ite community was very sparse, he began by saying, "We Shi'ites are like you, the Jews. We are waiting for the hidden Imam just as you await your Messiah. We believe in the principle of 'live and let live.' My duty as a man of God is to safeguard my community until the coming of the hidden Imam, and we have no quarrel or conflict with you Israelis."

The conversation lasted two hours, but his first statement has remained engraved in my memory to this very day. Later my superiors in the intelligence community told me I shouldn't waste time or resources on that man because he has no real intelligence information; however, that same man became my mentor and the very best teacher I could find to explain to me the complexity of the Shi'a community in Lebanon. He also became a close friend during the entire time I served in Lebanon. The information he possessed on the Shi'a community in Lebanon and on the complicated structure of Lebanese politics was more precious to me then (and certainly today) than all the other "hot" information I obtained as a case officer.

The character and words of that modest, wise, and pleasant man left such a strong impression on me that I took advantage of every opportunity during my service in Lebanon to visit him and hear more stories and insights about the history and complex nature of the Shi'a community in Lebanon.

Only later did I understand how right he was. If Israel had only taken the trouble to learn the nature of the Shi'a community in Lebanon, the Israeli government would have understood that, of all the sects, factions, and streams existing in that conflict-ridden country, the Shi'a actually had the greatest potential to become its strategic ally.

With great patience, my Lebanese friend described to me the complexity of the Muslim world and of the Arab world, and the place of the Shi'a community in that quagmire. He explained that not all Arabs are Muslims, and not all the Shi'ites are extreme Israel-haters. Although in most Arab states, Islam is the dominant religion, he said, most Muslim countries in the world are not Arabs. In almost all of them, Sunni Islam is dominant. In Iraq, Bahrain, and Lebanon, the majority is Shi'ite, but other communities rule those countries.

He also told me about the largest non-Muslim communities that exist in some of the Arab countries: about the Christian Copts in Egypt, about the Maronite Christians and the Druze in Lebanon, about the Christians and members of other religions in Sudan, and about the Alawites in Syria (a community that broke off from Shi'a Islam and became an independent religion).

"If the West in general and Israel in particular are genuinely interested in creating a real, stable, and long-term dialogue with the Arab world," my Lebanese friend said, "you have to start by taking a good look at the parts that make up the picture as a whole, and stop seeing the Muslim world—and in our case Lebanon and the Shi'a community—as one single entity."

In one of our many talks, my learned friend wanted to prove to me that he was not expressing only his own views, but that they were based on things said and written, as he noted again and again, "by wiser men than me." Of course, I read the writings that he recommended, if only to flaunt the fluency in Arabic of a young Israeli intelligence officer. I'll never forget how embarrassed I was when I had to admit I did not know who Moshe ben Maimon, bin Abdullah, man of Cordova, the Israeli, the man whose wonderful writing I had just proudly finished reading aloud, was. My friend was not surprised that I had fallen into the trap he had laid for me. With a broad smile, he said that man was one of the greatest philosophers of both Arab culture and European culture, one of the most important and admired figures in Judaism, about whom it was said, "from Moses to Moses, there have been none like Moses," and who was also called "the great eagle." He was talking about the Rambam, Moshe bin Maimun, Maimonides, or, in his Arabic name, Moshe ben Maimon, bin Abdullah, man of Cordova, the Israeli.

"A man's wisdom is not measured by his origin, religion, or status," my Shi'ite friend said as he walked me to my car after one of our meetings. "We the Muslims have learned from you Jews from the dawn of our history, and we continue to this day. We draw upon and learn from your wisdom and your experience, and, perhaps no less important, from your mistakes, too."

While he was warmly shaking my hand before I got into my car with the Lebanese plates used by the Israeli intelligence section, my host concluded, "Only when you learn to know us, the Shi'ites, the way we know you, the Jews, will you discover that we have more similarities than differences. Only when the Western world in general, and Israel in particular, understand that the way to a real dialogue with the Arab world can only take place through direct contact with Muslim religious leaders, only then, Inshaallah, the days of the Messiah may come, yours as well as ours."

I often think of those meetings and the many conversations we had, and I ask myself what happened to that man. Did he continue to lead his people according to his peaceful, noble, and intelligent faith? Or was he swept up by the vehement events and the evil winds of extremism and hostility between Israel and the Shi'a community—winds we stirred up out of our ignorance and arrogance—and today is one of Hassan Nasrallah's army of preachers? Did he survive at all? I do not know. To tell the truth, I'm afraid to know.

A MURDER IN THE MOSQUE;
A MASSACRE IN KARBALA

The Shi'ite clergyman's words continued to echo in my head for many years after I completed my work in Lebanon and moved on to other posts in other places in the world, including Arab countries.

During all those years, I was constantly troubled by several questions: Why did Israel choose to ignore the Shi'a community in Lebanon, to neglect it, even to offend it, instead of looking deeply into the possibility of turning it into an ally?

Why did Israel choose to view the Shi'a community in Lebanon not from its own perspective, but through the eyes of the Christians, the enemies of the Shi'ites? How could the Israelis fail to see that the immediate interest of the Christians—to get rid of the Shi'ite threat in Lebanon—was not consistent with Israel's interests?

I do not disagree with the fact that the Christian community was our best and largest ally in Lebanon. But just as the Christians knew how to promote their interests, which were not always compatible with ours, we could have done the same regarding the Shi'ites.

More than once I asked myself: How is it possible that what a young lieutenant with no experience in the Lebanese arena understood from informal talks with a minor Lebanese figure, was not understood (or worse, was not taken into account) by a long series of Israeli generals and experts who were active in Lebanon for years and professed to know every stone and every house in that country?

This time, too, did we fall into the same trap—called "arrogance made in Israel"—that we fell into time after time throughout our country's brief history, each time forgoing the need to really get to know the players and the rules of the game in the Middle East?

To try to answer these questions seriously, we need first to follow the different stages that Shi'a has gone through since it was founded and until now—both in the religious sphere and in the political sphere—and to understand its place in the morass of regional politics between Israel, Iran, Syria, and the Western countries.

The story of the Shi'a community—from its inception in the seventh century up to the 1960s—is a story of betrayal, political dispossession, and an ongoing sense of inferiority. In the eyes of the Shi'ites themselves, it was a story of a people seeking justice from a world that wanted to annihilate them.

The Shi'a emerged from a controversy that broke out among Muslims over the issue of who would succeed the prophet Muhammad after his death in 632. One group claimed that the legal successor was Ali Ibn Abi Talib, the prophet's cousin. Ali was forced to wait three "terms" until he finally gained the desired title of caliph of the Muslims, but he did not enjoy his lofty position for long. In 661, he was murdered in the al-Kufa mosque in southern Iraq. Members of the Umayya family, who ruled Syria at the time, exploited the situation and transferred the caliphate to their country. Twenty years after Ali's death, a group of his supporters from al-Kufa in Iraq—known as the "Shi'at 'Ali" (the faction of 'Ali), or, in short, "Shi'a"—encouraged his second son Hussein to take the caliphate back from the Umayya family. From then on, the Shi'a decided that the leader of their community would be one of Muhammad's descendants and would be called "Imam."

In 680, Hussein—permeated with a sense of mission and equipped with a promise of support by the al-Kufans—left the city of Al-Medina and traveled to Karbala in Iraq, to lead the battle over the caliphate. But when the signal was given, Hussein found himself alone on the battlefield, because the al-Kufans had betrayed him and violated their promise to join him in the revolt.

The small group of fighters with Hussein at its head was massacred by the Umayyad army.

This battle did not have an immediate political repercussion at the time, but for the Shi'a community it became a formative event. This defeat made the Shi'a the minority stream in Islam versus the Sunni majority for the next thousand years or so.

The death of Hussein and his loyal followers as martyrs led to a rapid increase in the number of those opposed to the rule of the Umayyad house, who now concentrated around Ali's descendants. He is considered a sacrificial martyr by the Shi'a, and his grave in Karbala is a pilgrimage site.

JABEL AMEL'S LONELINESS

According to the figures from the Pew Research Center's Forum on Religion and Public Life, since the start of the twenty-first century, Lebanon has been one of the most overcrowded countries in the Middle East. It has more than four million inhabitants that break down into seventeen communities, the largest of which is the Shi'a community, with more than a million people.[1]

Until a century ago, the Shi'a were a marginal community, the most neglected and discriminated against in the land of the cedars, not only from a religious and political standpoint but also economically. The Shi'ite inhabitants in Jabel Amel (the Lebanese part of the Galilee mountains) and Bekaa—the two largest concentrations of Shi'ites at the time—complained constantly to the Ottoman authorities about the heavier taxes levied on them compared to the other communities, as well as about discrimination in the division of government resources. In their level of education and income, the Shi'ite inhabitants of Jabel Amel and Bekaa also lagged behind the other parts of Lebanon.

As the Shi'ites see it, the hostility toward Jabel Amel was basically religious. This claim is supported by the fact that every force that passed through the area or conquered it made sure to burn the Shi'ite libraries in it. The Mamluks did that, the Ottomans did that, and, in the modern era, the process continued. In 1920, the French ordered the burning of the library of the religious scholar Abd al-Hussein Sharaf a-Din. The Israeli government, too, they claim, acted in a similar fashion in 1983, when it directed the Israeli military to burn down the al-Amin library in the city of Chakra, although factually this is untrue.[2]

Lebanon was born out of a battle and that is how the country has lived to the present day. In 1860, the Druze in Lebanon began rebelling against the Maronite Christians. The riots spread to Syria and finally turned into Muslim attacks against Christians. Five Christian powers of that period—England, France, Austria, Russia, and Prussia—accused the Ottomans, who ruled the area, of weakness and of encouraging the riots against the Christians, and compelled them to accept an arrangement according to which a force of representatives of the powers would be sent to restore order in Lebanon. In actual fact, only the French sent forces. In 1861, the pressure of the powers led to the establishment of a new territorial unit, called the Special District of Mount Lebanon or "the autonomous Sanjek of Lebanon." In 1914, the district was rescinded by Turkey, but during the fifty years of its existence, the Maronite Christians became the main shapers of Lebanon's character, while at the same time recognizing the existence of Druze and Muslim minorities. Demographically, the population in the Special District of Mount Lebanon was 80 percent Christians (58 percent of whom were Maronites), 12 percent Druze, 4 percent Sunni Muslims, and 5.5 percent Shi'ites.

On August 31, 1920—after the collapse of the Ottoman Empire in World War I and under the pressure of the Maronites in Lebanon—the French founded Greater Lebanon, shaped on the basis of the Maronites' interests. France, which received the mandate over Lebanon as part of the division of the booty between the victorious powers after the war, enjoyed the support of the Christians in Lebanon, but in Syria, France was forced to fight, from the start of its rule there, against local nationalist groups that were opposed to foreign rule. In 1944, Lebanon was declared an independent state by the Arab League, but to this very day Syria regards Lebanon as part of Syria, taken away in an unnatural step by the French.

On the domestic front, the establishment of Greater Lebanon changed the rules of the game. Until the nineteenth century, most of the struggles were between the Druze and the Maronites over the control and character of the district of Mount Lebanon, while, in the south of the country, the Shi'ite community lived in dismal conditions, totally uninvolved in the power struggles.[3] In 1926, when the new Lebanese constitution was published and elections were held, the Shi'ite district of Jabel Amel was also recognized as an integral part of Lebanon. In addition, Beirut and the district of Sunni Tripoli were added to the Special District of Mount Lebanon.

The expansion of Lebanon's territory changed its homogeneous character, and it became a multiethnic country, with equal numbers of Christians and non-Christians. The stability of the country was ensured by a division of the positions of power, defined in advance and based on a permanent ethnic key.[4] This system existed over several years, while leftist and Muslim elements wished to see it annulled and the constitution reformulated. The demographic-ethnic key for determining the division of power in the country was based on a traditional estimate according to which the Christian communities together constitute about 53 percent of the population, the Sunni Muslims about 20 percent, the Shi'ite Muslims about 18 percent, and the Druze about 6 percent.

The Lebanese constitution states that the president, the chief of staff, and the head of the secret services are Maronite Christians; the prime minister is a Sunni Muslim; and the minister of defense is a Druze. Each of the other communities is given representation in the form of government ministers, and the speaker of the parliament is a Shi'ite. Although over the years, the composition of the population changed, the formula for dividing power and government offices has remained basically the same up to the present day.

While the Sunni Muslims wanted to make Lebanon part of the all-Arab system as well as part of the historical Syrian state, in order to fix their status as a majority, the Maronites exerted pressure to keep Lebanon outside of the Arab bloc. The compromise that led to calm and stability was reached when the Sunnis relinquished their dream of a "Greater Syria" and the Maronites relinquished their ties to France and agreed that Lebanon would become a member of the Arab League in 1945.[5]

No one asked the Shi'ites.

Unlike the Christians and the Sunnis, the Shi'a community in Lebanon never gained a preferred status, nor did it have any backing by a world power or an international political element. It always remained a minority in all of the frameworks, districts, or states created in the area of Lebanon, and was discriminated against in comparison to the other communities. The major struggles in Lebanon left the Shi'ites outside the center of events.

THE RISE AND DISAPPEARANCE OF MUSA SADR

The process of secularization of Arab society in the early twentieth century did not leave out the Shi'a community in Lebanon. More and more young Shi'ites from families of the economic elite, as well as from middle-class and even lower-class families, moved to secular occupations, which they preferred to religious studies. It is estimated that from the end of the 1930s to the early 1940s, the Shi'a community in Lebanon, which then numbered 155,000 persons, had only forty-two religious scholars ("Ulama")—many of whom lacked the qualifications required of teachers of religion and religious judges. Only fifteen of them had been trained at Najaf, then the largest Shi'a center for advanced religious studies.[6]

Until 1969, the year in which the Supreme Shi'ite Islamic Council was founded, the Shi'a community in Lebanon did not have a religious or political institution, which wielded any influence, to deal with their affairs vis-à-vis the Lebanese government and the other communities. But their critical problem was the lack of a role model, a Lebanese leader they could follow and emulate, someone who could also provide them with answers and solutions to controversial religious and civilian issues.

In answer to their prayers, that leadership vacuum was about to be filled by a young thirty-one-year-old Shi'ite, Musa Sadr, who would, within a few years, change the face and status of the Shi'a community in Lebanon.

* * *

The imam Musa Sadr was born on March 15, 1928, in Qom in Iran, to a family that originated from Jabel Amel in southern Lebanon. His lineage goes back to the seventh imam of the Shi'a—a fact that lent him a special status in the Lebanese Shi'a community. Musa Sadr acquired his education in *madaris* in Qom, but he was not satisfied with only religious studies and graduated from the law faculty and the department of political economy at Teheran University.

In 1954, Sadr arrived in the city of Najaf in Iraq to further his religious studies, and at the end of four years of study, at the age of thirty-one, he moved to Lebanon to serve as the Shi'ite mufti of Tyre. Within a few years, the impressive-looking Sadr acquired a large group of supporters. Although he was not regarded as a major religious scholar (*mujtahid*),[7] nor was he the author of great religious essays, an important prerequisite for gaining influence and esteem among religious figures in Iran,[8] he was adept at exploiting his lineage and charismatic personality to bring about a substantive change in the thought and behavior of the Shi'a community in Lebanon.

Musa Sadr understood that the Shi'a community was not enjoying equal rights in Lebanon, that it was under the protection of the Sunni community, and that it was ruled by a small number of well-connected Shi'ite families. His first objective was to create communal institutions that were not answerable to the large Shi'ite landowner families. He embarked on fund-raising campaigns among Shi'ite Lebanese communities in West Africa and, within a short time, succeeded in establishing religious, cultural, and educational institutions in all the centers of the Shi'ite population in Lebanon.

Shi'a communities in West Africa were established a century ago. Members of the Shi'a community were searching for a way to escape the cycle of poverty and humiliation in Lebanon and embarked on ships that were supposed to take them to the promised land—America. Those ships stopped at the west coast of Africa, and the Shi'ite passengers were told they had arrived in America. After they disembarked, they were forced to manage somehow under difficult conditions, and lived in remote villages among the African population. Many members of the Shi'a community from Lebanon still live today in West African countries. Some of them are well off financially and control quite a few economic sectors in those countries. I visited Sierra Leone in December 2007, as part of my duties as director-general of the Israeli Diamond Institute. I was invited to meet with the president-elect of the country and his deputy, and at the time, I also met members of the Shi'a community there, third and fourth generations of Shi'ite families that had emigrated from Lebanon. I was amazed to find that they had preserved their customs and spoke Arabic with a Lebanese accent, as if they were still living in Lebanon.

Imam Musa Sadr turned to these communities and asked them to financially support his activities in Lebanon, and they responded generously. In the last three decades, those communities have undergone a radical change like other Shi'ites throughout the world; to our regret, some of their ties to Musa Sadr were replaced by a connection to Hezbollah. Information published in recent years indicates that members of the West African communities are providing massive economic support to Hezbollah.

Back in 1969, however, Imam Musa Sadr was appointed head of the Supreme Shi'ite Islamic Council, which was founded on the basis of a law passed by the Lebanese parliament to deal with all the affairs of the Shi'a community. Sadr's appointment did not enjoy the support of the traditional Shi'ite leadership, whose members preferred to act within the accepted religious frameworks, while Sadr was in favor of blurring the line between the sacred and the secular. Consequently, the Shi'ite politicians did their utmost to obstruct Sadr, even going so far as to claim he was an agent of the Lebanese intelligence services—but to no avail.[9]

The second chapter of the process introduced by Imam Sadr began to unfold. At the end of 1974, he founded a political movement given the name the Movement of the Deprived, which advocated the end of social dispossession, the political system of ethnic communities, feudalism, and discrimination among citizens.[10] The movement's main aim was to strengthen the Shi'a community in Lebanon, but Musa Sadr's attempt to introduce reform into the traditional structure of the Shi'a community was met with firm opposition by the older Shi'ite leadership. When the civil war in Lebanon broke out on April 13, 1975, Musa Sadr's position grew weaker, and the process of firmly establishing the Shi'a community in the land of cedars drew to a halt. At the start of the war, Imam Sadr adopted a neutral position and even initiated several public moves to stop it. In late June 1975, he went on a hunger strike in the al-Amalia mosque in Beirut to protest the violence spreading throughout Lebanon. Among those who came to visit him then were the heads of the communities in Lebanon, including Yasser Arafat and the Syrian foreign minister, Abd al-Halim Khaddam, who served as a mediator between the factions in Lebanon on behalf of Syria.[11]

Musa Sadr ended his hunger strike after only five days when he felt he had achieved his aim—separating the Shi'a from the war in Lebanon. But unfortunately Lebanon is not India and Musa Sadr is not Mahatma Gandhi. A few days after he ended his fast, an event occurred in the Bekaa area that forced Sadr to reveal his militant posture: twenty-seven fighters of a new, previously unknown organization called Amal were killed while training with explosives.[12] The imam was forced to admit openly for the first time that the Shi'a had an armed militia, and that he was one of its founders.

When he was caught "red-handed" as having been involved in arming the Shi'a community, Sadr declared that Amal was founded because the Shi'a had to ensure the safety and survival of the community, just as all the other ethnic communities in Lebanon had done in the 1970s. In fact, a political movement in Lebanon could only exist if it had a military militia.[13]

The literal meaning of "Amal" is "hope," but in this case, it was also the initials of the phrase "the Lebanese Opposition Brigades." The militia was formally declared by Imam Sadr on July 6, 1975. Throughout the entire civil war,[14] Amal was the strongest Shi'ite militia, and it gained the support of Syria and Iran. Later it became a political party, holding about 10 percent of the seats in the Lebanese parliament. It is not surprising, then, that Imam Sadr was regarded as one of the most important figures in the history of the Shi'a community in Lebanon, and perhaps in the entire Arab world.

Musa Sadr was the first man in the modern era who successfully challenged the perception that then prevailed in the Shi'a community, according to which the Shi'ites are inevitable victims who will be redeemed only with the coming of the disappeared Imam (*Mahdi*). Until then they must reconcile themselves to their bitter fate, or at least to try to introduce change only through peaceful means. Within only twenty years, Musa Sadr managed to significantly improve the situation of the Shi'a in the Lebanese internal arena, and owing to his activity, they gained the status of a community with equal rights within the political and religious fabric of Lebanon.

On the Palestinian issue, Sadr's views can be divided into two time periods: Up to 1970 he spoke about a common fate shared by the Palestinians and the Shi'ites, and maintained close ties with the Palestinian leaders, including Yasser Arafat. But his support and identification weakened after 1970, when the headquarters of the Palestinian organizations moved to Lebanon (after being expelled from Jordan) and began acting against Israel from Lebanese territory. The Israeli retaliation actions in south Lebanon, during which Shi'ites were harmed, angered Sadr, who, on more than one occasion, said that the Shi'ite identification with the Palestinians was not meant to be at the expense of the Shi'ites.[15]

Musa Sadr was not prepared to allow the Palestinian struggle against Israel from south Lebanon to give them control over the region. In a speech he delivered in Beirut on March 21, 1978, following the Litani operation, he pointed an accusing finger at the rich Arab world, which, according to him, had stood by passively while damage was being inflicted on the inhabitants of Lebanon. But he believed the real danger to Lebanon in general and to the Shi'a in particular came from the Palestinians whose war against Israel from south Lebanon had led to the Israeli invasion and the destruction of the south.

On August 25, 1978, Imam Musa Sadr went to Libya on a visit. That is where he and his two escorts disappeared, and their fate is unknown to this day. But he was not forgotten. Thirty-three years after that mysterious affair, when riots broke out in Libya in 2011, Hezbollah and the Lebanese government supported international actions against Muammar al-Qaddafi's regime and also demanded an investigation into Musa Sadr's disappearance.

Sadr's disappearance in 1978 aroused anxiety within the Shi'a community in Lebanon, but a few years later, two Shi'ite religious figures undertook the leadership of the community. This time the rules of the game and the interests were totally different from those that determined Musa Sadr's actions. These new rules of the game would change not only the status and image of the Shi'a community but also the face of Lebanon, of the Middle East, and of the whole world.

THE CHOICE OF SHEIKH FADLALLAH

On February 1, 1979, at 9:33 a.m., an Air France plane landed at the Teheran airport. It carried one of the most influential figures in modern human history, a man who significantly changed the dialogue that had existed until then between the Western world and the Muslim world, and, to the same extent, between the Arab world and the rest of the Muslim world.

On the day when Khomeini returned to Iran and took over power in that country, a change in perception occurred both among the Shi'ites in Iran and within many Shi'a communities throughout the world. It took the form of unrest, and also sowed seeds of revolt against different forces that overshadowed the Shi'ites.

Khomeini began to plant these seeds in Iran many years before he was exiled, but it was during the years of his exile that his popularity took on momentum and led to his return and rise to power in February 1979.

Unlike many Shi'ite leaders in the world, Khomeini believed that every Muslim government that does not act "in the right way" should be overthrown, and that under his leadership Iran had a key role to play in overthrowing those governments. "The right way," in Khomeini's view, was not only to enforce the Sharia laws but also for every Muslim country to totally cast off any dependence on non-Muslim powers.

It did not take long before Shi'a communities in the Muslim world responded to his call. In 1979–1980, riots took place in the oil-rich area of eastern Saudi Arabia, most of whose inhabitants are Shi'ites. In 1981, an abortive attempt at a coup took place in Bahrain, and in 1983–1984, Shi'ites carried out several attacks in Kuwait.

The change in perception in the Shi'ite community, especially in the Gulf states, was also given expression in early 2011, when a wave of riots broke out in the Arab world. Most of the inhabitants of tiny Bahrain are Shi'ites, and they took to the streets in processions and demonstrations, calling for a change in government and the overthrow of the Sunni royal house.

These riots began to spread eastward, to the eastern district of Saudi Arabia, where the Shi'ites are the majority, and throughout Saudi Arabia calls went out for a day of rage on March 11, 2011. A top-secret memorandum sent by the Saudi minister of the interior to police commanders on the morning of the planned day of riots makes it clear that, in the Saudis' view, this was a religious war and not demonstrations calling for economic change:

Friday
Hijri calendar, 6.4.1432
(11.3.2011)
The Kingdom of Saudi Arabia
Ministry of the Interior—top secret
Internal Security Forces—Memorandum number 38432-9913882

To: Police commanders in the following areas:

Al-Riatz, Mecca, al-Medina, Kha'il, al-Katzim, the northern borders, al-Juf, Tabuk, a-Sharkia, Asir, Najran, Jassan, commander of special emergency forces.

Following our earlier letters in the matter of what is called "the hanin revolution" that were disseminated through the spider network [the Internet] by anonymous people whose purpose is to breach security; this is a deviant group sabotaging the country. Do not treat them mercifully. Beat them with iron fists and all officers and soldiers have permission to shoot at them. This is your country and your religion and if anyone wants to change or harm it, you are obliged to prevent him from doing so.

Many thanks and I wish you every success.
Minister of the Interior
Naif bin Abd al-Aziz al-Saud

It is clear from the memorandum that the Saudi minister of the interior had given permission to every officer and every soldier to open fire on the demonstrators, even after the United States objected strongly to violent measures against peacefully protesting demonstrators. The Saudis regarded the riots as a religious war and did not intend to obey directives coming from the United States and to follow the path of Hosni Mubarak.

Three days later, on March 14, 2011, after the Saudis succeeded in getting through the day of rage without any damage being caused, they, together with the other Gulf states, turned their attention to the situation in Bahrain. On that day, Saudi military forces crossed the sea to Bahrain, along with forces from the United Emirates. Warships from Kuwait patrolled around

Bahrain to prevent weapons from being smuggled in from Iran and, in particular, to enable the Bahrain army to ruthlessly suppress the riots. Within a few days, the danger passed in Bahrain as well, and the king of Bahrain issued a statement thanking the Gulf armies that had helped Bahrain cope with an attempted coup by "external factors" (a reference to Iran).

Iran could not sit by quietly; the public and diplomatic protests led to the recall of the ambassador from Bahrain (a severe act of diplomatic protest), but apparently, Iran understood that at that point in time it was unable to act any differently.

As of this writing, a Saudi military force of hundreds of soldiers is stationed in Bahrain for the purpose of ensuring calm. The headquarters of the Saudi forces is located several hundred meters from the local parliament building in the most conspicuous manner to serve as a clear-cut message—that Saudi Arabia will not permit the Sunni government in Bahrain to fall.

* * *

Ayatollah Ruhollah Mousavi Khomeini's concept, in many senses, amounted to a revolution in Shi'a theological thinking. It advocated an activist approach calling on the Shi'ites to change the reality/situation rather than to wait for the revelation of the disappeared Imam.[16] Khomeini also went so far as to create an ideal model for a government in the Islamic state that is following the right path. This model is *velāyat-e faqīh*[17] ("state of the jurist" or "state of the jurisprudent"). This concept was influenced by Plato's *Republic*, which describes an ideal state divided into several classes. The "philosophers"—namely, wise, knowledgeable men—are the ruling class. The next class below them comprises the "guardians," who protect the rule of the philosophers. Khomeini developed this concept in a more militant spirit, and the model has been implemented in full in Iran: the religious scholars (*ulama*) are the "wise men" who rule the new state, and the "guardians" in this case are the revolutionary guards.[18]

Khomeini's concepts were influenced and shaped by his aspirations, and these went beyond the leadership of the Shi'ite world. He wanted to lead the entire Muslim world, and hence often used a unique terminology that he developed for that purpose. For example, he defined his revolution as "Islamic," and not "Shi'ite," as a signal to the Sunni world.[19] He refrained from dealing with any religious issues that were likely to arouse a controversy with Sunni Islam and focused on secular matters, such as opposition to imperialism, the West, and Israel.

One of Khomeini's greatest opponents in the Shi'a world was Ayatollah Abu al-Qasim al-Khoei, who advocated a defensive, passive approach. According to his concept, only the revelation of the 12th Imam would bring about the yearned-for redemption and justice. He stated that Khomeini's theory was a deviation from Shi'a, and called on the Shi'ites to disregard it. Consequently, the Shi'a world was divided between these two approaches. [20]

In 1970, a shift occurred in the rivalry between the two Ayatollahs. While Khomeini was forced to remain in exile outside Iran, dependent on the financial contributions of his followers in Iran, Iraq, and Lebanon, Khoei became the most important religious leader in the Shi'a world; he began to act resolutely to establish societies and charitable funds, to build institutions throughout the Muslim world, and to appoint representatives on his behalf in each country.

When the civil war broke out in Lebanon in 1975, which also resulted in a difficult refugee problem in the Shi'a community, Khoei ordered the establishment of a fund to aid refugees and appointed Mohammad Hussein Fadlallah as his representative. Fadlallah, whose standing in the community was at a low ebb, exploited the appointment to improve it. [21]

No one knows why Khoei preferred Fadlallah over Musa Sadr, except for the fact that the former had studied at Najaf and was a refugee himself, after having left the Naba'a quarter in Lebanon together with all the other Shi'ites. Khoei said that, as a refugee, Fadlallah would understand the plight of the other refugees. But in an area like the Middle East, loyalties are also like legal tender. Although Khoei strengthened Fadlallah's standing in Lebanon and enabled him to return to center stage, Fadlallah did not hesitate to take the first opportunity to betray his benefactor. In 1979, after the revolution in Iran, he went over to Khomeini's camp[22] and, three years later, helped the new leader to found, together with others, a new movement in Lebanon, which would later became one of the most violent terror organizations in the world—Hezbollah.

ISRAEL AGAINST THE SHI'ITES AND VICE VERSA: A SELF-FULFILLING PROPHECY

In 1982, four years after the mysterious disappearance of Imam Musa Sadr and three years after Khomeini's rise to power in Iran, while Lebanon was still up to its neck in a civil war, a new element cropped up on the Lebanese scene. Within a few years, it would succeed in placing the name of the Shi'a community and of Lebanon on all news broadcasts everywhere in the world, but not in a favorable context. Hezbollah would succeed not only in splitting the Shi'a community within itself and within the Muslim, Arab, and Western world, but also in leading Lebanon once again into a period of bloodshed.

Hezbollah, founded under the auspices of Iran, was based at first on Musa Sadr's approach, but very soon turned to modes of action contrary to the peaceful means that he advocated and in keeping with the approach of its first spiritual leader, Mohammad Hussein Fadlallah. The disparities between these two leaders reflected the changes, among others, that occurred during those years within the community toward Israel.

Musa Sadr believed that, in order to maintain its independent character, the Shi'a community in Lebanon should focus on itself, its needs and interests, and to keep those separate from the Arab, Islamic, Middle Eastern, and world contexts. Fadlallah, in contrast, had a totally different approach, one based on Khomeini's concepts, according to which the specific interests and needs of the Shi'a community are secondary to its obligation to become the leader of all Muslims.

At first, this "imperialistic" approach did not gain popularity among the Shi'ites in Lebanon, who were preoccupied with their own troubles and were not eager to become involved in the wars of others. But every Arab leader in the Middle East knows very well that the best card to play in order to improve his standing and gain support for his positions is to clash with Israel. And on the night of March 14, 1978, such an opportunity presented itself to Fadlallah.

Three days after the terrorist attack on a bus on a coastal road, in which thirty-seven Israelis were killed, Israel Defense Forces (IDF) launched the Litani operation. Although the goal was to damage the infrastructure of the Palestinian terror organizations operating in southern Lebanon, Fadlallah exploited the opportunity to intensify the fear of Israel among all Lebanese, and claimed that Israel's aim was to conquer parts of southern Lebanon. Hence, he argued, it was not merely a fight against the Palestinians but also a struggle by Israel against the entire Islamic world.

Fadlallah was short, stocky, and not very impressive looking, but he was a skilled preacher. His rich Arabic and his rhetoric capabilities, which he had acquired during his studies at Najaf, helped him win over his audience. He had a unique style of preaching that opened with quotes from the Quran, which made his listeners deeply attentive and lent him the status of an authority on the holy book.

Afterward, he'd move on to deal with current affairs in a down-to-earth language comprehensible to everyone. By the time the question-and-answer period arrived, he had the audience under his spell. He also peppered his answers to questions with long quotes from the Quran. His ability to respond rapidly with clear, spontaneous answers on Islamic and political issues from the Quran won him respect and admiration in comparison to other religious scholars who found it difficult to answer questions from the audience without preparing in advance.

Fadlallah arrived in Beirut in 1966 and settled in the poor neighborhood of Naba'a in the eastern part of the city. The Shi'ite immigration to Beirut began in 1940 as a result of the economic crisis in southern Lebanon, and it was not welcomed by the Sunni residents of western Beirut. For that reason, the Shi'ites settled mainly in Naba'a, where they were joined in 1948 by the

Palestinian refugees. At first Fadlallah established a *husseiniya* in the neighborhood, as a cultural, religious center for the Shi'ites, next to the Shi'ite mosque that serves the members of the community as a place to mourn the death of Imam Hussein. Later he founded a cultural society called "the family of brotherhood," which ran clinics and youth clubs as well as a middle school for religious studies called the Islamic Sharia Institute. The best students in this institution were sent to further their knowledge in seminaries in Najaf. Fadlallah disseminated his teachings among the broad Lebanese public through the *Al-Hekma* newspaper published by the society.

As soon as he arrived in Lebanon, Fadlallah concluded that the main target audience he needed to invest his efforts and resources in was the young generation. He believed that the main reason for the decline of the Shi'a community in Lebanon was the young people's indifference to religion, because they had been exposed to "bad culture" and had not received answers to the religious questions that came up in their daily lives.

Fadlallah met frequently with the young Shi'ites, who were then under the influence of Gamal Abdel Nasser's brand of pan-Arabic ideology. According to it, despite the official independence that Arab countries had received, imperialism actually still ruled the Arab world. [23]

In Fadlallah's view, imperialism is, in fact, the cardinal problem of the Arabs in general and of the Shi'ite community in particular. In his book *Islam and the Logic of Power*, [24] Fadlallah explains that the accumulation of military power need not serve a specific group or community, but rather the aims of Islam in its war with the heretics and imperialism. According to Fadlallah's approach, the internal conflict in Lebanon is only a spark of a world-embracing struggle of Islam against imperialism. In contrast to Musa Sadr, who regarded the armed Shi'ites as the protectors of the community in its internal struggles in Lebanon, Fadlallah viewed them as soldiers in the Islam army against the opponents of the faith. [25]

In the civil war in Lebanon, Fadlallah was forced to leave his home in the Naba'a quarter, to abandon his center in Beirut, and to move southward in search of a new place for his activity. Seemingly that was a low point, but in fact, as soon as he was appointed by Abu al-Qasim al-Khoei as head of the fund to support Shi'ite refugees in Lebanon, he began to gain stature and power. It was the first time he had acquired the acknowledged status of a leader on the national-communal level. [26]

In April 1979, two months after Khomeini's rise to power in Iran, the members of the Shi'a community in Lebanon took to the streets and, in a show of self-confidence, called for the establishment of an Islamic state in Lebanon. At the same time, Iran began to send official and unofficial representatives to Lebanon, as emissaries spreading the revolution.

Fadlallah joined them and became their ally. [27] Those Iranian emissaries were not fluent in Arabic and were unfamiliar with the lives of the young

Shi'ites in Lebanon. There was no one more appropriate to act as a link between Iran and the Shi'ite youth than Fadlallah, who knew how to talk to those youngsters in their language.[28]

At first, Fadlallah acted intensively to change the modes of operation of Amal and to adapt it to the all-Islamic aims dictated by Teheran. Finally, he and the Iranian emissaries despaired of changing Amal, and Fadlallah was forced to give his consent and support to the founding of Hezbollah, although officially he chose to remain outside the organization, to avoid creating a split in the Shi'a community.[29]

Although he was defined by many as the spiritual leader of Hezbollah, Fadlallah maintained his independence, and for that paid a heavy price.[30] He had only limited influence on Hezbollah's activity, if any at all. Experts estimate that there was cooperation between him and the organization, but that the emissaries from Iran did not feel very obligated toward him, and as Hezbollah grew stronger, even that degree of obligation lessened.

On the Palestinian issue, Fadlallah, as I noted, interpreted the situation differently than Musa Sadr. He called on the members of the Shi'a community to focus on the major enemy—Israel—and to apply their force against her. In a speech he delivered at Bint Jbeil in 1972, he claimed that politicians who believed that the exit of Palestinian fighters from the south would solve the problems of the Shi'ites were wrong. In his view, Israel did not attack south Lebanon because of the Palestinians, but because Israel wanted to conquer south Lebanon, just as it had conquered large areas in previous wars.[31]

His militant words were like music to the ears of the young Shi'ites, who wanted to see themselves playing in a larger arena than their communal field. These were the same young men who joined the left-wing movements and the Palestinian organizations in Lebanon, since Sadr's sectorial and isolationist approach did not attract them.[32] Obviously, living in close proximity to the Palestinian population in the Naba'a quarter enhanced Fadlallah's support for the Palestinian cause, in contrast to Sadr's qualified views on the subject.

The Israeli invasion of Lebanon in 1982 and the IDF's entrance into Beirut brought Fadlallah even closer to the Palestinian cause, and he called for Shi'ite solidarity with the Palestinians. At first, there was no response to that call, since even before the IDF invasion, the Shi'ites had begun objecting strongly to the Palestinian hegemony in southern Lebanon, and armed Amal members even attacked Palestine Liberation Organization (PLO) men there and in Beirut.[33] But as the IDF prolonged its stay in Lebanon, the Shi'ites began to place more trust in the gloomy prophecies Fadlallah had voiced years earlier, warning that Israel's intent was to conquer the lands of Lebanon, and not only to prevent Palestinian attacks from its territory. Tragically enough for both sides, that was a self-fulfilling prophecy. The more the

Shi'ites violently opposed the Israeli invasion into Lebanon, the deeper the hold of the IDF in that country became. The wall of mutual hostility between Israel and the Shi'a grew higher and also "justified" itself. There was just one thing we forgot to do throughout all those years of bloodshed: talk to the Shi'ites.

ARE THERE ANY MODERATE SHI'ITES LEFT (OR HAVE WE TURNED THEM ALL INTO EXTREMISTS)?

There was one main reason for Israel's mistaken behavior toward the Shi'a community in Lebanon in particular and the Shi'a in the Arab world in general: We, like most of the Western world, including the United States, have viewed them, and continue to view them, through the eyes of other factions that are frightened by the growing Shi'ite power. We adopted the anxiety that is felt by the Sunni Muslims and the Maronite Christians in relation to the Shi'ites. A simple analysis would have made clear to us that the Shi'a is not necessarily Israel's enemy. Its major struggle is over its place in the Islamic world in relation to the Sunnis, and Israel was at the most a pawn in this struggle, one used by both sides.

It is true that the Christians were our ally in Lebanon for many years, but that does not mean we were obliged to adopt their entire worldview, particularly when it relates to the Shi'a in Lebanon. Our natural tendency is to enter an alliance with a certain element and, at the same time, to adopt its worldview vis-à-vis its opponents. In Turkey, for example, we adopted the worldview of the Turks against the Kurds, although the Kurdish people were a friend of the Jewish people.

We were so panic stricken by the Iranian Shi'a, beginning with Khomeini's rise to power and continuing with Mahmoud Ahmadinejad's Iran, that we failed to notice that both of them were using Israel only in order to obtain legitimacy for their attempts to become the leaders of the Muslim world; most of the Shi'ite religious scholars throughout the world do not support this approach, but rather adhere to the traditional Shi'a approach, which calls for no political intervention until the appearance of their Messiah—the disappeared Imam.

The State of Israel denounced Ahmadinejad in every possible forum, but did not take the trouble to send a message of conciliation to the Shi'a in general, or a message of approval of their progressive approach, and certainly not a message of appreciation for the fact that Jews in Iran have enjoyed respect throughout history. In the loud anti-Iran declarations, which made no distinction between an opportunistic and dangerous enemy like Ahmadinejad and the Shi'ites in general, we played into the hands of our most extremist enemies and confirming the truth of their vilification of Israel.

When Israel invaded southern Lebanon, it missed an opportunity to enter into an alliance with this community, which, at the time, was the enemy of our enemy—the Palestinians. Instead of using as leverage the aid we gave the Shi'ites by ousting the Palestinians from the villages of the south and destroying what was then known as Fatahland, we preferred to allow the Christians to rule over the Shi'a community in southern Lebanon, thus continuing the condescending attitude the Lebanese Shi'ites had been the object of throughout history.

As more time passed, and the population saw that we intended to stay in Lebanon for a long time, we were dragged into a military struggle against Amal, Musa Sadr's organization. That was an organization we should not have been fighting; instead, we should have been holding a dialogue with it. By defeating Amal, we ended up freeing the stage for Hezbollah, which concurred with Khomeini's approach (i.e., the most important thing is the struggle against imperialism and Israel and not the immediate interests of the Shi'a community).

Anyone even somewhat familiar with the Middle Eastern arena clearly understands that the days when the Shi'ites played a marginal role in Islam, or in the regional morass, are gone. Today, that community is a major player, and not just in the political sense.

Today Iran is the one keeping Bashar al-Assad's regime in place, financing what is left of his crumbling army, paying the thousands of Hezbollah members fighting alongside him, and continuing to finance the vast operation—what some call a state within a state—that Hezbollah has established in Lebanon. And on the Palestinian front, Iran is a primary financier of the Islamic Jihad organization, making it possible for the organization to establish an orderly military setup as well as administrative institutions such as communication centers.

Consequently, it is imperative that Israel do its best to find the way to renew its relations with that community—in Lebanon, in the other parts of the Arab world, and in Iran.

In my view, the only path that can lead to that is a change in the Israeli perception. Even today, we have seen the entire Shi'a community in the same negative light, and never considered the possibility of creating channels of dialogue with moderate elements in the community, and there are quite a few of those.

Since completing my military service and throughout the years of my diplomatic service, I have met quite a few Shi'ites who impressed me with their reason and moderation, among them businessmen and academics. One of those people who remain engraved in my memory is Professor Mahmud Ayub. The talks between us began with great hope and ended, I must admit, with a large, distressing question mark hanging over them.

I met Professor Ayub ten years after I was discharged from the IDF, when I was a vice-consul of Israel in Philadelphia. One of the first things I did when I began in that position was to find out which local university offers courses in religion, and I found my way to the department of religion at Temple University, then headed by Professor Ayub. Before I met him, I collected some background information about him and was glad to discover that he is a Shi'ite intellectual originally from southern Lebanon. That information was consistent with the profile of the person I was seeking as a partner for dialogue that would lead, or so I hoped, to closer ties between Israel and academics from Islam in general and from the Shi'a in particular.

At our first meeting, which took place in his office at the university, Professor Ayub shared some of his biographical details with me, including the fact that he had six children. He did, however, hesitate at first to tell me that he was a Shi'ite from southern Lebanon. Only after I related some of my good memories from Lebanon, and he felt comfortable in my company, did he share with me his memories from the land of his birth.

I found my talks with him fascinating. They took place in Arabic, the language I like best after Hebrew, and I was also enormously interested in his views and positions, although I disagreed with some of them. But more than that, I felt that these talks were, in fact, a continuation of those I had held ten years earlier with the Shi'ite religious scholar from southern Lebanon. In this case, too, I felt that the talks grew out of a dialogue and a desire for mutual understanding, and were not taking place from a position of power or on the basis of a struggle.

In one of our meetings, Professor Ayub surprised me with a tempting suggestion—that I should enroll as a student in his department and write a doctoral dissertation under his guidance, a comparative study of Shi'a and Judaism.

"I have no doubt," Ayub said to me, "that a study of this kind, carried out by a Jew, will evoke much interest in the academic world and in general." Before I even had a chance to consider the proposal, he added, "Don't worry about any bureaucratic obstacles here at the university. Such a study is very important, and if necessary, I will personally help you overcome any such obstacles."

Although the suggestion was tempting and also flattering, I knew from the outset that I could not accept it, because of my heavy workload as a vice-consul. Several months later, although I had been compelled to reject his suggestion, I was glad when Professor Ayub accepted my invitation and came to celebrate the Israel Independence Day party held at a hotel in the city.

To my regret, the special connection between the amiable Shi'ite professor and me was severed when I completed my duties in Philadelphia and returned to Israel, but several years later, I came across his name again, this time in less favorable circumstances. On January 7, 2008, I was amazed to read an announcement published by the board of governors of Temple University, stating that it had decided to reject a donation of $1.5 million for the establishment of a chair in the name of Professor Ayub, who had retired in the meantime. The reason for the refusal, it turned out, was that the organization behind the donation, the International Institute of Islamic Thought, was on the U.S. State Department's blacklist of organizations that support terror activities.

During those years, a real revolution took place in the United States, which began in the wake of the September 11, 2001, attacks. Many longtime residents of the United States, who were openly and legitimately engaging in their professions, including Professor Ayub, became enemies in the eyes of U.S. citizens. To this day, I do not know what the connection was between Professor Ayub and that organization suspected of supporting terrorism, but I confess I find it hard to see a link between the amiable academic, with rather moderate views, in whose company I spent many pleasant hours, and the support of terror.

On the one hand, I may just be naive, and perhaps that very civilized professor, who had invited me to do a doctorate under his guidance and who celebrated Israel's Independence Day, was, in fact, an agent of an extremist Islamic organization who had been planted in the West and exploited its liberality. On the other hand, it is equally reasonable to assume that the United States is sometimes overly rash in painting all the Shi'ites with the same brush. The danger in this case is that we are, with our own hands, burning the bridges between peoples and religions, pushing the moderates into the arms of the extreme, and creating a fanatic, faceless enemy whom we fear.

THE BOTTOM LINE:
IRAN IS NOT AHMADINEJAD!
IRAN IS NOT AHMADINEJAD!

What is true when it comes to the Lebanese Shi'ites, is even truer in relation to Israel's attitude toward Iran. Israel should not judge the Iranian people only on the basis of its extremist leadership.

In the last three decades, since Khomeini's rise to power, Israel has regarded Iran and its people and leaders as Israel's greatest enemy. Time after time, Israeli officials have spoken about Iran as if it were a single entity: "The world must stop Iran," "The international community must impose sanctions on Iran," and the like.

Israel needs to understand that just as it is impossible to relate to the Israeli public as a single entity, because it is actually a fervent, even stormy "bazaar" of different, contradictory views and ideas, this idea holds true for Iran as well.

The Islamic Republic of Iran is not a homogeneous unit. It has many groups that do not regard Israel as an enemy, but actually understand very well that the anti-Israel line of their leaders is meant to serve the political purposes of the Ayatollah's rule. Proof that Iran is far from being "one voice" can be found in the riots that broke out in the streets of Teheran in June 2009, immediately after the election results were published, announcing Ahmadinejad's victory. Hundreds of the supporters of the reformist candidate Mir-Hossein Mousavi, who understood that the election results were falsified, went to Valiasr Boulevard in central Teheran, where they clashed with policemen under clouds of tear gas. The next day the riots spread to Sharif University in Teheran, and there, too, the students clashed with security forces; when members of the revolutionary guards entered the campus area, the president of the university announced his resignation. In parallel, Ahmadinejad ordered the arrest of his rivals in the elections—Mousavi and Mahdi Karroubi. Many of their supporters were also arrested and transferred to Evin, the infamous prison in Teheran. Although these riots did die out, since then the voices of the Iranian reformists calling for Ahmadinejad's removal grew stronger, culminating in the recent elections held in Iran in 2013 when Hassan Rouhani, considered the most moderate among the candidates, was elected president. It is impossible to know whether he will, in fact, lead a significant turnabout in Iran or will merely serve as a president devoid of any authority, while the Supreme Leader of Iran, Ali Khamenei, is pulling the strings with the help of the revolutionary guards.

In early 2011, the wave of riots sweeping across the entire Middle East also shook Iran, actually the only non-Arab country affected by that wave. To my regret, no significant international support was extended at that time to the demonstrators. The Israeli journalist Ari Shavit calls that phenomenon a "post-colonial complex," which leads the enlightened West to be critical and heavy handed toward its friends (Hosni Mubarak is an excellent example) and gentle and anemic toward its enemies.[34] It is easy for that same enlightened West to come out against Benjamin Netanyahu, but it's hard for it to oppose Bashar al-Assad, who, in March and April of 2011, ordered his army to open fire against his own people, who were demonstrating; more than one hundred thousand Syrians have been killed by his army, and the number increases daily.

When our leaders ignore these differences, and lump the Iranian people together with their extremist leaders, the Iranians also think of Israel as one mass, and as their enemy. Then Ahmadinejad's goal and his like—to unite his people under his rule in their common hatred of Israel—is achieved. So it is very important, in making declarations and speeches, to stop attacking

"Iran" and to concentrate our criticism on the present Supreme Leader of Iran, Ali Khamenei.

With the help of Voice of Israel broadcasts in Persian we should continue transmitting messages of conciliation and coexistence to Iran, directly into the ears of its inhabitants. On June 27, 1999, the *Teheran Times* printed a news item that stated the Majlis (the Iranian parliament) had prohibited senior Iranian journalists from giving interviews "on radio stations hostile to Iran."[35] This resulted from the success achieved by the Voice of Israel in Persian in acquiring an audience in Iran, also through telephone interviews. In my view, the broadcasts should not be in the form of propaganda, but rather should explain what the Iranian people have in common with the Israeli people. We need to improve the level of these broadcasts also through the Internet and satellite communication.

From a religious standpoint, an interreligious dialogue between Jewish and Shi'ite religious scholars should be encouraged. It will not be easy, since Israelis are fixated on the idea that the Shi'a is more extreme than the Sunna, and that the Shi'a as a whole is represented by Khomeini and Ahmadinejad. The initial stage is to hold a dialogue with Shi'ite imams living in the West. News of that dialogue will reach Iran, and if we have enough patience, we will be able to build a bridge to that community, which is so far and yet so near to us.

The interreligious dialogue with the Shi'a should be conducted by leading rabbis, even the chief rabbis. Judaism has close ties with Islamic thinkers who originated in Iran, particularly from the philosophical and theological aspect. As that same Lebanese Shi'ite religious scholar taught me, the simplest examination of our sources will reveal the interrelationships and the cross-pollination that existed between Maimonides and Islamic religious scholars from Iran. These overlapping points should be given greater public expression, in the same breath as our attacks on Ahmadinejad and leaders like him as the archenemies of the twenty-first century.

While we, as Israelis, naturally tend to adopt moves that produce immediate results, usually political or military, in this case, our attempt to rehabilitate relations with the moderate factions of the Shi'a will, unfortunately, require many years, and even then it is doubtful whether we will be able to repair the damage that has already been caused. Settling differences and building trust is a long, ongoing process, but it is important to make the effort and it may pay in the end. The only question is whether in the Iranian case and in the Lebanese case we haven't already missed the boat.

Chapter Six

An Interfaith Dialogue

The only way to cool down the bonfire of jihad and hatred is actually through the synagogues and the mosques.

In October 1996, I returned to Israel at the end of my three-year assignment as the Israeli vice-consul in Philadelphia. My family and I were glad to get back to Israel, but our happiness, like that of all the Israelis at the time, was mixed with sadness and a sense of despair. Those were very trying times, with suicide bombings taking place inside Israel's territory. In the first three months of that year, Hamas had carried out four such attacks, killing fifty-nine people.

It was the third wave of suicide attacks that Israel had experienced from 1993 to 1996, from the time that terror organizations began to use suicide bombers inside Israel. The first wave came as a reaction to the Oslo agreement signed in September 1993. The second was in reaction to the massacre by Baruch Goldstein at the Makhpela cave in Hebron in February 1994. The third wave—which occurred in February–March 1996—was a reaction to the targeted killing of the "engineer," Yehiya Ayyash, in January 1996. It was the shortest but the cruelest of them all.

The first attack in this wave occurred on February 25, 1996, on the number 18 Egged bus in Jerusalem. Twenty-five people were killed. A week later, on March 3, another suicide bomber blew up on this same bus line in Jerusalem, this time killing eighteen people. The following day, on March 4, 1996, a suicide bomber blew up near the entrance to Dizengoff Center shopping mall in Tel Aviv, this time killing thirteen Israelis, most of whom were teenagers.

In March 1996, another extreme and dangerous element was added to these attacks, one which would change the picture of terror in the region and in the rest of the world. In a sermon, broadcast live on the Qatari TV channel Al-Jazeera, before tens of millions of viewers worldwide, the Egyptian sheikh, Yusuf al-Qaradawi, one of the greatest Sunni theologians in the Muslim world, perhaps even the most important one, stated that the suicide missions carried out by Hamas in Israel are not considered acts of terror but rather "Jihad for the sake of Allah."

"The suicide bombers who were killed in these actions were acting to protect the land and the honor against the Israelis who have stolen Palestine," al-Qaradawi stated in his sermon. "Consequently, they are not suicide bombers but *shahids* ('holy ones') who laid down their lives in a Jihad."[1]

This was not the first time, and certainly not the last, in which a Muslim religious leader made such a statement. On March 6, 1995, the Hamas leader, Sheikh Ahmed Yassin, declared that every suicide bomber who receives the blessing of an authorized Muslim sheikh before leaving on his mission will not be considered a suicide bomber, but rather a *shahid* who has fallen in a jihad. But in the eyes of many in the Muslim world, particularly those who are active in the various terror organizations, the sermon given by Sheikh al-Qaradawi—who is viewed weekly on the program by about forty million Muslims throughout the world—is regarded as a genuine religious ruling that approved the actions of the suicide bombers in the name of Islam.

This was an additional big step in turning the Israeli-Palestinian conflict into a religious war—a dangerous war by far more difficult to settle than any other political conflict. In my view, this is a war that could have been avoided, or at least restrained, and perhaps still can be. In this chapter, I will try to show, based on several moves that I was privileged to take part in, how, with a consistent, sincere effort, it is possible to build preliminary initial bridges from synagogues to mosques, and vice versa.

THE POSITION OF ADVISER ON
ISLAMIC AFFAIRS WAS CANCELED
DUE TO A LACK OF BUDGET

Upon my return to Israel, I quickly learned through my own experience how deplorably we have neglected the dialogue between the Muslims and ourselves. At the end of my mission in Philadelphia, I was posted to the interfaith department of the foreign ministry. I was pleased to be assigned that post because I hoped that in that department I could continue to work on developing links between Israel and the Arab and the Muslim world.

Before I took on that position, I held talks with employees of the department, and one of the things I learned was that in the past it had also included

an adviser on Islamic affairs, an academic who occasionally attended interfaith conferences held in states friendly to Israel. I was encouraged. Shortly
afterward, I found out that this person was, in fact, a kind of clandestine
adviser who held both Israeli citizenship and citizenship in another country,
and that the fact of his employment in the Israeli foreign ministry was never
publicized so that he could continue attending academic and interfaith conferences without being labeled as a representative of the Israeli government.
In other words, his attendance did not involve the official participation of the
State of Israel in these conferences; instead, he was there to create contacts
and collect information.

Shortly after my return, before I had time to unpack all the crates in my
old-new home, I was summoned to an initial meeting with Avi Benyamin,
who then ran the department. At that meeting, I officially learned what I had
previously heard: the interfaith department of the foreign ministry focused
primarily on contacts with the Christian world, and no dialogue—open or
discreet—was held with Islamic elements, not in Arab countries or anywhere
else. Even the work of the adviser on Islamic affairs had been discontin-
ued . . . for budgetary reasons. Although this was only an introductory meeting, I decided to utilize it in order to present my new boss with the operative
plan I had prepared in advance to strengthen ties between Israel and Islamic
religious elements. Then, as I still do today, I believed that through an interfaith dialogue, Israel could not only enlarge the circle of friendly Arab and
Muslim countries but, equally important, weaken the power of leading Muslim religious leaders who use the Quran and Islam as a means of encouraging
suicide attacks and other acts of terror against Israel, under the heading of "a
holy war."

In Israel, and perhaps in the West as a whole, there is a simplistic tendency to automatically attach the extremist or fundamentalist label to every
Muslim. When did you last hear or read about moderate Islam? The very
definition of Islam in its entirety as extremist taints the religion as a whole,
and only encourages antagonism and suspicion of its most moderate followers. Anyone who understands that he will be labeled, in any case, as an
extremist is likely, in his rage and frustration, to become one.

I explained to the director of the interfaith department that, for every
religious leader like al-Qaradawi, who exploits Islam to encourage suicide
attacks under the cover of a holy war, there is another Muslim leader who is
firmly opposed to such views.

To illustrate my words, I gave him a document I had prepared, containing
a list of Muslim religious leaders from Arab and other countries—not all of
them friendly to Israel and not all of them maintaining diplomatic relations
with us. Along with biographical details about each of these men, the document contained quotations from things they had said over the years, particularly in recent times. Their common denominator was their firm objection to

the use of Islam as a tool to justify acts of terror. Some of them even came out openly against religious leaders who supported those who planned and executed the attacks.

"Why should a Muslim cleric in an Arab or Muslim country that is not friendly to Israel agree to enter into a dialogue with us?" the director of the department asked me. "What interest can we serve for him?"

I found the answer to that question in an announcement published a few weeks earlier by the Supreme Council of Egypt for Islamic Affairs—a governmental body subject to the Office of Religious Endowments (the Waqf) of Egypt. It was publicized at the end of the eighth conference of the General Committee of the Council, held in Cairo at the end of July 1996, on the topic "Islam and the Future of the Cultural Dialogue." Muslim delegations from seventy-one countries throughout the world participated.

"The committee stresses the values common to all cultures, in particular the faith in Allah and the dissemination of morals, respect of all human beings, recognition of their rights and especially the freedom of belief and the freedom to hold religious rites."[2] These words opened the concluding statement, signed by Dr. Mahmud Hamdi Zakzouk, the Egyptian minister of endowments and president of the Supreme Council for Islamic Affairs. Zakzouk continued:

> It is every man's right to take part in making fateful decisions that affect the society in which he lives, and he is entitled to a life of respect and a just division of happiness. The Committee calls for closer relations between the different cultures, for they complement one another and act together for the good of humankind.[3]

The announcement went on to state that the Committee feels it is important to acknowledge the difference between the various cultures and the different monotheistic religions—in order to maintain an equal dialogue among the parties. In addition, the Committee called for the abandonment of a "policy of cultural, racial or religious arrogance."[4]

As for the acts of terror being perpetrated in the name of Allah, the statement said:

> The Committee notes that the monotheistic religions denounce violence and terror, and it is impossible to ascribe these accusations to Islam, just as it is impossible to link the legal right of defense against aggression—a right recognized by international treaties relating to the oppressed and conquered peoples—with the atrocious acts committed through religious or racist fanaticism, which hide under the cover of religion.[5]

Regarding the Palestinian issue, the Committee stated:

The Committee regards the failure of efforts to solve the Palestinian problem as one of the gravest problems that threaten co-existence between the different peoples. The Committee welcomes the decisions of the recent Arab summit (the Cairo summit) on the matter of Palestine and the future of holy Jerusalem.[6]

Further on, the Committee expressed its concern regarding the position of the Israeli government, "which is opposed to the right of the Palestinian people to self-determination and the establishment of its independent state with its capital, Jerusalem."[7]

In addition to this declaration, at the end of the conference, the participants published an open letter under the heading the "Cairo Declaration." Its alleged intent was to stress the importance of the interfaith dialogue and the intercultural dialogue, but, in fact, it reflected the fear of the states participating in the conference in the face of the growing power of Islamic fundamentalism and their opposition to the use of religion as a pretext for acts of terror:

A clear distinction should be drawn between the purpose of religions and the waves of extremism sweeping across many countries in the world. Extremism in religious thinking or religious understanding, and the attendant fanaticism, isolationism and terror, have no connection with religion, even if those disseminating it assign themselves religious titles and for the sake of their own aims adopt mendacious, glittering slogans. Dialogue is a cultural element while extremism is an element that is hostile to culture and progress. The Committee stresses that extremism, violence and terror are exceptional phenomena that require all possible efforts to cope with them and to oppose their dissemination.[8]

> O mankind! We created
> You from a single (pair)
> Of a male and a female,
> And made you into
> Nations and tribes, that
> Ye may know each other[9]

In our view, this verse reflects the fact that all persons come from one source and that is the truth that ought to reside in our minds. There are no people who are better than other peoples. All are the creatures of God, who gave them understanding and honor and made them superior to the beasts. The Committee calls on all intelligent men and women in the world to stand shoulder by shoulder for the sake of peace. If we truly want to have peace in the world, then we must not return life back to the hostility of the distant or the near past and to the horrible results it caused.[10]

The message that came forth from this conference was one of hope. It was a brave message that called for a dialogue between Islam and the other monotheistic religions, even though the final statement included sections that were critical of Israel.

A very respectable group of Muslim communities throughout the world seemed to be genuinely reaching out to the non-Muslim world. This feeling is validated by the fact that this was a statement issued at the end of a conference held at the initiative and under the official auspices of Egypt, the largest Arab country.

Nonetheless, in the culture of the Middle East, you can never be content with words written or spoken; you also have to search, understand, and analyze the things that were not said, what was hinted at between the lines, for whom the words were intended, and, no less important, the time and place where they were spoken.

Although at the end of the conference, the participants called for interfaith brotherhood, it was not by chance that Egypt chose to host such a widely attended conference, since the words spoken there did not come out of nowhere, nor were they meant for Western ears, but rather for Arab ears.

"And it is here," I said in 1996 to the director of the interfaith department of the foreign ministry, "exactly at this point in time, when the moderate Arab states are extending a hand for peace to the other religions—particularly out of a fear that the spread and rising power of extreme Islam in their midst—we can clearly see the interest that Muslim religious leaders have in holding a dialogue with Israel. Even more important, this is also our window of opportunity to respond to this reaching out and to open an interfaith dialogue with the Muslim world, and not to allow Islamic radicalism to take over Islam and subjugate it to its revolutionary political aims."

Over the years, I did maintain such contacts with prominent Muslim religious leaders in various places in the world, either as an Israeli diplomat or wearing other hats. I initiated some of these and was invited to others, but in each of them I acted out of a deep conviction that if there is a key in the Middle East that can open the door to a sincere, genuine dialogue between us and the Muslim world—then it is the interfaith dialogue. In my view, only by force of such a dialogue is it possible to weaken, and finally uproot, the perception disseminated by extremist Muslim religious leaders throughout the world, according to which the Jews are the source of all the Muslims' problems, and that the Israeli-Arab conflict is a religious war in which acts of terror and suicide bombings are permissible. For centuries, Jews and Muslims lived side by side, with good neighborly relations, with absolute freedom of religious practice in most Arab and Muslim countries. The claims of the sheikhs al-Qaradawi, Yassin, and their like—that the Quran permits the killing of Jews—are not only lies but also meant to serve personal political aims that are light-years away from the real, important need of the two religions—to lead their lives in peace.

SHEIKH TANTAWY'S LETTER

One of my first actions upon beginning my job in the interfaith department of the foreign ministry was to get the Sephardic chief rabbi on board with my efforts to develop ties with Muslim religious leaders.

One of the things that Muslim religious leaders often say is that they have no problem with Judaism—a monotheistic religion that acknowledges one God and hence is a legitimate religion—but only with Zionism and the State of Israel.

As strange as it may sound, Judaism and Islam are much closer to one another than either one is to Christianity. The Islamic adherence to absolute monotheism has always been highly regarded by Jewish religious leaders, and Islam sweepingly accepts all the Jewish prophets. In Christianity, however, the Holy Trinity somewhat challenges the monotheistic principle, and both Judaism and Islam find it rather objectionable.

I went to meet Rabbi Eliyahu Bakshi-Doron in his office in the Great Synagogue in Jerusalem. During our meeting, I learned (to my surprise) that he knew my father, Yitzhak Aboudara, may he rest in peace. "Although your father did not observe all the commandments," the rabbi said to me, "he has earned a special place in my heart." In 1970, Rabbi Bakshi-Doron served as the rabbi of the Ramat Yosef quarter of Bat Yam, and my father was then deputy mayor of the city. The rabbi asked for my father's help in solving a problem that disturbed the people in his neighborhood: every Friday evening, the neighborhood synagogue changed its function—a blanket was placed over the Holy Ark and the synagogue turned into a discotheque.

I recall my father asking me once to accompany him there one evening so he could see with his own eyes what was going on. Indeed, the synagogue became a discotheque every Friday night at 9:00 p.m. My father was shocked, and I remember that, too. On the following Sunday, my father issued an ultimatum to the mayor of Bat Yam: if the discotheque was not closed down, he would resign and his faction would become a combative opposition. From that day, Rabbi Bakshi-Doron told me, the desecration of the Sabbath in the synagogue ceased.

We both remembered the story, and after a few minutes, I felt comfortable enough to raise my proposal for our first joint initiative: an exchange of letters with one of the most important, most influential Muslim religious leaders in the world—the rector of Al Azhar, Sheikh Muhammad Sayyid Tantawy (who passed away in March 2010).

In addition to his official position, Tantawy was also known as the leading spiritual authority in the Sunni Muslim world, and some even regarded him as the most senior Arab Sunni authority. But I was not interested in Tantawy because of his high position, mainly because he often used it to voice extremist statements calling for jihad and also justifying acts of terror and violence in the name of Islam. At the time, when I searched the foreign ministry's computerized system of cables with the name "Tantawy," dozens of cables from our embassy in Cairo came up, quoting his harsh incitements against Israel on various occasions.

For example, in an interview he gave to a *Le Soir* journalist in June 1997, Tantawy was asked to relate to his call to the Muslim world to wage a jihad against Israel, with the aim of destroying the Jewish character of Jerusalem.

In the *Le Soir* article, Tantawy was quoted as saying, "The term Jihad is a unifying element for the Muslim community, when there is a need to defend the honor, the morals, the religion or the land, the Muslim joins in a Jihad." However, Tantawy also said, "The term Jihad does not mean the killing of innocent persons or an unrestrained attack, but rather defense of the Muslim nation."[11]

Three years later, while I was still serving in Qatar as the head of the Israeli delegation, I was amazed to read quotations from an interview with Tantawy on October 10, 2000, when the Al Aqsa Intifada was at its height, in the *al-Khaleej* newspaper that is published in the United Arab Emirates. Sheikh Tantawy was asked what he thought of the calls of religious leaders "to revive the spirit of jihad in the hearts of the youth of the Islamic nation, in order to fight aggression and to liberate the pillaged land,"[12] and whether he believed the Muslims should declare a jihad against Israel.

"Jihad for Allah's sake is one of the virtues that every Muslim should seek at all times," the sheikh replied, "and it is the duty of every man capable of carrying it out. Dozens of Quran verses and dozens of prophetic Hadiths mention the virtue of Jihad for the sake of Allah. Consequently, Jihad for the purpose of blocking aggression and liberating the occupied land is the duty of every Muslim everywhere and at all times."[13]

"Does this mean that fighting the Jews is a duty, so that the land can be liberated and Israel restrained from its tyranny and enmity?"

"Allah the Almighty says in His book, 'Fight in the path of Allah those who fight you and do not transgress, for Allah does not love transgressors.' Fighting Israel is an obligation in support of the oppressed, and it is fighting in order to repel the aggressors. As long as the Jews are aggressors and pillage our rights and spill our blood, it is our duty to fight them. If they stop fighting, recognize our rights, and return the pillaged land to us, then it is our duty to treat them well and adhere to our [good] treatment of them."[14]

In the Muslim world, the sheikh of Al Azhar is regarded as a "government-sponsored" cleric, because he was appointed to his position by the president of Egypt. Consequently, he exerts far less influence than authentic religious leaders who gain in popularity owing to their writings, lectures, or their broad knowledge of Islamic theology. For example, hundreds of thousands of Egyptians (unofficial sources spoke of about two million) came to Tahrir Square to hear al-Qaradawi's sermon. It is doubtful whether that crowd would have come to hear the sermon of any of the heads of Al Azhar, past or present.

Nonetheless, at a time when Israel is under attack by all leaders of the Arab spectrum, journalists gleefully pounce upon a statement like that by a cleric close to the moderate Egyptian government.

Tantawy's vacillation between support for suicide bombings and "we have to adhere to our good treatment of them" was neither new nor surprising to me. In every visit by a sheikh in Europe, in the United States, or elsewhere outside the Muslim world, his words always carried a tone praising the interfaith dialogue, perhaps as a tactical move meant to take some of the sting out of the criticism of Islam in the international arena.

Moreover, although he often uttered blatantly hostile words against Israel, the elderly sheikh did not eschew meetings with Israelis. On December 16, 1997, he met in Cairo with Rabbi Yisrael Meir Lau, then Israel's Ashkenazi chief rabbi. This meeting provoked a long, drawn-out controversy between opponents and supporters in Egypt. In 1999, Tantawy was invited by Rabbi Shmuel Sirat to participate in an interfaith conference he planned to hold in France. For years, Rabbi Sirat—then the chief rabbi of French Jewry and the head of the commission on an interfaith dialogue in the Alliance organization—was active in promoting cooperation between Jewish and Muslim clerics with the aim of furthering peace. Tantawy made his participation contingent on the participation of clerics from Jordan and the Palestinian Authority, and finally accepted the invitation.

At that stage, I still had not managed to delve into Tantawy's considerations or his true motives, but I had the feeling that it was important to act in conjunction with him, so I asked Rabbi Bakshi-Doron to sign a letter I had formulated in his name. The letter related to the common aspects of Judaism and Islam and the essence of religion—to do good and to act for the sake of the good. It argued that the suicide bombings were totally antithetical to that essence. One of the principles that singles out religions in general and Islam and Judaism in particular, the chief rabbi wrote, is that of the sanctity of life, which the suicide bombers disastrously violate.

The rabbi signed the letter, and it was sent to its destination. Tantawy's reply arrived very quickly. In it, he noted that, despite his identification with the Palestinian interest and his shock at the atrocities the Palestinian people were undergoing at the hands of the Israelis, he—as the head of Al Azhar—was resolutely opposed to suicide bombings.

The exchange of letters between the two leading clerics was widely published in the Egyptian and the Israeli media, and resonated throughout the entire Muslim world. One of the first reactions to the letters was that of the head of the southern division of the Islamic movement in Israel, Sheikh Abdullah Nimer Darwish, who published a statement firmly opposing suicide bombings and accusing extreme leaders for misleading the younger generation of Muslims by convincing them that the only way to oppose occupation is through suicide bombing. [15]

In interviews to the Israeli media, Sheikh Darwish said on more than one occasion that the jihad is cultural and not military. Although I thought that statement was meant especially for Israeli ears, it cannot simply be dismissed, and it was very important, particularly in the stormy period in which it was made. As of this writing, Sheikh Darwish serves as chairman of the Adam Center for Dialogue between the Three Religions and declares that he firmly believes in the rule of law and in integration into institutions of the State of Israel. Three decades ago, that same Nimer Darwish founded a terror organization called Usrat al-Jihad (The Family of Jihad) whose aim was to establish an Islamic state based on the Sharia in Palestine. In 1981, Darwish was arrested along with several of his friends, convicted of membership in a terror organization, and served a prison sentence until 1985, when he was released as part of the Jibril deal. After his release, he concentrated on public activity and began to express opposition to the involvement of Israeli Arabs in violent actions.

From all this it is definitely possible to conclude that all the paths of Islam do not inevitably lead to extremism.

MAULANA QADRI'S SUIT

My second cooperation with Rabbi Bakshi-Doron took place in 1997. One day I learned from the Asia department of the foreign ministry that the Israeli embassy in London had been approached by Maulana Ajmal Qadri, a high-level Pakistani religious leader from the Jamiat Ulama-e-Islam (Assembly of Islamic Clergy, hereinafter JUI), which later won the elections in Pakistan. As soon as I heard that, I understood how important his visit to Israel would be, and I immediately set about organizing it. Previously, our contacts with Pakistan had never been on the religious plane, but rather in the framework of political meetings with the heads of Pakistan. Those meetings were always accompanied by the furious voices of religious leaders in Pakistan, who regarded them as damaging to the very foundation of Islam. Consequently, I thought Qadri's arrival was a significant breakthrough. Moreover, his conciliatory approach and his membership in JUI were important. That Muslim religious organization had split off in 1945 from another party called Jamiat Ulama al-Hind (Assembly of Indian Clergy), after the latter supported the Indian National Congress movement against the Muslim League on the question of Pakistan's separation from India.

During his visit, Qadri surprised me when he told me that he and his colleagues had been opposed to Pakistan's separation from India, because it stemmed from political, not religious, considerations, and the Muslim clerics preferred to remain in India. According to him, if Pakistan had remained part of India, the Muslims could have converted to Islam many adherents of other religions, and hence they opposed the separation.

Until the 1970s, the organization was scarcely active on the local political scene in Pakistan because of its firm opposition to the modernist policy of the then president of Pakistan, General Ayub Khan, whose government fell in the early 1960s. In elections held in 1970, the Islamist party entered the political arena for the first time, and since then has been playing a key role in the government. It is a religious party that has worked to turn Pakistan into a state based on religious law. The organization was considered religiously rigid, and since its establishment, it has helped found thousands of religious schools in Pakistan, more than any other religious movement. The media has reported quite often that it maintains contacts with the Taliban organization in Afghanistan.

To enable Qadri to visit Israel without arousing the wrath of his colleagues in Pakistan or of other elements in the Muslim world, I contacted an Islamic college in Israel and arranged an official invitation for him to visit it to dedicate a new library. But as an official guest of the Israeli foreign ministry, Qadri and his entourage stayed at the Laromme Hotel in Jerusalem. I myself served as their personal escort during the three days of their visit.

After he attended the library dedication ceremony, I introduced Qadri to several members of the academic staff of the Hebrew University who specialize in Islamic law, and later to Rabbi Bakshi-Doron. The meeting between the two clerics took place in the offices of the chief rabbinate in Jerusalem, and Qadri insisted that it be open to the press. A young journalist from the Galei Tzahal radio station and a *Ma'ariv* correspondent on religious affairs arrived to cover the meeting. The following day, an article was published in *Ma'ariv* that aroused much criticism in Pakistan.

At the end of his meeting with the chief rabbi, we took Qadri and his entourage to pray at the Al Aqsa mosque on the Temple Mount. At the entrance to the mosque, he asked that I enter with him. I thanked him for the invitation but explained that since it is a place holy to Islam, I would be glad if he would visit the mosque in the company of members of the Wafq. And that's what happened.

After the visit to the mosque, Qadri told me that, throughout the tour, the Wafq people complained about the religious oppression they were suffering at the hands of the Israelis. "At a certain stage, I stood up," he said, "looked them in the eyes and told them that I suggest they open their eyes and look at other parts of the Muslim world; perhaps then they will understand the true meaning of religious oppression."

From that moment, Qadri said with a smile, all the Wafq members scattered, leaving him and his escorts in the middle of the mosque. That enabled them to enjoy a quiet prayer service and to fulfill the commandment of "Umra"—a pilgrimage to the Al Aqsa mosque.

The following day, news of Qadri's visit to Israel was published in the Pakistani press. The foreign minister of Pakistan, with whom Qadri had met to coordinate his visit in advance, now harshly attacked him and said that upon his return to Pakistan he would be arrested, since his visit had not been approved by the government. In the article, Qadri was quoted as having said that in this era, the Muslim world ought to help solve the Palestinian problem by fully recognizing the State of Israel. I feared for his life, but he reassured me, saying, "There'll be a lot of noise and it will pass. Every significant move begins with a small step, just as I did by coming here, and I know exactly what I am facing."

The following day, Qadri flew directly to London, and, as far as I know, after spending a few months in Sweden with the communities of his followers, he returned to Pakistan. Eleven years after that visit, in November 2008, I learned that the newspapers *Pakistan Observer* and the *Pakistan Times* had reported that a Pakistani delegation of 174 clergymen, businessmen, and senior members of the Pakistani government, headed by Maulana Ajmal Qadri, had visited Israel. The delegation had arrived from Pakistan through Abu Dhabi and Jordan, and its members met, among others, with Prime Minister Sharon, Foreign Minister Silvan Shalom, and the Palestinian president, Mahmud Abbas.[16]

The item in the *Pakistan Times* stated, "This was Qadri's third visit to Israel in recent years, and the visit is important because it took place in view of the improved relations between Israel and Pakistan."[17]

Although the Pakistani foreign ministry denied that the Pakistani government had known about the visit, had sent the delegation, or had financed the visit, the news item stated that "the visit was with the knowledge of the Pakistan government since prior to the delegation's departure for Israel, Qadri had issued a local press release about the visit." The item concluded by noting that while there was some controversy as to who knew about the delegation's visit and who approved it, the prevailing view is that it was a trial balloon sent up by the Pakistan government to "test the temperature of the water."[18]

As I said earlier, during Qadri's first visit to Israel, I had the privilege of serving as the personal escort of this impressive cleric. We spent long hours together, during which he showed genuine readiness to understand Israeli society and culture, and never stopped asking questions about a wide variety of topics, ranging from religion and state to culture and philosophy.

On the last day of his visit, when we were about to leave for the airport, Qadri suddenly opened his suitcase, pulled out one of his traditional suits (made in Pakistan), and handed it to me.

"I don't have a gift to give you, and I would like to give you one of my suits as a token of my appreciation for the effort you made and because you are a true brother."

I thanked him, and since we are about the same size, I was able to wear the suit at cultural events in the years to come.

Not only did this visit succeed in creating a link between a Pakistan cleric and a chief rabbi in Israel, but, on the operative level, Qadri's statements were also added to other moderate statements by others in the Muslim world deriding the use of Islam as a pretext for acts of terror against Israel. This is one more piece of evidence showing that the interfaith dialogue has the power to change positions and perceptions even among those whom we perceive to be extremist and basically anti-Israeli.

YOU CAN GO, BIN LADEN

My experience with Qadri was not my only one with clerics from Pakistan. One of my first aims when I arrived in Hong Kong in 2001 as Israel's consul-general was to make contact with one of the local Muslim communities—made up mostly of people from Pakistan. Most of the worshipers at the Great Mosque on Kowloon Island were of Pakistani origin, as was the local imam.

When I asked people in the Jewish community about the mosque and the Muslim community, they squirmed. Some of them quoted from an article printed in the local English newspaper *SCMP*, about U.S. investigators who came to Hong Kong after the 9/11 attack to follow up information that a Taliban leader had visited Hong Kong before the attack to raise money. Most of the people I asked simply said it was an extremist community, and that it was dangerous to even get close to the area of the mosque—a statement firmly reiterated by the consulate's security officer.

But that situation did not last very long. A new rabbi was appointed to the Reform congregation in Hong Kong—Rabbi Lee Diamond from Israel, who had newly emigrated from the United States. Rabbi Diamond turned out to be a great guy, who was proud to represent the State of Israel and undertook to hold an interfaith dialogue in Hong Kong.

About a year after I was appointed as consul-general, the rabbi told me he had met the imam of the Great Mosque in Kowloon, who seemed like a very pleasant, impressive man. I was glad to hear that, and I asked Rabbi Diamond to invite me and the imam to the same event, which he did. I met a young, impressive cleric, very knowledgeable about his religion, and, above all, a lover of mankind.

We talked during the affair, and when it was over, we remained nearly the last ones in the hall of the Jewish community center in Hong Kong. We spoke about theological subjects, but we mainly did our best to get to know one another. Before we were about to part, the imam said, "I have always dreamed about making a pilgrimage to the sites holy to Islam in Jerusalem and I would be very glad if you could help me fulfill that wish." I replied that not only would I be happy to help him realize his dream, but I would also be glad to accompany him on his visit to Israel. And that is what actually happened.

To avoid an unpleasant incident at the Ben Gurion airport—which is often the case when guests from abroad are interrogated and searched—I invited the imam to fly with me to Israel as the guest of the foreign ministry. I made sure the relevant authorities at Ben Gurion airport knew about his arrival—I sent them several cables and received their confirmation by cable.

To my regret, my fears of an incident at the airport were confirmed. After we landed, I went with the imam to the border control station, handed over our two passports, and said that he was an official guest of the foreign ministry.

"You can go through, but he has to pass a security interrogation," the policewoman said politely, looking at the imam. I responded by telling her I was a diplomat and the man I was accompanying was a guest of the foreign ministry, and insisted that she check with the ministry's situation room. After we waited about twenty minutes, the commander of the police station at the airport came over to us, handed the imam his passport, apologized for any inconvenience, and wished him a pleasant stay in Israel.

On the way to the Zion Hotel in Jerusalem, the imam noticed that I was upset because of the incident. "My friend," he said, "you should know that a few months ago I visited Egypt, and at the Cairo airport I was delayed for no less than four hours, and under far less comfortable conditions than the ones at Ben Gurion airport. So please don't be upset. As far as I'm concerned, everything is fine."

The imam asked to spend his first day in Israel, which was a Friday, walking around alone and going to prayer services in Jerusalem. We agreed to meet on Sunday to go on a tour together. I gave him my business card and urged him to call me at any time if he needed anything at all.

His first call for help came a lot sooner than I had anticipated. On Saturday at 11 in the morning, while I was at a friend's house near Kfar Saba, I received a phone call from him, and I could tell from his voice that he was shaken. It turned out that while he was walking the streets of Jerusalem, some policemen from the Border Police asked him to show some identity papers. Within a few seconds, the imam from Hong Kong found himself facing the barrel of an Israeli weapon. While he was trying to explain to me, in a voice shaking with fear, what had happened, I suddenly heard the policeman say in a belligerent tone, "Put the phone down right now!" After the imam followed his instructions, I heard the policeman cocking his weapon menacingly to show he meant business.

We were cut off. I immediately called the imam's cell phone, and I was delighted when he replied. "Please put your phone on speaker," I asked in English, and when he did, I started yelling angrily into it:

"Listen up, you big hero. The man you just arrested is an official guest of the State of Israel. He is the leader of the Muslim community in Hong Kong. I strongly suggest that you release him immediately and give him his passport. If you don't, I promise you I'll make sure you're put on trial for this and for the disrespect you show to people."

There was silence on the other end of the line, and two seconds later, I heard the policeman say to the imam, "You can go, bin Laden." I was deeply embarrassed and blamed myself for having left him alone that Saturday. You can make the very best efforts, but one fool can spoil everything with one stupid act.

When we met the next day, I could see that the episode of the previous day had not dampened his spirits. To pacify me, he said that the incidents at the airport and in the streets of Jerusalem had illustrated how sensitive the situation was in Israel.

Before I completed my mission in Hong Kong, I met with the imam several more times, and he continued to advocate his conciliatory worldview and to preach peace and call for an interfaith dialogue in his sermons in the mosque.

What makes this story important is not the visit I organized for the imam in Israel, but the fact that leaders like this young Pakistani cleric do exist in the world and head large Muslim communities like the one he led in Hong Kong, which numbered tens of thousands of Muslims. Supposedly he had no reason to like me or Israel, but he understood the importance of interfaith dialogue and that leadership in an Islamic community can be built on non-radical elements. He delivered the Friday sermons in the main mosque of Hong Kong, attended by thousands of Muslim worshipers from various countries: Afghanis, Syrians, Pakistanis, and others. I had many good meetings with Christian leaders in Hong Kong, but the connection with the imam was, in my view, especially important.

WHEN THE MUFTI OF ISTANBUL
PRAYED AT THE WAILING WALL

As soon as I took up my post in the interfaith department in 1996, I marked Turkey as one of the main target states with which Israel ought to improve interfaith relations. When I presented this idea to my fellow employees at the foreign ministry, quite a few eyebrows were raised.

"Why should we invest energy in Turkey?" I was asked. "It's a secular country that is friendly to Israel; it even cooperates closely with us on security issues."

That was true in 1996, but unfortunately no longer true today. For decades, Turkey has been becoming more and more fundamentalist, and this is becoming a very clear trend. Islam has gained popularity at a higher rate there than in any other country in the world.

In 2009, there were more than 85,000 active mosques in Turkey—one for every 1,000 inhabitants (in contrast to one hospital for every 60,000 inhabitants). This is the highest proportion in the world of mosques in relation to the population. Today in Turkey, there are about 90,000 imams—more than doctors or teachers. In addition, Turkey has thousands of *madaris*, religious schools, and about 4,000 official governmental frameworks for teaching the Quran. In addition, there are unofficial frameworks for religious studies; it is estimated there are twice as many as the official ones.

In the first four and a half years of government headed by Recep Tayyip Erdogan, the leader of the Justice and Development Party (AKP), the expenses of the Ministry of Religious Affairs grew fivefold and its budget is larger than the combined budgets of eight other ministries.[19]

In addition, in Turkey more people participate in the Friday prayer services in the mosques than in Iran, and Sunni Islam studies are compulsory in the public schools, in contravention of the rulings of the European court of human rights and the Turkish Supreme Court, which forbade the Turkish government from imposing these studies on students. These rulings were not to the liking of Prime Minister Erdogan or Minister of Religions Ali Bardak, who were furious at these two institutions for not having first consulted Islamic clerics.

Moreover, in the early 1990s, Turkey had enormous influence on the republics of Central Asia, which had just gained independence from the Soviet Union, and whose original tongue was from the family of Turkish languages. After the fall of the Soviet Union, Turkey became a model of emulation for those republics and acquired the status of "the America of Central Europe." Turkish shopping centers and retail chains opened up throughout Central Asia, bringing religious influence along with them. Those Central European republics—which had had secularism imposed on them by the Communist regime—were thirsting for the Islamic sources and religion. The revival of their original languages and their national culture constituted a kind of defiance toward the population of Russian descent, which had immigrated to their area with the encouragement of the previous Communist government. You might say this is the basis for the tense relations between Russia and Turkey, which stem from the contest over influence on the Central Asian republics, which are also expressed in the struggle in the island of

Cyprus, with Russia supporting the Cypriots and Turkey continuing to support Turkish Cyprus.

These democratic regimes of Central Europe regarded Turkey as a role model in the religious sphere as well. Turkey, as a secular Islamic state, was a counterweight to the Iranian influence, which was pushing for an Islamic religious form of rule in the spirit of the Iranian Ayatollahs. But it's not clear that they are trying to imitate Turkey today, in view of the Islamic extremism led by Erdogan and his party.

In March 1996, the president of Turkey, Suliman Demirel, and the minister of religion, Nuri Yilmaz, visited Israel. During the visit, Yilmaz agreed to send representatives to a Jewish-Muslim, or Israel-Turkish interfaith seminar. The seminar took place in April 1997, and I was assigned to organize it.

The Turkish delegation was headed by the mufti of Istanbul, Salhatin Kaya. Not only did he hold an official senior position, but Kaya was also regarded as an important authority on Sharia in the Muslim world. Other members of the Turkish delegation would address him with the honorary title *Hocam*, which means "my teacher."

Another member of the delegation was Professor Serpatin Guluk, a native of Izmir, who was a senior lecturer at the theological university of Konia and a member of the advisory council on religious affairs of the Turkish foreign ministry. In advance of his trip to Israel, Guluk, a thorough, meticulous man, had prepared a one-hundred-page document dealing with issues common to Judaism and Islam. It was personally submitted to the then president of Israel, Ezer Weizman. The third guest was Professor Saban Kuzgan from the theological university in Elazig. Professor Kuzgan served for two years in Kuwait, on behalf of the Turkish foreign ministry. He learned Arabic there, and during his academic studies, he also learned Hebrew.

The Turkish delegation landed in Israel on Sunday, April 13, 1997, and was received by me and my counterparts from the Turkish foreign ministry. On one of the four days of their visit, I took the guests to the Temple Mount, a visit coordinated with the directorate of the Wafq. A representative of the ministry's official guest bureau joined the group.

At a certain stage of the tour on the Temple Mount, when they got to the section known as Solomon's Stables, the Wafq representatives turned to the Turks and said they were not prepared to allow the "Jew"—namely, the escort from the foreign ministry—to join them at that site. They also spoke to the man directly and asked him to leave and to return to pick up the guests after the tour.

When the mufti of Istanbul heard that, he was furious and informed the Wafq men explicitly, "Either all of us or none of us." The Wafq men refused to change their position, so the three Turks and the escort left without so much as blinking an eye, forgoing the opportunity to view that beautiful underground space, with its lovely arches, pillars, and spacious halls.

When they left the mosque, the Mugrabi gate, which is usually closed, was opened especially for them. As they walked down the incline leading to the plaza of the Western Wall, the Wafq escort explained that the Western Wall is the wall to which the prophet Muhammad tied his mare, Al-Buraq, and to this day, the wall is named after her. The Turks, who were not content with that explanation, turned to the escort from the foreign ministry and asked what the source of the wall's sanctity for the Jews is, and whether it is a vestige from the days of the First or the Second Temple. Needless to say, the Wafq people were not at all pleased with those questions.

At the plaza of the Western Wall, the guests asked for skullcaps. They wore them, mingling with the many Jewish worshipers who were there at the time and together went over to the wall. Then the mufti of Istanbul turned to the Israeli escort and apologized for the incident that had occurred a few minutes before at Solomon's Stables.

"That behavior does not show much wisdom and it is offensive," the mufti said about the Wafq men's refusal to allow the Jew to be present. The mufti explained that he did not want to get into an argument with the Wafq people, and not simply because he knew it would do no good and because they were, after all, their guests. He avoided a clash mainly because he did not want to spoil the overall good atmosphere that had prevailed during the visit to this place so sacred to the two religions.

At the end of the visit to the Temple Mount, the guests were taken to meet the president of the Sharia court of appeals and other officials in the Sharia court system (like the rabbinical courts, they have an official status in Israel). During the meeting, the mufti asked how the courts functioned in Israel and particularly about their autonomy. He reacted to most of what he heard with a smile, as if he seemed to be thinking: You have no idea how much freedom you enjoy here.

This part of the visit, however, was only a preamble to the interfaith dialogue seminar with representatives of Judaism. I organized the seminar in a lovely building in Jerusalem called Beit Shalom (house of peace), and invited some of the leading figures in the field, including Rabbi David Rosen, formerly chief rabbi of Ireland, one of the first to initiate an interfaith dialogue with the Vatican, who also was accorded an honorary title by the pope for his role in the Jewish-Catholic reconciliation process. I also invited Rabbi Dr. Ron Kronish, director-general of the Interreligious Coordination Council, which encompasses sixty organizations, all of them active in Israel. I brought a translator, a new immigrant from Turkey, to the seminar so that members of the Turkish delegation could express themselves freely.

As the seminar progressed, it became more intensive, and the mufti and his two escorts were obviously taking interest in everything that was said. The atmosphere was also very congenial.

Toward the end of the seminar, the mufti asked to be interviewed on Istanbul's popular radio station. The interview lasted about half an hour, and the translator who was working with us told me that the mufti had gone out of his way to praise the hospitality he and his colleagues had received, the freedom of religion enjoyed by the Muslims in Israel, and his impressions of his visit at Al Aqsa. When he returned to Turkey, the mufti was also interviewed by the print media, and another brick was laid into the wall we wanted to build against the Islamic extremism that was calling for suicide bombings. It was important that the people in Turkey as well as in the Central Asian republics understood that there was no religious conflict between Judaism and Islam beyond the flourishing joint economic projects. However, to our regret, today the citizens of Turkey are hearing other voices. Hardly a week goes by without Ergodan virulently attacking Israel while exploiting the restraint of Western and American leaders, who would have placed on trial any political figure in their countries who expressed himself with that kind of invective.

HOJA EFFENDI SPEAKS
THE TRUTH AS ALWAYS

On June 4, 2010, when most leaders in the Arab and the Muslim worlds were attacking Israel because of its actions in the incident that was given the name "the Turkish flotilla," out of all the hateful, critical voices, only one, to everyone's surprise, dared to come out against the organizers of the flotilla. That was the voice of the most influential religious leader in Turkey, Imam Fethullah Gülen.

"The fact that the organizers of the flotilla did not try to come to some arrangement with Israel before deciding to transfer goods to Gaza, shows that they were challenging the Israeli government, and it was clear that would lead to a bad end," Gülen was quoted as saying in an article in the *Wall Street Journal*. Imam Fethullah harshly criticized the organizers of the flotilla for having failed to reach some agreement with Israel; he added that every time a relief organization turns to him regarding help for the Palestinians, he asks them to reach an agreement with the Israeli authorities. [20]

I met Gülen—one of the most important religious leaders in Turkey, with millions of followers and who calls for moderate, spiritual Islam—in Turkey on February 25, 1998, as part of an official visit I arranged for Rabbi Bakshi-Doron in that country. The idea of setting up a meeting between the chief Sephardic rabbi of Israel and the most important religious leader in Turkey came to me one day while I was skimming through several leading Middle Eastern newspapers.

In one of them, I saw an item stating that Gülen had been invited to meet with Pope John Paul II, after he had met the previous year with Cardinal John O'Connor in New York. I thought: If the imam is going to meet with the pope, why shouldn't he meet with the chief rabbi in Israel?

There was some difference of opinion in Israel about holding such a meeting. Our embassy in Ankara was opposed, because it wanted to avoid annoying the secular military establishment in Turkey. On the other hand, the consul-general in Istanbul, Eli Shaked, was in favor of such a meeting and also coordinated it. There were also varying opinions in the headquarters of the foreign ministry, so I was pleased when our view was finally accepted and the decision was made to promote the meeting.

I already knew about Gülen's existence by then, but I had never delved deeply into his views or actions. This time, as part of my job in the interfaith department, I read about him thoroughly and understood that he was exactly the man I was seeking for this kind of connection: an impressive, important Muslim leader, enormously influential in Turkey and the Central Asian republics, where he established hundreds of schools after the fall of the Soviet Union. At the height of his activity, so I learned, Gülen controlled an empire that comprised a huge Islamic bank, a TV station, a popular newspaper called *Zaman*, and many economic institutions. Many regard the movement he founded, the Gülen movement, as one of the largest social movements in the world.

No one knows exactly how many supporters the movement has because members need not register, but the estimate is many millions in Turkey, Central Asia, and elsewhere in the world.[21] The Gülen movement consists mainly of students, teachers, businessmen, journalists, and other professionals, organized in a flexible network. Since its establishment, the movement has founded schools, universities, labor unions, charitable organizations, real estate funds, pressure groups, student organizations, radio and TV stations, and newspapers. Schools and businesses are organized locally and maintain contact with a network of similar institutions throughout the world. After having studied its effects in Holland, the Dutch minister of the interior stated it was more like a group of autonomous institutions weakly connected with one another, rather than a real movement.

An article in the British *Economist* once stated that perhaps the Gülen movement should be recognized as the leading Muslim network in the world.[22] That same article noted that, owing to Gülen's tributes to science and his advocacy of the interfaith dialogue and multiparty democracy, he has earned the praise of many non-Muslim organizations in the world. Professor Nilüfer Göle, a prominent Turkish-French sociologist from the École pratique des hautes études in Paris, defined Gülen's movement as "the most global movement in the world."[23] One of the movement's main characteristics is that it is based on faith, but is not restricted to one specific faith. There are quite a few Christians and adherents of other religions among its members, but I do not know if there are any Jewish members.

When I arrived with Rabbi Bakshi-Doron at Imam Gülen's office, we were amazed to discover a court that was very similar in appearance to a Chasidic court. Dozens of people were gathered at the entrance to the building. They led us to a small room, where about twenty men stood around one man who looked like a guru and recorded every word he said. Fethullah Gülen went out of his way to create a good atmosphere for the meeting, and Rabbi Bakshi-Doron reciprocated.

The conversation began with a historical survey by each of the leaders of the good relations that had prevailed between Jews and Turks, and after half an hour, it moved on to current topics. Imam Gülen related to the problem of the suicide bombers, and stated resolutely that those who claim that this form of terror is the fulfillment of a religious commandment do not understand and are misleading the followers of Islam. He also cited examples from the Quran of peaceful and conciliatory approaches that exist in Islam, and stressed that the movement he heads has always strongly advocated the principles of peace, interfaith dialogue, and brotherhood among the nations.

The rabbi, for his part, emphasized the respect that Judaism exhibits toward the sites holy to Islam and the fact that the Israeli ministry of religions invests in Muslim religious institutions. The rabbi said that the case of Israeli rule is the first time a new ruler has not destroyed or harmed holy places, and is enabling unfettered freedom of religious practice.

At the end of the meeting, Rabbi Bakshi-Doron gave the imam a copper relief of Jerusalem, and the imam gave the rabbi an exceedingly beautiful ancient jug from the early Ottoman period, decorated with Islamic motifs and painted red and white.

This meeting was covered with large headlines in the Turkish press, but later that same year, Turkish military elements, apprehensive about Gülen's rising popularity, began to bring pressure to bear on him. Gülen, who got the hint, left for medical treatment of his diabetes in the United States and has never returned to Turkey. During the years of his stay in the United States, elements close to the secular government in Turkey have spread rumors that Gülen is living in the United States under the auspices of the CIA. In the United States, Gülen carried on as he had in the Central Asian republics; he established a network of sixty-five schools in different states. Today he lives in Pennsylvania. To my regret, since his meeting with Rabbi Bakshi-Doron, the Israeli connection with him has been broken.

Fethullah Gülen is regarded as the father image of the present Turkish prime minister, Recep Tayyip Erdogan. Gülen's movement, which influences millions of Turks, supported Erdogan's Party of Justice and Development (AKP) in the elections it won in 2003.

Its enormous influence on the ruling party was very evident after the flotilla. When Erdogan's deputy, Bulent Arinc—a harsh critic of Israel—was asked about Fethullah Gülen's criticism of the flotilla to Gaza, he replied, "*Hoja Effendi* [Fethullah Gülen's title] speaks the truth as always." Erdogan's deputy did not want to publicly clash with Gülen and therefore acquiesced to his criticism. But eventually, the relationship between the two broke down and Fethullah Gülen came out against Erdogan in the local elections in 2014. And while many thought Erdogan would lose, it turned out that he was more popular than Gülen, and after those elections, Erdogan's party announced his candidacy as the next president of Turkey; on August 10, 2014, he won the election and was announced as the next president of Turkey.

Later, during the chief rabbi's visit with Gülen, we traveled to Ankara where we met with the then president of Turkey, Suliman Demirel. After the president and the rabbi exchanged a few polite remarks, Rabbi Bakshi-Doron said he wanted to tell the Turkish president an anecdote from the shared history of Jews and Turkey:

> You know, Your Excellency, religious leaders in Israel no longer enjoy the status they had in the past. In your time, during the Ottoman Empire, the chief rabbi was known as the *Hakham Bashi*, the wisest of men, and this was a very significant status under Turkish rule. Allow me to tell you a story about an epidemic that raged in Tiberias around 1890. Four people died, and in keeping with the procedure that existed then in the Ottoman Empire, a letter was sent to Constantinople informing the government. The man who received it was an official who apparently misunderstood its contents and issued an instruction on behalf of the Ottoman government that all inhabitants of Tiberias be confined within the city boundaries and then the city with all of its inhabitants be set on fire, to prevent the epidemic from spreading toward other parts of the empire. When the Jews heard of this instruction, they raised a loud outcry. The *Hakham Bashi* sent an urgent letter to the sultan urging him to rescind the rash order. The sultan did accede to his request and, as a result, the lives of thousands of people were saved.

President Demirel looked straight at Bakshi-Doron and replied, "My dear sir, the status of religious leaders in Israel today is immeasurably better than it would be if you were ruled by Turkey today, so do not regret that we no longer rule over you."

This was the time of the secular government which was supported by the army and felt confident about its power. Turkey of the twenty-first century is a totally different country, and the process of religious extremism goes hand in hand with anti-Israeli political extremism. Today Turkey, along with Qatar, supports the Hamas movement against Egypt and the other Gulf states. Turkey is also in an ongoing conflict with the new government in Egypt, strongly opposed the overthrow of Morsi, and refused to accept the legitimacy of Abdel Fattah el-Sisi's election as president.

THE SANCTITY OF LIFE CONVENTION

In October 1997, I had another important meeting with a high-ranking Muslim religious leader, this time with Abdurrahman Wahid of Indonesia, then head of the Sunni Islamic movement—called "Nahdlatul Ulama" (NU) (Awakening of Religious Scholars), which has thirty million members—and later president of Indonesia.

Abdurrahman was invited to Israel to participate in a conference of the Peres Peace Center, and I was asked to escort him during two days of his stay. While we were on the Jerusalem tour I had arranged for him, I asked him who the Indonesians regard as the most popular cleric who decides on religious matters. When he replied that would be none other than Sheikh Yusuf al-Qaradawi—the man who had issued the ruling permitting suicide bombings—an idea popped into my head. I then asked him if he would agree to sign a joint declaration with Rabbi Bakshi-Doron calling for the sanctification of life in Islam and Judaism.

Abdurrahman agreed. We were supposed to meet that afternoon with Rabbi Bakshi-Doron in the offices of the rabbinate. I suggested to the Indonesian leader that he rest a bit before the meeting, and he readily agreed. After parting from him, I dashed over to the foreign ministry. When I got there, I shut myself inside my office, asked not to be disturbed, and formulated the treaty. I got hold of a parchment-like page, and on it printed in English the wording of the joint declaration that bore the heading "Convention on the Sanctity of Life":

Convention on the Sanctity of Life

As believers in one God who is good and does good, and whose will it is to preserve the world that He has created, we herewith declare that the belief in the sanctity of human life is an integral part of Judaism and Islam.

We call upon all true believers to recognize and preserve the supreme value of human life and to refrain from harming defenseless people.

May the Almighty, Creator of the Universe and all that is in it, instill the recognition of this sublime truth in the hearts and minds of all His creatures.

Rabbi Eliyahu Bakshi-Doron   Abdurrahman Wahid

Rishon le-Zion and Chief Rabbi   Chairman of the NU organization
of Israel

At their meeting, the two men signed the convention in front of cameramen representing the media. This was the first time a declaration of this kind had ever been signed, coming out against suicide bombings and defining them as opposed to the will of God, to the basic teachings of Islam and Judaism. It was a moving event, and afterward, on our way to the hotel, Abdurrahman told me that he felt he had done something very important, which represented the view of the overwhelming majority of Muslims, who do not agree with suicide bombings, which taint all of Islam, and do not want to be identified with or defined by them.

When Abdurrahman returned to Indonesia, I framed the declaration, and since then it has been hanging on the walls of all of my offices.

The signing of the convention by Abdurrahman Wahid and Rabbi Bakshi-Doron was given broad media coverage in Indonesia and throughout the Arab world. It was very important because of its timing, particularly because of the position it took against the religious rulings that supported suicide bombings, and all the more so because it was signed by the leader of an Islamic movement numbering thirty million members, who was elected two years later as the first president of Indonesia, after the fall of Suharto's regime. In my view, it was one more testament to the fact that a dialogue between religious leaders is capable of engendering real change; forgoing such a dialogue could lead to catastrophe. If we could only persuade other important religious leaders like Abdurrahman Wahid, such as Gülen and even Tantawy, in his qualified approach, to stress the sanctity of life, we might even succeed in saving lives.

* * *

Throughout human history, religion has played a key role in internal and regional disputes. In the Middle East, where most of the countries are Arab, Islam is the major religion, and, alongside it, Christianity, Judaism, and other religions have existed, at times in peace and coexistence, at other times in conflict or even at war.

In the last one hundred years, this region has suffered from wars and struggles, internal and external, as well as from instability and security, economic, political, and social unrest, which has seriously disrupted the lives of all the inhabitants of the regions, of all religious persuasions. In nearly every crisis, revolution, or war that struck the region—not only between Israel and its neighbors but also during inner-Arab or inner-Islamic crises—religion has played a central role, whether as the cause of the crisis or as the fuel intended to justify and prolong it.

In the 2000s, religion has become a more central factor, and religious extremism has wielded more influence over regional and global crises. In the various countries, Islamic radicalism has increasingly gained strength as a result of some common causes. The majority of governments in Arab countries have failed to improve the economic situation, the quality of life, and the standard of living of their people. This has led, among other things, to the bankruptcy of Arab nationalism of the brand of secular radicalism. Economic hardships, a sense of deep frustration, and dissatisfaction vis-à-vis quite a few Arab governments that were regarded by their citizens as corrupt led to a growing rise in Islamic sentiment throughout the Middle East.

The trend of extremism, or "Islamization," has filtered down to all strata of the population, both in Arab countries, in the other Muslim countries, and in Western states that have large Muslim populations. This vacuum, created by the people's mistrust of their leaders, has been filled by the advocates of radical Islam, drawn from the model of the Muslim Brotherhood, on the one hand, and of Iran on the other. The Sunni and Palestinian Hamas movement and the Shi'ite Hezbollah organization have, in recent years, begun to participate in the political arena, exploiting their growing popular support, in order to realize their vision of establishing Islamic religious states throughout the Middle East.

But in many cases, the call for the establishment of an Islamic religious state and the use of all means to achieve that goal—including a holy war (jihad) and suicide bombings—is really only a pretext for achieving completely different goals, which are not related to religion. One of these cases is the Israeli-Palestinian conflict, which was never a religious conflict and never broke out because of gaps or controversies between Islam and Judaism, as many Muslim religious leaders, who rigorously oppose the use of Islam to justify the killing of innocent people, have stressed.

In order to divest the conflict of any religious claims—which are used by extremist terror organizations and clerics who lead these or are identified with them—we need to strengthen the interfaith link between Judaism and Islam. Perhaps we can then also undermine the power of the extremist movements that meddle in the conflict in order to achieve their own goals. Dr. David Rosen, the president of the International Jewish Council for Interreligious Relations and one of the advocates of interfaith diplomacy, said, "If one does not want religion to be 'part of the problem,' then one must empower the religiously responsible voices and ensure that 'religion is part of the solution' advancing a spirit of cooperation and mutual respect."[24]

This is also the worldview that has deeply affected my thinking since childhood, when I heard my father tell wonderful stories about the neighborly relations, friendship, and coexistence between Jews, Muslims, and Christians in Egypt, in the first half of the twentieth century, before Gamal Abdel Nasser's rise to power.

My faith in the power of interfaith dialogue to bridge the gaps and differing positions between the two ethnic groups was reinforced during my service in Lebanon as an intelligence officer, as well as in unit 504, when I spent a great deal of time with Muslim clerics. Finally, when I became a diplomat in the Israeli Ministry of Foreign Affairs, I made every effort to further this aim wherever I was stationed throughout the years, whether in Arab or Western countries.

Now, oddly enough, when the voice of radical Islam is growing louder, I have even more faith in the potential of the interfaith dialogue with Islam and the importance of including this approach in the overall array of strategic and diplomatic efforts that Israel uses toward countries in the region in order to blot out the voices calling for murder and terror in the name of Islam. Most important, an interfaith dialogue can draw the religions closer and is an important means of drawing the countries and peoples closer. Hence, in my view, all the sides ought to officially include religion and the major religious players of both religions in their diplomatic efforts.

I am not naive enough to think that an interfaith dialogue in itself can lead to the resolution of the Israeli-Palestinian conflict. It is completely clear to me that this approach can only have a limited effect; nonetheless, I have no doubt that it could be very beneficial if it is made part of Israel's attempt to build a bridge over the stormy seas and burning earth that separate us and most of the Arab countries and the Muslim world.

It is not an unrealistic utopia.

On January 3, 2005, a conference was held at the Egmont palace in Brussels, its purpose being to encourage Jewish and Muslim clerics to become involved in resolving the bloody conflict between the Israelis and the Palestinians. More than two hundred rabbis and imams attended. One of the conference's peak moments was when Jewish and Muslim clerics decided unanimously to observe together a moment of silence in memory of the fallen. Precisely at noon, all the participants stood around the table in the lavish conference room. Rabbis and imams stood together, bowing their heads, in total silence, in memory of the victims of the conflict.

Right after the three minutes of silence, the huge space of the hall was suddenly filled with the sound of a Hebrew prayer in memory of the dead, recited by the chief rabbi of Haifa, Rabbi Shlomo Shlush. All those present in the hall—Jews, Muslims, and Christians—said "Amen" at the end of the prayer. Then the former mufti of Istanbul, Zimer Omar Farouk Turan, declaimed some verses from the Quran. This moving event closed when the chief rabbi of Rishon le-Zion chanted a psalm in a voice choked with tears.

After the prayers, the hundreds of clerics remained standing. Many of them had a hard time concealing their emotions.

"That was an historic moment," Rabbi Shmuel Sirat, former chief rabbi of France and one of the conference's organizers, said. "It proves that rabbis and imams can act to achieve a united aim. Throughout all my years as a rabbi, I have never witnessed a moment like this one. And I say in the words of the prayer: '[The Almighty] who has kept us alive, and has preserved us, and enabled us to reach this time.'"

Hojat al-Islam Muhammad Mehatali, a senior Iranian cleric, looked at his colleagues in amazement. "These moments were the highlights of the whole conference," he said. "Where have you ever seen Muslims and Jews praying as if they were one family?"

The conference concluded with a pledge that all the Jewish and Muslim clerics would work individually and jointly to put an end to bloodshed between Israelis and Palestinians and would struggle with all their might against hatred, ignorance, and extremism on both sides. When the declaration was read, the participants got to their feet and applauded for a long time.

I chose to cite this conference as an example of the great potential that lies in an interfaith dialogue, not only because it was, apparently, the first time that so many Jewish and Muslim clerics had gathered together under one roof, but mainly owing to the reason for their participation in this conference. Throughout the four days of the conference, the Muslim clerics repeatedly gave vent to their distress at the fact that their religion, Islam, was sending people to kill in its name, and stated that anyone who took the life of others in the name of religion was violating God's commandments.

"We are all sons of one father, Abraham the Patriarch," Rabbi Eliyahu Bakshi-Doron said. "So how is it that every Palestinian suicide bomber yells '*Allahu akbar*' before he blows up?"

Sheikh Talal Sidr of Hebron moved the audience when he called on them to visit every mosque and synagogue to preach peace and dignity. "This is the divine commandment; we must educate a generation to peace and love," he said.

"How is it that every Jewish prayer ends with the word *peace* and every Muslim prayer ends with the word *peace* and we are killing each other?" asked Sheikh Abdul Jalil Sajid, the imam of Brighton, England.

"Without the approval of the religious leaders, the secular elements will not succeed in making peace," Kamal Riyan, a leader of the Islamist movement in Israel, told the participants. "Unless the religious embrace the process of peace and reconciliation, there will be no peace in the Middle East."[25]

As I have said, I am a great advocate of meetings of this sort, but in the very same breath I have to say that we must not err by thinking that this is a magic solution to the relations between Israel and the Muslim world—certainly not in the present situation, in which religion in the Middle East is a divisive element rather than a uniting one. In fact, there is no widespread agreement as to the real potential of such moves. Dr. David Rosen and others claim that the interfaith dialogue is a significant factor that carries real weight and can help draw the sides closer, and even promote regional peace. However, quite a few scholars and Orientalists express their doubt about its effectiveness.

There seems, however, to be no disagreement about two facts: First, the interfaith dialogue is an additional channel toward mutual recognition and understanding, one that should be introduced into the broad strategy for resolving the Israeli-Palestinian conflict, even if it is a slow process. Second, the State of Israel is not investing enough time and effort in examining this option.

In early 2007, the secretariat of the European Union adopted a resolution, according to which the term "Islamic terror" should not be used, but rather the term "terror by people misusing Islam." The idea on which this resolution was based was that no religion permits the killing of innocent people, and that anyone who uses the name of Islam to justify terror and killing is distorting its message.

In response to this resolution, in an article that examined the present weakness of the central stream in Islam versus the radical stream, Shmuel Bar, a senior research fellow in the Institute for Policy and Strategy in the Interdisciplinary Center in Herzliya, who holds a PhD in the history of the Middle East from Tel Aviv University, wrote the following:

> Western political society tends to assume there are pragmatic and rational reasons for terror acts, and if the political complaints are properly handled, the phenomenon will dwindle. But when the roots of terror are not political, it is merely naïve to expect that political gestures will cause the radicals to change their approach. Attempts to deal with the terrorist threat as if it were cut off from its intellectual, cultural and religious origins are doomed to failure. The war against terror begins on the religious-ideological level and must adopt suitable methods. It is necessary to deal with the cultural and religious sources of Islamic radicalism to make it possible to develop a long-term strategic for coping with the terrorist threat that stems from them. [26]

While Bar recommends an examination of the cultural and religious origins of Islamic radicalism in the context of preventing terror, Orientalist professor Immanuel Sivan recommends (with some reservations) that the use of the interfaith dialogue as a means of reducing Muslim anti-Semitism should be reconsidered.

In a position paper that Sivan published in December 2009 titled "Muslim Anti-Semitism: A Challenge and Possible Responses," he described and analyzed the hatred of Jews in the Muslim world, discussed the dangers it posed, and suggested ways to thwart or restrain it. Among these, Sivan included the intercultural and interreligious dialogue between Judaism and Islam.

"To what extent can this response be accompanied by the 'soft power' of discourse and dialogue? Even optimistic advocates of dialogue admit that the results until now have not been very encouraging." With these words, Sivan tried to curb the enthusiasm of the proponents of dialogue.[27] I do not share his skepticism, but I do admit that the challenge is not a simple one. Years of incitement by charismatic and unrepressed clerics have permeated the political conflict between us and the Arabs with religious elements. On our side, too, there is no dearth of rabbis who have used religion as an ax to grind and found in it legitimation for every act of hatred. Conciliation is to be found in the mosques and synagogues of the more moderate imams and rabbis. Based on my admittedly limited experience, there are more moderate clerics than we might suppose, and they are concerned enough to join the effort to try to remove religion from the cycle of bloodshed. Unlike their brethren who fan the flames, they do have a God.

I believe that interfaith dialogue and international pressure can definitely influence the positions of the most radical people. I have chosen to close this discussion in the name of the incorrigible optimists with two current examples.

In this chapter, I have already mentioned the former sheikh of Al Azhar, Dr. Muhammad Sayyid Tantawy, as one of the prominent religious leaders in the Islamic world that was in the habit of using his status and position to make extremist declarations calling for jihad and legitimizing acts of terror and violence in the name of Islam, even though he was not always consistent in his positions.

In July 2009, about a month after Barack Obama's visit to Cairo, the elderly sheikh, who died in March 2010, published an article in the periodical *Magalat Al-Azhar*, in which he praised the speech that the U.S. president delivered during his visit. Tantawy wrote in his article:

> Cairo welcomes you . . . all human beings are brothers in humankind and they should learn to know one another, to be sincere towards one another, to bring to one another from the beneficence that Allah has given, to cooperate with integrity and faith and not with sin and aggression . . . dialogue is the best way to arrive at the general good. . . . We Muslims advocate cooperation and solidarity between the civilizations.[28]

In his greeting, Tantawy commended Obama for his initiative in opening a new page in the relations with the Muslims, and also expressed his support for Obama's call to the Palestinians to abandon violence along with his call for the United States to act for the establishment of a Palestinian state. In his article, the elderly sheikh also advocated the punishment of extremists who murder innocent people, the preservation of the rights of minorities, freedom of religion, and women's rights. [29]

Nine months before he passed away, the sheikh correctly read the map of the region and the world, and in particular understood the difficult situation the Muslim world found itself in, to a great extent "thanks" to him and to religious leaders like him, who had dragged their religion, which forbade killing the innocent, into the black hole of terror. Now, employing his well-known zigzagging positions, he tried to improve his position, or, at the very least, the status of the religion of which he had been such an important leader, until his death.

Two months later, on September 12, 2009, a special program was broadcast on the MBC channel on the occasion of the eighth anniversary of the 9/11 attack. On it, the man who came out against acts of terror was none other than Sheikh Salman al-Ouda, a senior Saudi cleric and the overall supervisor of the website Islam Today. He expressed his strong disapproval of al-Qaeda and terror, and called on Iman al-Zawahiri, the present-day leader of al-Qaeda, to reconsider the extreme ideology of his organization. [30]

It was virtually an earthquake. For years, Sheikh al-Ouda had adhered to the most extreme position. In the past, he had been one of the leaders of the extremist Saudi Islamist movement Sahwa ("Awakening") and, in November 2004, had signed, together with twenty-five Muslim clerics, a ruling calling for jihad against the U.S. forces in Iraq.

In 2005, there was an abrupt shift in his positions. That year, although he continued to support opposition to the coalition forces in Iraq, he openly attacked Osama bin Laden. A year later, in September 2007, on the sixth anniversary of the attacks on the Twin Towers and the Pentagon, he addressed bin Laden, warning him that if he persisted in his acts, he would be responsible for the death of millions of people, and the time would come when he would be judged by Allah.

On another occasion, al-Ouda said on the MBC channel:

> The Muslims are the only nation whose sons kill one another. There is no other nation in the world—not the Jews, nor the Christians, nor the Buddhists or the pagans—whose sons do that—let us not throw stones at the houses of others . . . in the final analysis, that will harm us, as the saying goes: if you live in a glass house, don't throw stones on others. We say that to Iran and to every Arab or Islam state, for it is possible to say about our houses, more than about (others houses) that they are made of glass. . . . Some of the overall Islamic suffering is caused by (internal) fighting, the Arab and Islamic mentality and the desire to divide things further (and to incite) more problems in this Arab and Islamic (region) . . . until when will people continue to hold on to weapons, as if they are the only tool for achieving their aims. [31]

In an article published on October 3, 2009, on the Islam Today website that he supervises, al-Ouda called on the clerics to refrain from participating in an extremist religious discourse, and urged them to unequivocally and strongly denounce the murderous acts of terror perpetrated in the name of Islam, in order to save the "foolish youths" who follow behind the terror organizations. Here is a translation of a few excerpts from his article:

> I have called and still call on our clerics and faithful propagandists to call things by their true names and to remove the divine, holy name of "Jihad" from the actions of the murderous organizations, which kill innocent people and undermine the security of Islamic states or of other countries with which we have agreements. . . . We should explicitly denounce evil crimes in the world, which are perpetrated in the name of Islam or in the name of Jihad, and to strip them of the masks that their names provide them with, whether they be called al-Qaeda, or Jihad organizations, or military or fighting organizations, or the Islamic state. [32]

Al-Ouda spoke these words distinctly and bravely. In Israel of 2015, is there anyone who is listening?

Chapter Seven

A Smart Middle East

I remember precisely when I completed the first draft of the Hebrew original of the book you are holding now. It was the evening of September 5, 2010, a few days after the first meeting between Prime Minister Benjamin Netanyahu and the head of the Palestinian Authority, Abu Mazen. The atmosphere, according to the reports in the media, was warm and friendly. It was so warm that even Amr Moussa, the secretary-general of the Arab League at the time, the man in whose honor Egyptians sang "I hate Israel, I love Amr Moussa," began speaking out loud about full normalization.

Another item that appeared on the news website Ynetnews the same day heralded the coming of the Messiah. Its headline read, "A Lebanese Mufti: Ahmadinejad, You Talk, But Do Nothing." You had to rub your eyes in disbelief. Two days after Abu Mazen called the former Iranian president "a thief of power," Sheikh Muhammad al-Jozo, the mufti of Mt. Lebanon, bitterly jeered at him, "Launch your missiles, Ahmadinejad, destroy Israel, wipe her off the map and together with her, the Arabs in Palestine." The mufti also did not hesitate to speak freely about the organization that existed under Iranian auspices: "Hezbollah, your forward base in Lebanon, the one who raised the heads of the Arabs so high—until they no longer had heads . . . how long will you go on trading in the blood of the Palestinian people? How long will you continue with your imaginary demonstrations and battles that only exist in the media, and which harm the Arabs and serve the interests of the Persians in the region?"[1]

How easy it was to bask in those refreshing voices, which we had so yearned to hear. Now, as I sit in front of my computer, in October 2014, completing the English translation and updating this book, the Middle East has again reshuffled the cards. In Syria, more than one hundred thousand citizens were killed by Bashar al-Assad's armed forces and Hezbollah fighters who joined the battle to support him. A new faction of fundamentalist Sunni Arabs, called ISIS, has risen in Iraq and Syria, described as even worse than al-Qaeda. We have yet to see how this world threat plays out. In Egypt, Hosni Mubarak is still in prison together with Mohamed Morsi, representative of the Muslim Brotherhood, who was elected and then ousted from power by the newly elected president, Abdel Fattah el-Sisi. Even America, which tried to oppose el-Sisi and ignore him, finally had to come to terms with the rising new leader of Egypt. And after the United States, together with Qatar and Turkey, tried to achieve a cease-fire between Hamas and Israel, only Egypt—el-Sisi—was capable of gaining a cease-fire in Cairo on August 5, 2014, and it remains to be seen if any permanent agreement comes out of it. And Abu Mazen, who established a government of technocrats together with the Hamas, was forced to see how that government never came into effect after ideological and tactical disagreements with Hamas, while he was dragged into supporting Hamas in the "Protective Edge" operation; it seems that his major aim is to achieve the status of an autonomous state in the United Nations (UN) even if a peace agreement is not signed with Israel. That is his goal and with that alone he wants to enter the pages of history . . .

But before we fall into a deep depression, we should bear in mind that neither the slight complacence of September 2010 nor the dismal moroseness of August 2014 are reliable guides to help anyone safely traverse the deserts of the Middle East. The well-known Israeli manic-depressive tendency, the impulse to leap rapidly from the euphoria of hope to the depths of despair, from the peals of peace to the drumbeats of war, from regarding every Turkish raft as an existential threat and every handshake by Abu Mazen as an eternal peace treaty—that is the very first thing we have to learn to shake off. It's time to grow up.

Second, we have to learn from the mistakes of the past; otherwise, we are condemning ourselves to repeat them again and again. And here is a summary of some of these lessons:

1. *When we approach a negotiation with our neighbors, for good or for bad, we have to thoroughly study the cultural bases that make up their worldview.* Because of our condescension and arrogance, we think we understand them, but we do not. We have to go back to the schoolroom—to study not only Arabic but also Islam, Arab culture, and the history of the Middle East. In the introduction to this book, I wrote how Yehudah Hubashi once said to me, "Listen, when we were weak, we were strong." I really liked that insight, but after I thought about it some more, I decided to change it a bit: "When we were weak, we were smart."

   At the beginning, we were weak and therefore we were forced to be smart. We were forced to play the diplomatic game at the UN, to make the impossible happen and to acquire approval for the establishment of the state. We were forced to act wisely and creatively, but now that we are stronger, no one forces us to be smart. No one forces us to learn. This change in status has led to arrogance, condescension, one-sidedness—and, in their wake, also disappointments, frustrations, and despair.

"So what is new about that?" a member of the forum I was addressing once asked me impatiently. "I worked for quite a few years in China, and there, too, we were required to learn the local cultural code. Why is it different in this case?"

"You're right," I replied. "The problem is that every businessman who goes to China knows that he has to learn the cultural codes before he can sell them as much as a match, but we are convinced that we understand the Arabs from our first day of military service." In the Chinese we are ready to invest, but what about those with whom we live in the same geographical space? What about the people with whom we are engaged in a bloody, long-enduring conflict? What about those people with whom we will have to make peace in order to live in real peace in our country? In them, we invest less.

2. *The name of the game is resourcefulness and resolve.* We have to replace our automatic isolation with a persistent, consistent effort to create cooperative endeavors, not only for partial and tactical needs, not only to achieve overall peace agreements. In our isolationist policy we are like a child who invites his friends to play with him and, when they refuse, says, "Who needs you, anyway?"

It is this approach that led us to a unilateral withdrawal from Lebanon in the darkness of night and to a disengagement from Gaza. In both cases, we left while scattering groundless threats that we would "go berserk" if there was any provocation from the area we withdrew from. In Lebanon, we did not go berserk until we really did, while in the Gaza Strip we continued to be on the receiving end of Qassam rockets, or, to be more exact, the settlements around Gaza were the ones who continued to suffer from the Qassams; in the last two military battles with Gaza, the center of Israel became a target as well.

Sooner or later, we will have to understand that our neighbors do not really perceive these unilateral withdrawals as a policy based on power, but simply as cowardice, as our desperate desire to flee from more determined forces that are prepared to sacrifice their lives although they have much smaller numbers and less equipment than we do. It is true that, in our region, it is difficult to arrive at understandings that can enable more controlled withdrawals. We don't always immediately see the partners for such moves, but quite a few Arab states would have been happy to act as our brokers for such withdrawals. Why should we forgo making such an attempt in advance and give a prize to Hezbollah or Hamas? Additional unilateral steps are a dubious luxury that we cannot afford.

3. *We have to lower our profile in relation to normalization.* We have to convert our bombastic statements about a new Middle East into a silent, consistent process of integrating. This is where we most need silence, simply total silence. There is no room for ambitious, global plans. To integrate into the Middle East, we simply need to act—to act in small, modest projects, systematically and continuously, until one day the existence of many such paths of action will naturally turn into a complete picture.

We also must aspire to integrate into the Middle East as an important country, but not as a light unto the nations. The nations want to see their own light, not ours. The Arab world is changing and revising, despite its dislike of rapid changes, but at its own pace.

For years, Israel has been the glue that unified the Arab world—in its hatred of the State of Israel. It is not possible to easily or quickly rid oneself of this function in the Middle East. Cooperative ventures, which at the time were the crowning glory of normalization, such as the Egyptian gas deal, became a weapon to be wielded against the previous Mubarak government and, at the same time, of course, against Israel. We should not refrain from such cooperative efforts in the future; however, we have to take into account that peace is made not only with leaders but, first of all, with people, and that the task of making it does not end with the signature of an agreement, but only begins there. This is an arena we cannot abandon, despite all the insults and obstacles.

4. *We should relate to economic sanctions as a tool with very limited power.* This tool is not effective against states and entities that do not respect personal property, against extremist regimes that rely on God's will instead of drawing their legitimacy from the citizens' well-being. That is why it did not work in Gaza, or in Iran, to end its nuclear program.

Along with the question of effectiveness, there is always the question of morality. Economic sanctions are indeed a tool that does not endanger our soldiers—hence its popularity—but it can make us insensitive. In our desire to change the other side's policy without harming our armed forces, we create an economic siege on millions of people. Anyone who thinks that siege will cause the people to overthrow their government has been proven wrong, and anyone who favors tightening the siege until all of Gaza screams is guilty of immorality. In that context, I want to say one clear thing: I do not want to draw any comparisons with other Western countries. I do not want to explain why we are the most moral in comparison to others; I do not want to resort to the excuse that other nations commit war crimes. I want to be moral, period.

5. *It is important that we burn into our memory the way in which we missed out on gaining the Shi'ite community as a possible partner in Lebanon, and turned it into the spearhead of the war against us in the north.* That is so we do not repeat the same mistake with other groups and communities. In such a complex place as Lebanon, so full of conflicting interests, which is true of the Middle East in general, we have to choose our allies intelligently, without arousing demons that are already there. If we know how to identify, respect, and promote our allies in time, we won't meet them later opposite us on the front line.

6. *Although today religion is the fuel poured on the bonfire of the conflict, if we are smart in our behavior, it can become the water that cools it down.* In order to remove religion from the political conflict, it is important to start holding a dialogue with the moderate clerics so their voice will be heard—and, at the same time, ours as well. We must not relinquish the religious arena only to the extremist Muslims. We have to get the chief rabbis and other important rabbis actively involved in the task of conciliation.

7. And here is another lesson that emerged in the wake of the Arab Spring in the Arab world, and I confess that, although I have acted according to it during my entire professional life, I did not fully appreciate it until now: *Our negotiations with Arab countries cannot be conducted only in closed rooms, on the highest levels*, and as I've said, they should not end with the signing of one or another political agreement. The dialogue—as angry, offensive, blatant, and frustrating as it may be—has to be ongoing, and it has to be with the entire Arab public, of course through the Arab media, which has become a vehicle of unprecedented influence.

The Arab peoples have taken to the streets, have overcome the obstacle of fear, have overthrown governments, and have proven that they are not impressed by the manipulative attempts of their leaders to blame Israel for the riots. We have to reach out to them in every possible way, and the most effective way is via television and media broadcasts. And we should do that in Arabic.

* * *

Besides the lessons to be learned, I am guided by one principle in our relations with our neighbors, and that is modesty. That does not mean we have to give up our uniqueness or who we are. The man has yet to be born who can succeed in robbing the Jewish people of their identity, and as we know, many have tried. But when we behave modestly, we are not belittling ourselves. Life is complicated. When we see a condescending person, we have a low opinion of him, because we actually appreciate a person who behaves modestly. It is no different when it comes to relations between nations. The State of Israel should be smart in its behavior, and that begins with deflating our ego and acting mature.

In the relations between us and our neighbors, we must not try to lord it over them or patronize them. Nor should we engage in brutal purposefulness, based on a cold, calculating balance of interests. The Israeli culture of getting straight to the point threatens to engrave in the minds of the world an image of us as direct, blunt, interest-driven, and only desirous of achieving our selfish ends. Paradoxically, when that is how we are perceived, our chances of preserving our interests are minimized, not maximized.

* * *

In conclusion, I will offer a short story:

One night in 1986, when I was serving in Marj Ayun in southern Lebanon, an intelligence officer came into the room. We introduced ourselves, and when he heard my previous surname, Aboudara, he asked, "Are you related to Yitzhak Aboudara from the import business in Tel Aviv?" I replied, "Yes, he's my father." And I told him that my father had passed away four years before. I was surprised that he knew him.

"Your father was an amazing man," he said, sadly. "I met him on the last Friday before Rosh Hashanah, eight years ago. I'd put off till the last minute buying gifts for the employees in my factory, and I was racing around from shop to shop in Tel Aviv, looking for nice enough gifts that were within my budget. I arrived at your father's place of business at noon, an hour before closing time, exhausted, sweating, upset, and hopeless. I was sure I wouldn't manage to buy the gifts before the holiday.

"Your father welcomed me with a smile, while I, without even so much as a 'Shalom,' just blurted out the following words: 'My name is so and so, I have a factory with eighty workers in Pardess Hanna and I need gifts for Rosh Hashanah for such and such a budget. Do you have anything to offer me?'

"Your father smiled at me, placed his hand on my shoulder, and said in a calming voice, 'I do, my young friend, but about work we'll talk later. Maybe first, you will drink some coffee?'"

Notes

1. A DIALOGUE OF THE DEAF

1. Amira Galin, "The Influence of Culture and the Israeli Aspect," in *The Dynamics of Negotiations—from Theory to Application* by Amira Galin, 9th ed. (Tel Aviv: Ramot, May 2003), 209–10 (Hebrew).

2. Raymond Cohen, *Culture and Conflict in Egyptian-Israeli Relations: A Dialogue of the Deaf* (Bloomington: Indiana University Press, 1990), 170.

3. Shlomo Ben Ami, *A Front without a Rearguard: A Voyage to the Boundaries of the Peace Process* (Tel Aviv, 2004), 26 (Hebrew).

4. Gilead Sher, *The Israeli-Palestinian Peace Negotiations: Within Reach 1999–2000* (Tel Aviv, 2001), 44 (Hebrew).

5. Ben Ami, *A Front*, 41.

6. Ibid., 116.

7. Raviv Drucker, *Harakiri* (Tel Aviv, 2002), 14 (Hebrew).

8. Ibid., 17.

9. "You Will Never Get a Better Offer: Excerpts from the New Book by Ehud Olmert—What Really Happened in the Negotiations with the Palestinians," *Yedioth Ahronoth*, "Seven Days" supplement, January 27, 2011, 38–40 (Hebrew).

10. "Editorial," *Al-Ahram*, Winter 1992.

11. Mustafa Kabha, The War of Attrition as Reflected in Egyptian Sources (Tel Aviv, 1995), 126–27 (Hebrew).

12. Mohamed Hassanein Heikal, "*Alajras tedak!*," July 31, 1970, http://nasser.bibalex.org.

13. "Barak: 'Assad Is a Strong, Serious and Reliable Leader,'" *Globes*, January 25, 2000 (Hebrew).

14. Charles Hauss, *Comparative Politics: Domestic Responses to Global Challenges* (Belmont, CA: West/Wadsworth, 2000), 467.

2. UNILATERAL STEPS

1. Ron Miberg, "Welcome to the New World Reality," *Maariv*, September 23, 2013 (Hebrew).

2. Lev Grinberg, "They Can't Handle the Truth: Why Israel Can't Get over Its Ongoing Leadership Crisis," *Haaretz*, December 12, 2014.

3. "Palestinian Responses to IDF Withdrawal from Southern Lebanon," June 6, 2000, www.memri.org.il.

4. Ibid.

5. Ibid.

6. Ibid.

7. Shlomo Ben Ami, *A Front without a Rearguard: A Voyage to the Boundaries of the Peace Process* (Tel Aviv, 2004), 116 (Hebrew).

8. "Palestinian Responses."

9. Ibid.

10. Alex Fishman, "That's What a Unilateral Withdrawal Looks Like," *Yedioth Ahronoth*, June 2, 1999.

11. North Africa, Syria and Lebanon Department of the Ministry of Foreign Affairs, "The Evacuation of Jezin by the SLA," cable sent to all Israeli delegations abroad, June 3, 1999, 2.

12. Resolution 425 is the March 1978 decision that led to the establishment of the United Nations Interim Force in Lebanon (UNIFIL), intended to achieve three aims: to confirm the IDF's withdrawal from Lebanese territory after the Litani operation; to restore peace and security along the border between Israel and Lebanon; and to assist Lebanon in regaining its effective control over the evacuated area.

13. Deputy Director General for International Organizations, "To the Question of the Withdrawal from South Lebanon," circulated classified cable to all Israeli missions abroad, March 23, 2000, 1.

14. Ibid., 2.

15. Ibid.

16. Ibid., 3.

17. *This Morning*, radio program hosted by Arie Golan, Reshet Bet, Israel Broadcasting Authority, March 29, 2000.

18. Deputy Director General for International Organizations, "To the Question of the Withdrawal from South Lebanon."

19. Ram Erez, ed., "Civil-Military Relations in Israel: Influences and Restraints," in *The Withdrawal from Lebanon: A Case Study in the Relations between the Civilian and the Military Echelon in Israel* (Tel Aviv: Jaffe Center for Strategic Studies, November 2003), 34 (Hebrew).

20. Ibid., 36.

21. Ibid., 37.

22. Winograd Commission to Investigate Events in the 2006 Campaign in Lebanon, "Testimony of Gen. Amos Malka before the Commission," January 30, 2008, 8, www.vaadatwino.co.il/statements.html.

23. Hossam Tamam, "A Reading into Al-Qaradawi-Muslim Brotherhood Relation," July 18, 2008, http://www.ikhwanweb.com/article.php?id=17396.

24. *Al-Misri al-yom* (Egypt), September 2, 2006.

25. Walla News, "Barak: We Will Have to Carry Out More Unilateral Moves," October 29, 2010, http://news.walla.co.il.

3. A DEMON CALLED NORMALIZATION

1. Shimon Shamir, "A Meeting of the Peoples," Symposium on the Normalization Process (Tel Aviv: Shiloah Institute, March 17, 1981), 6.

2. Itamar Rabinovich, *Peace and Normalization, Waging Peace: Israel and the Arabs 1948–2003* (Tel Aviv, 2004) (Hebrew).

3. Abba Eban, speech given at the Geneva Peace Conference, December 21, 1973, https://www.jewishvirtuallibrary.org/jsource/Peace/geneva.html.

4. "Editorial," *Al-Ahram*, Winter 1992.

5. Shimon Peres, *The New Middle East: A Framework and Processes in an Age of Peace* (Bnei Brak, 1993) (Hebrew).

6. Ibid., 65.

7. Ibid., 68.

8. Ibid., 61.

9. Ibid., 48.

10. Ibid., 104.

11. Ibid., 168.

12. Mohamed Hassanein Heikal, *Autumn of Fury: The Assassination of Sadat* (London, 1984), 61.

13. Ibid., 61.

14. "Peace Treaty between Israel and Egypt," March 26, 1979, http://www.mfa.gov.il/mfa/foreignpolicy/peace/guide/pages/israel-egypt%20peace%20treaty.aspx.

15. David Sultan, *Between Cairo and Jerusalem: Normalization between Arab States and Israel: The Egyptian Case* (Tel Aviv: Tel Aviv University, 2007), 21.

16. Said Yakin, *A Study on the State of Arab-Israeli Normalization* (Ramallah, 2003) (Arabic).

17. Ibid., 5.

18. Ibid., 7–9.

19. Ibid., 71–72.

20. Ibid., 144.

21. For further discussion regarding the case of Egypt, see Sultan, *Between Cairo and Jerusalem*.

22. Sultan, *Between Cairo and Jerusalem*, 49.

23. Fuad Ajami, *The Dream Palace of the Arabs* (Tel Aviv, 2000), 263 (Hebrew).

24. "The Bombs of Normalization," *al-Rayah* (Qatar), August 11, 1999.

25. Amer Tahbub, Op-Ed piece, *al-Rayah* (Qatar), October 28, 1999.

26. The act of leaving a temporary appointee expresses the dissatisfaction of the hosted country.

27. This figure was never published, and members of the local Israeli delegation learned about it through rumors.

28. Like the first Intifada in 1987, it seemed that the course of events was out of control and that an escalation was taking place between the sides that would not lead to a rapid end to the problem.

29. These supportive messages were sent to the U.S. embassy through the State Department.

30. The German chancellor was brought to Qatar to promote the granting of contracts to German companies in preparation for the Asia Games, which were scheduled to take place in Qatar in 2006. The German ambassador asked to meet with me after the visit, and said that the chancellor had asked him to update the head of the Israeli delegation in Qatar about the meeting and the Qatari reply, according to which they intended to maintain relations. It was obvious that he was grudgingly reporting to me on the meeting, since he felt that, by raising the Israeli issue, the chancellor had adversely affected the German agenda and had digressed from the main reason for his visit to Qatar. I did not look surprised by the update, and he did not look pleased with the need to provide an update, the instruction for which had come from "above his head."

31. At a dinner in the home of the U.S. ambassador, at which she hosted Tanner and me, Tanner said that the Qataris had been surprised by the argument that connected a U.S. academic institution to links with Israel.

32. Israel Economic Mission in Doha, "Qatari Press Review," cable sent from Doha to the ministry in Jerusalem, *al-Rayah*, October 30, 2000, 1.

33. The Qatari government invested $2 billion in renovating Qatar. The project included building vast housing complexes in preparation for the conference; planting tens of thousands of new, full-grown palm trees along streets and roads; practical support for the construction of commercial centers; and providing bank guarantees to companies wanting to build large projects.

34. "Qatar: Severing Relations with Israel," *Yedioth Ahronoth*, November 10, 2000 (Hebrew).

35. "Although the Delegation Has Closed Down, the Israelis Are Still in Qatar," *Yedioth Ahronoth*, November 2, 2000, 6 (Hebrew).

36. U.S. Department of Defense, "Secretary Cohen Press Conference in Doha, Qatar," November 18, 2000, www.defense.gov.

37. This is a verbatim translation of the Arabic into English. Abu Muhammad Abudallah Ibn Muslim Bin Qutaybah al-Dinawari, *A Collection of Stories—Uyun al-Akhbar*, Part One, Dar al-Kutub al-Elmeya [the house of Books of Knowledge] (Beirut, Lebanon, 1985).

38. *Ha'aretz*, December 21, 1994 (Hebrew).

4. ECONOMIC SANCTIONS

1. Dianne E. Rennack, "Economic Sanctions to Achieve U.S. Policy Goals: Discussion and Guide to Current Law," Congressional Research Service [CRS] Reports Military and National Security, October 20, 1997, www.fas.org.

2. Jona Lendering, "Megarian Decree," Livius, Articles on Ancient Greece, www.livius.org.

3. Gary C. Hufbauer, Jeffrey J. Schott, Kimberly Ann Elliott, and Barbara Oegg, *Economic Sanctions Reconsidered*, 3rd ed. (Washington, DC: Peterson Institute for International Economics, November 2007), 1.

4. Gary C. Hufbauer, Jeffrey J. Schott, and Kimberly Ann Elliott, *Economic Sanctions Reconsidered* (USA Institute for International Economics, 1990), 9.

5. Joy Gordon, "Economic Sanctions, Just War Doctrine and the 'Fearful Spectacle of the Civilian Dead,'" *Cross Currents* 49, no. 3 (1999).

6. Hufbauer, Schott, and Kimberly, *Economic Sanctions Reconsidered*, 11.

7. Ibid., 10.

8. Ibid., 63.

9. Ibid., 36.

10. Peter Fitzgerald, "The Impact of Economic Sanctions," in *UK: Stetson University College of Law Volume II: Evidence* (London, May 9, 2007), 2.

11. Ibid., 51.

12. Shmuel Sandler, *Basic Concepts in International Relations* (Tel Aviv, 1999), chapter 15 (Hebrew).

13. Amos Nadan and Eldad Pardo, "Rethinking Economic Sanctions on Iran," *Tel Aviv Notes*, August 22, 2007, 1.

14. Ibid., 4.

15. Hufbauer, Schott, and Kimberly, *Economic Sanctions Reconsidered*, 91.

16. Kimberly Ann Elliott and Peter P. Uimonen, *The Effectiveness of Economic Sanctions with Application to the Case of Iran* (Washington, DC, 1993), 404.

17. Although the Israeli government adopted only three decisions on this subject, the executive bodies dealt with it on a daily basis, the main one being the Coordinator of Government Activities in the Territories (COGAT).

18. Prime Minister's Office, "Statement by the Acting Prime Minister at the Opening of the Cabinet Meeting," statement to the press, January 29, 2006, http://www.pmo.gov.il.

19. Ibid.

20. Prime Minister's Office, "Government Resolution no. 4,705," February 19, 2006.

21. The Quartet is the foursome of the United States, the European Union, Russia, and the United Nations. The forum was established in Madrid in 2002 as a result of the regression in the peace process in the Middle East.

22. Reut Institute, "The Cessation of Transfer of Funds Will Not Quash the Palestinian Authority under Hamas Control," *Basic Warning Document*, March 2006, 2 (Hebrew).

23. Ibid.

24. International Fact-Finding Mission, International Federation for Human Rights, "Failing the Palestinian State, Punishing Its People: The Impact of the Economic Strangulation on

Human Rights within the Occupied Palestinian Territory," report no. 459, October 20, 2006, 27, www.fidh.org.

25. Ibid., 10.

26. Anat Kurz, "The Israeli-Palestinian Arena: Straddling Escalation and Calm," *Strategic Assessment* 9, no. 4 (2007): 17.

27. Ibid., 5.

28. Prime Minister's Office, "Government Resolution no. 4,780," April 11, 2006.

29. In one of the discussions held at the Prime Minister's office with the National Security Council, the head of the PM's office, attorney Dov Weisglas, said that the Palestinians would not starve but would be very thin. There is no documentation for that statement except for the fact that it was reported by one of the participants in the discussion, and was the general spirit of the views expressed in the discussion.

30. Eli Avidar, "The Struggle against Hamas," memo sent to the Foreign Minister, Jerusalem, May 3, 2006.

31. Ibid.

32. International Federation for Human Rights, "Failing the Palestinian State," report no. 459, 28.

33. Prime Minister's Office, "Government Resolution no. 54," May 21, 2006.

34. Ibid.

35. International Federation for Human Rights, "Failing the Palestinian State," report no. 459.

36. Although the United States has a firm position on the issue, it was compelled to fall into line with the other three members of the Quartet: the European Union, Russia, and the United Nations.

37. Temporary International Mechanism (TIM), June 2006, http://ec.europa.eu.

38. International Federation for Human Rights, "Failing the Palestinian State," report no. 459, 6.

39. This is an update to government resolution 4,705, of February 19, 2006, which totally freezes the transfer of tax monies to the Palestinian Authority.

40. Prime Minister's Office, "Government Resolution no. 917," December 24, 2006.

41. "You Will Never Get a Better Offer: Excerpts from the New Book by Ehud Olmert— What Really Happened in the Negotiations with the Palestinians," *Yedioth Ahronoth*, "Seven Days" supplement, January 27, 2011, 38–40 (Hebrew).

42. Ibid.

43. Prime Minister's Office, "Government Resolution no. 1,407," March 18, 2007.

44. Prime Minister's Office, "Government Resolution no. 1,851," June 24, 2007.

45. Shaul Mishal, "The Agony of Victory," *Strategic Assessment* 9, no. 1: 10.

46. Amir Kulick, "Actions Not Talk," *Strategic Assessment* 10, no. 4: 54.

47. Prime Minister's Office, National Security Council, "Project of Hamas' Growing Strength in the Gaza Strip," 2006, 2.

48. Mark Heller, "The Hamas Victory—Initial Reactions," *Strategic Assessment* 8, no. 4.

49. Hufbauer, Schott, and Kimberly, *Economic Sanctions Reconsidered*, 51.

50. First Class, "Dahlan at the Fatah Rally: 'Hamas Are Murderers,'" January 7, 2007, newsIco.il.

51. Mohammad Yaghi, "Palestinian Public Opinion: A Year after Hamas's Victory," policy no. 1191 (Washington Institute, January 30, 2007).

5. THE SHI'A

1. Tracy Miller, "Mapping the Global Muslim Population: A Report on the Size and Distribution of the World's Muslim Population," Pew Research Center's Forum on Religion and Public Life (Washington, DC, October 7, 2009).

2. Ramez Rizk and Gibal Amal, *Jabal Amel tarikh wa ahdat* (Lebanon: Dar al-Hadil, 2005), 216–17 (Arabic).

3. Yaacov Shimoni, *Arab States* (Tel Aviv, 1959), 41 (Hebrew).

4. Ibid., 47.

5. Ibid., 477–78.

6. Ibid., 133.

7. The Shi'a, unlike the Sunna, regarded *ijtihad* (renewal) as an important element. A Shi'ite cleric was esteemed if he was a *mujtahid*—an authority who hands down religious rulings based on textual sources. Martin Kramer, *Fadlallah: The Compass of Hezbollah* (Tel Aviv, 1998), 14.

8. Fouad Ajami, *The Vanished Imam, Musa al-Sadr* (Tel Aviv, 1978), 50–51 (Hebrew).

9. Ibid., 108–9.

10. Shimon Shapira, *The Imam Musa Sadr* (Tel Aviv, 1986), 17.

11. Ajami, *The Vanished Imam*, 190–92.

12. Ibid., 193.

13. Kramer, *Fadlallah*, 25.

14. The civil war in Lebanon broke out on April 13, 1975, and continued until October 13, 1990, when East Beirut was conquered by the Syrian army. See also Shimoni, *Arab States*, 490.

15. Ibid., 186.

16. Nasr S. V. Reza, *The Shia Revival* (New York: W. W. Norton, 2006), 72–73.

17. Ibid., 144.

18. Ibid., 126.

19. Joseph Kostiner, "Shi'i Unrest in the Gulf," in *Shi'ism, Resistance and Revolution*, ed. Martin Kramer (Boulder, CO: Westview Press, 1987), 183.

20. Ibid., 125, 144.

21. Martin Kramer, ed., *Shi'ism, Resistance and Revolution* (Boulder, CO: Westview Press, 1987), 27.

22. Reza, *Shia Revival*, 144.

23. Ibid.

24. Rodger Shanahan, *The Shi'a of Lebanon: Clans, Parties and Clerics* (London: I. B. Tauris, 2005), 153.

25. Kramer, *Shi'ism*, 24.

26. Shanahan, *The Shi'a*, 146.

27. Kramer, *Shi'ism*, 22.

28. Ibid., 31.

29. Ibid., 33–34.

30. Shanahan, *The Shi'a*, 155.

31. Kramer, *Shi'ism*, 22.

32. Ibid.

33. Ibid., 35.

34. Ari Shavit, "Jenin, Jenin," *Ha'aretz*, April 7, 2001, part 2, 1.

35. *Teheran Times*, June 27, 1999.

6. AN INTERFAITH DIALOGUE

1. Nahman Tal, "Israel and the Terror of the Suicide Bombers," *INSS* 5, no. 1 (June 2002): 25–32.

2. Center for Political Research in the Israeli Ministry of Foreign Affairs, "Islam and the Future of the Cultural Dialog," cable sent to the Interfaith Department, November 11, 1996, 1, section 2. This cable is a synopsis of an announcement issued by the General Conference of the Supreme Council of Egypt for Islamic Affairs.

3. Ibid.

4. Ibid.

5. Ibid.

6. Ibid., 2, section 2.

7. Ibid.

8. Ibid., 2, section 3.

9. This verse is from the Sura Al-Hujurat (The Apartments) in the Quran, which was the Committee's motto.

10. Center for Political Research in the Israeli Ministry of Foreign Affairs, "Islam and the Future of the Cultural Dialog," 2, section 3.

11. Press brief from the Israel Embassy in Brussels, "Interview with Sheikh al-Azhar," published in *Le Soir*, June 24, 1997, 1, section 5.

12. "Leading Egyptian Cleric Calls for Jihad," MEMRI Special Dispatch no. 137, October 13, 2000. This article was first published in the United Arab Emirates paper *Al-Khaleej* and later published in *Al-Hayat Al-Jadida* on October 10, 2000.

13. Ibid.

14. Ibid.

15. Sheikh Abdullah Nimer Darwish, personal communication with the author, December 10, 2014. This was not a one-time statement by Darwish. In 2012, he gave an interview to an Israeli Arabic channel and said, "There are terrorists who try to convince the people that they represent Islam . . . while, in fact, they practice terrorism because of sociological complexities they suffer from." "Sheikh Abdullah Nimer Darwish—Terrorism," televised interview in Arabic, May 3, 2012, http://www.youtube.com/watch?v=Houx4WoqOo.

16. "Pakistan's Maulana Ajmal Meets Palestinian President, Israeli PM," *Pakistan Times*, November 18, 2005, http://pakistantimes.net.

17. Ibid.

18. Ibid.

19. Rachel Sharon-Krespin, "Fethullah Gulen's Grand Ambition," *Middle East Quarterly*, Winter 2009, 55–66.

20. "Reclusive Turkish Imam Criticizes Gaza Flotilla," *Wall Street Journal*, June 4, 2010, http://online.wsj.com.

21. *The Guardian* (London), September 1, 2000.

22. "Global Muslim Networks: How Far They Have Travelled," *The Economist*, March 8, 2008, http://www.economist.com/node/10808408.

23. "Turkish Schools World's Most Global Movement, Says Sociologist," *Today's Zaman*, October 6, 2008, http://www.todayszaman.com/newsDetail_openPrintPage.action?newsId=144416.

24. Rabbi David Rosen, "An Interfaith Path to Peace," transcript of World Interfaith Harmony Week 2012 Observance at the UN, February 7, 2012, http://www.upf.org/component/content/article/4778-world-interfaith-harmony-week-2012-observed-at-the-un.

25. Walla News, "Jewish-Muslim Brotherhood Began at the Brussels Conference," January 9, 2005, news.walla.co.il.

26. Shmuel Bar, "The Philosophical Roots of Radical Islam," http://www.kivunim.org.il.

27. Immanuel Sivan, "Muslim Anti-Semitism: A Challenge and Possible Responses" (Jerusalem, 2009), 16.

28. Muhammad Sayyid Tantawy, "Tamlat fi khatab al-ra'is barakh Ubama min mantur islami" (Cairo: *Al-Azhar*, August 2009).

29. Ibid.

30. "Senior Saudi Cleric Calls for Moderation, Criticizes Al-Qaeda and the Terrorism Perpetrated in Islam's Name," MEMRI Special Dispatch no. 2915, April 19, 2010.

31. Ibid.

32. Ibid.

7. A SMART MIDDLE EAST

1. Roe Nachmias, "A Lebanese Mufti: Ahmadinejad, You Talk, But Do Nothing," Ynetnews, September 5, 2010, http://www.ynet.co.il/articles/0,7340,L-3949757,00.html.

Index

CPSIA information can be obtained at www.ICGtesting.com
Printed in the USA
BVOW08*1142280415

397684BV00005B/5/P